Encounter with the Earth

Resources

Encounter with the Earth

Resources

Léo F. Laporte

University of California, Santa Cruz

Canfield Press San Francisco
A Department of Harper & Row, Publishers, Inc.
New York London

Sponsoring editor: Howard Boyer
Production editor: Pat Brewer
Artists: Larry Jansen, Pam Vesterby
Designer: Barbara Robinson
Copyeditor: Vickie Golden
Photo Researcher: Kay Y. James
Cover photograph: Kennecott Copper Corporation

Library of Congress Cataloging in Publication Data

Laporte, Léo F.
Encounter with the earth.

Includes bibliographies and indexes.
CONTENTS: v. 1. Materials and processes.—v. 2. Resources.—v. 3. Wastes and hazards.
1. Earth sciences. 2. Natural resources. 3. Pollution. I. Title.
QE28.L24 1975b 550 75-23034
ISBN 0-06-384781-7 (v. 2.)

This book was previously published as Part Two of *Encounter with the Earth* by Léo F. Laporte.

Encounter with the Earth: Resources

75 76 77 10 9 8 7 6 5 4 3 2 1

Credits begin on p. 175.

Contents

Preface

This book looks at the earth's resources, which support our lives and civilization. In the chapters that follow we establish the potentials and limitations of our resources: metals and nonmetals, energy, water, oceans, and soils. Our discussion is at the introductory level, requiring only an elementary knowledge of basic earth science concepts and principles. In the last chapter we explore some topical issues on resources. In particular, we review factors that influence the supply and demand of our resources in an attempt to demonstrate that answers to the question "How much for how long?" are complex and somewhat uncertain.

Too often, our discussions about resources take extreme positions: either we are about to run out of almost everything in the near future, or there's nothing to worry about because we can find more (haven't we always?)—anyway, technological advances will bail us out. As in most many-sided issues, especially those involving a large element of human choice, the solutions and predicted outcomes are not so clear-cut or predetermined.

Before lining up with either the Doomsday or Cornucopia schools, we want to develop an objective evaluation of our resources by describing what they are, how they occur, to what degree they are renewable or nonrenewable, and the best, current estimates of their abundance. With this background, we should be in a better position as citizens to plan our society's future course of action. To use an analogy, we could think of this as a description of the stage, props, and lighting available for the unfolding of the human drama. Once we know these things, we can write a limited number of scenarios appropriate for our stage, props, and lighting. Whether the story has a happy or tragic ending depends on what sort of script we write and how we all act out our assigned roles, rather than on the nature of the stage, props, and lighting themselves.

Remember, then, that the emphasis here is on the "goodies" stored within the earth; goodies that keep the human race going. Consequently, we draw on and relate basic earth science principles and concepts dealing with resources.

What are some of these principles and concepts? As we will soon see, economically valuable deposits of metals and nonmetals are the result of the same rock-forming processes that make crystalline and sedimentary rocks like granite and sandstone. Fossil and nuclear fuels, too, are merely special cases of ordinary geologic phenomena like sediment accumulation and lithification, and migration of subsurface fluids. The movement of natural waters determines the availability of water as a resource just as it shapes the land surface. Many of the same processes operating on land also occur within the sea, so that land-based resources formed by these processes are found within the oceans as well. Soils that provide our food and fiber develop from physical and chemical weathering of sediment and rock. Hence our perspective is to focus on the ways in which earth processes generate the great variety of resources so useful to humans.

Several unique elements have been incorporated in the book. Some of the social, economic, and political issues that are inevitably entangled with resources are introduced, and in some instances discussed at length. Each chapter includes a Viewpoint written by an authority in the field to expand on some element treated in the chapter or, in a few cases, to introduce another aspect or opinion. These Viewpoints were written to give the reader a sense of the ongoing search for strategies and tactics for living on a finite earth and to avoid cut-and-dried statements on particular issues or problems. Marginal notes throughout each chapter refer forward and backward to other sections of the book that relate to the discussion. Some marginal notes suggest topics for more open-ended discussions as well as projects that might be pursued. In addition, a summary, glossary, and list of suggested readings at the end of each chapter should be of use to the student. The book brings together from a wide variety of literature much data and many graphs and tables that are rarely available to teachers or students in the earth sciences. At the end of the book is a general glossary of basic earth science terms used in the book.

No textbook is written in a vacuum. Of necessity an introductory book that covers a wide range of subjects requires the generous help of many people. In particular, I wish to acknowledge the assistance of the many people who contributed opinions, ideas, or information as the book progressed. I am grateful to the following persons who commented on the initial organization and aims of the book: Robert E. Boyer, University of Texas, Austin; Edward A. Hay, De Anza College; Bernard

W. Pipkin, University of Southern California; Arthur N. Strahler, University of California, Santa Barbara; and J. T. Wilson, University of Toronto.

The full text was reviewed by the following persons, none of whom, of course, is responsible for any misstatements or inaccuracies: John G. Dennis, California State University, Long Beach; Richard R. Doell, U.S. Geological Survey, Menlo Park; M. Grant Gross, Chesapeake Bay Institute; N. Timothy Hall, Foothill College; Charles B. Hunt, Johns Hopkins University; John H. Moss, Franklin and Marshall College; Edward O'Donnell, University of South Florida; Kazimierz M. Pohopien, Mt. San Antonio College; Robert L. Rose, California State University, San Jose; and Henry I. Snider, Eastern Connecticut State College. Special thanks are given to the six persons who found time to submit interesting and insightful Viewpoints and thereby broaden the appeal and range of the text, and in particular, to my colleague Gerald Bowden for his trenchant wit in the accompanying cartoons.

Anyone who has written a book knows how crucially important the knowledge, skills, and patience of editors are. So I thank Pat Brewer, production editor, for her talent in putting it all together with imagination and taste. I cannot express fully my appreciation to Howard Boyer, project editor, who saw this book through from vague notions to completed text.

Santa Cruz, California — Léo F. Laporte
June 1975

Resources

Bingham copper mine, Utah.

Tailings from gold dredging operations in Dawson City, Yukon Territory, Canada.

Metals and Nonmetals 1

Resources are like air, of no great importance until you're not getting any.

Anonymous

The dawn of civilization dates back thousands of years, when our prehuman ancestors discovered how to make and use tools. Slowly at first, then more rapidly, humans came to rely on natural materials for hunting and agriculture, for shelter and public monuments, for art and religion. As we learned to exploit the environment more and more skillfully, we derived tools like stones and arrows, plowshares and barbed wire, pigments and paper, electric power and transistors from natural resources.

In this chapter we describe major mineral deposits upon which civilization so heavily relies. We'll discuss their formation, their regional and global distribution, and current techniques for their discovery and extraction. As we will see, geologic processes produce metallic and most nonmetallic deposits so slowly, in terms of our relatively brief tenure on earth, that they are almost all nonrenewable resources—generated once and for all human time. Moreover, the geographic distribution of mineral deposits is irregular because of the chance combination of special geologic circumstances that form them. Consequently, we not only should understand how geologic processes operate in general, but should also learn the special conditions responsible for production of specific metal and nonmetal deposits.

1-1 Putting a Value on Minerals

In ordinary rock, the average content of metal is far too low for mining and processing at reasonable profit. Although aluminum and iron average 8 and 5 percent, respectively, most metals occur in much smaller amounts in the earth's crust, usually ranging from less than one percent to a few parts per million. However, geologic processes like igneous intrusion, sediment deposition, and chemical weathering can concentrate metals locally and enrich their abundance by factors of hundreds of thousands of times, making their recovery economically profitable, as detailed in Tables 1–1 and 1–2. Such enriched geologic deposits are called *ores.* For example, hematite (Fe_2O_3) and magnetite (Fe_3O_4) are iron ore minerals that contain 70 to 73 percent iron by weight. Many rocks contain these minerals, but only in small amounts; such rocks do not form ores. In a few places, though, rocks are so rich in hematite and magnetite minerals that it is profitable to mine them for their iron content; such rocks are considered ores.

The percent of metal is calculated from the atomic weights of the constituent elements of the mineral. Iron's atomic weight is 56, while that of oxygen is 16.

Nonmetallic mineral deposits like sand and gravel, sulfur, salt, and phosphate rock also have economic value, as you can see in Table 1–3. Nonmetallic materials are used for cement, industrial chemicals, fertilizer, and many other things. Although they have less value pound for pound than metallic resources, they often occur in large enough volumes that their aggregate worth is considerable. While the word "ore" is by tradition and etymology (or is Middle English for metal) reserved for metallic mineral deposits, its economic implications—namely profitability of mining—do apply to nonmetallic mineral deposits like sulfur, gypsum, and gravel. So a large deposit of sand and gravel suitable for quarrying and

Table 1–1 Metallic Minerals

Metal	Percent in Crust	Minimum Percent in Ore	Enrichment Factor	Important Ore Minerals
aluminum	8	35	4	bauxite ($Al_2O_3{\cdot}nH_2O$)
iron	5	20	4	hematite (Fe_2O_3) magnetite (Fe_3O_4)
titanium	0.5	5	10	ilmenite ($FeTiO_3$)
manganese	0.1	25	250	pyrolusite (MnO_2)
chromium	0.02	20	1000	chromite [$Mg,Fe)Cr_2O_4$]
nickel	0.008	1	125	pentlandite [$(Fe,Ni)_9S_8$]
zinc	0.008	2.5	312	sphalerite (ZnS)
copper	0.005	0.5	100	native copper (Cu) chalcocite (Cu_2S) chalcopyrite ($CuFeS_2$)
tin	0.003	1	330	cassiterite (SnO_2)
lead	0.0016	4	2600	galena (PbS)
molybdenum	0.001	0.1	100	molybdenite (MoS_2)
tungsten	0.0001	0.5	5000	wolframite ($FeWO_4$) scheelite ($CaWO_4$)
mercury	0.00001	0.1	10,000	cinnabar (HgS)
silver	0.000007	0.01	1450	native silver (Ag) argentite (Ag_2S)
uranium	0.000002	.02	1000	uraninite (UO_2)
platinum	0.0000005	0.003	1700	native platinum (Pt)
gold	0.0000003	0.001	3300	native gold (Au)

Table 1–2 Sources and Uses of Selected Metals

Metal	Major Source	Principal Uses
aluminum	Chemical weathering of aluminum-bearing rocks	Metals, abrasives, chemicals, and refractories
iron	Sedimentary rocks (banded iron formations)	Steel and various alloys for construction, tools, and so on
titanium	Igneous and metamorphic rocks, placers	Alloys for aircraft and space vehicles, pigments
manganese	Sedimentary rocks	Shock- and abrasion-resistant steels, steel production
chromium	Igneous rocks	Stainless steel, cutting tools, wear-resisting alloys
nickel	Igneous rocks	Steel and other alloys, electroplating
zinc	Metamorphic rocks and hydrothermal deposits	Alloys, especially brass and galvanizing steel, pigments
copper	Igneous and sedimentary rocks; weathered copper-bearing rocks	Electrical wire, tubing, and various alloys
tin	Igneous rocks and hydrothermal deposits, placers	Tin can plating, solder, alloys, especially brass
lead	Sedimentary rocks	Storage batteries, leaded gasoline, pigments, alloys
molybdenum	Hydrothermal deposits	Alloys for hardness, toughness, and resistance to corrosion
tungsten	Metamorphic rocks and hydrothermal deposits	Alloys that are extremely hard and strong at high temperatures
mercury	Hydrothermal deposits	Thermometers, switches, batteries, catalysts, and paints
silver	Hydrothermal deposits and by-products of other ores	Coinage and sterling ware, photography, and electronics
uranium	Sedimentary rocks	Nuclear explosives and power generation
platinum	Placers and igneous rocks	Electrical contacts, catalysts, dentistry, and jewelry
gold	Hydrothermal deposits and placers	Monetary exchange, jewelry, dentistry, and electronics

use in construction is not, strictly speaking, an ore deposit because it is a nonmetallic resource. But whether it is an economic deposit depends on the costs of quarrying and shipping compared to current market value.

Economic value

Whether or not a mineral deposit can be exploited depends largely on economics. The cost of quarrying or mining an ore from the ground, the ease of extracting a metal from its ore, and the distance from the quarry

Table 1–3 Nonmetallic Mineral Deposits

Sources	Material	Uses
various	stone	ornamental and construction
loose sediments	gravel	road beds, cement
and sedimentary	sand	glass, cement
rocks	clay	ceramics
	lime	cement, agriculture
evaporite	gypsum	plaster
sedimentary	potassium	
rocks	sodium	chemical
	magnesium	industry
	sulfur	
guano deposits	nitrates	fertilizer
sedimentary rocks	phosphates	
	asbestos	brake linings, cement products
		insulation
igneous	mica	electrical industry
and	diamonds	
metamorphic	garnets	abrasives
rocks	corundum	

or mine to suitable markets are economic factors that help define an ore and economic nonmetallic deposits. Of course, spiraling demand for a certain metal may raise its price sufficiently so that what was once an uneconomic ore deposit becomes profitable to mine. For example, the rise in gold prices from $35 an ounce to more than $150 has made some previously unprofitable gold deposits worth mining.

New discoveries in mining and metallurgical technology have turned many previously worthless deposits into ores. Up until the 1940s, most mining took place underground: miners followed a thin, rich ore deposit into the earth. Today, above-ground, *strip mining* has become economically practical: gigantic, mechanical shovels strip away the overlying soil and worthless rocks and expose the ore below. Thus as richer, or higher grade, ores are used up, new metallurgical processes are developed to exploit lower grade deposits. One hundred years ago, ore grade of copper deposits was defined as 3 percent or more copper metal. But as high-grade copper ores dwindled and strip mining techniques improved, lower grade ores could be used. At the same time, methods for processing large volumes of low-grade ore also advanced so that the copper could be profitably extracted. Consequently, copper ore grade has dropped below 0.5 percent copper in many parts of the world. Thus what were formerly uneconomic deposits—although slightly enriched in copper—have become economic deposits, or ores.

Some nonmetallic deposits, like sand and gravel for construction, are used in such great quantities that their market prices are determined primarily by how much it costs to transport them. Usually they are not transported much more than 50 to 100 kilometers because it is cheaper to find a closer source of these materials. In short, an ore or (economic nonmetallic mineral) deposit is a rock whose desirable metal (or nonmetal) content can be sold at a price higher than the costs of extraction, processing, and transportation. These costs vary from place to place and time to time, so specific definitions of an ore or economic mineral deposit also change.

The high price of labor is chiefly responsible for these transportation costs.

Metallic ores

Although ore deposits are defined in economic terms, metallic ore minerals, like all minerals, are defined by their composition and structure. Therefore ore minerals are more widely distributed than ore deposits. Metallic ore minerals are of three main types: native metals, sulfides, and oxides. Native metals are not chemically combined with other elements, whereas in sulfide and oxide ore minerals the metallic atoms are chemically combined with sulfur or oxygen atoms (Table 1–1).

Native metals, which include gold, silver, copper, and platinum, may be disseminated throughout a rock as discrete particles. The rock, or ore deposit, is mined and crushed, then the metals are mechanically separated from the rock. Because these metals are virtually pure, native metal deposits are particularly valuable—assuming that the ratio of metal to rock is high enough to make mining a deposit economically worthwhile. Gold, sometimes mixed with silver, nearly always occurs as a native element. Many rocks contain gold, but either in such a low amount or in rocks so difficult to mine and process that they are not ores. Yet as the value of gold increases, more and more nonore deposits are reevaluated as significant sources of this precious metal.

Like native metals, sulfide and oxide ore minerals can be mechanically separated and concentrated from the rock in which they are found. Mechanical methods involve magnets, liquids of various densities, and vibrating tables, all of which take advantage of differences in magnetism and density of ore minerals to separate them from the worthless rock. For example, magnets can separate iron-bearing minerals from nonmagnetic rock. Inclined tables that vibrate can shake down denser, valuable minerals from less dense, useless ones. (As the tables shake, the dense minerals move down the table faster than the less dense ones, concentrating at the lower end of the table.) When crushed ore is dropped into liquids of a particular density, desirable minerals will sink (or float) while the worthless ones will float (or sink).

After mechanical concentration, the sulfur or oxygen in ore minerals must be removed chemically. Metallic sulfides are usually heated in the presence of abundant oxygen so that the sulfur in the metal reacts with the oxygen and forms sulfur dioxide gas. When the gas escapes, it leaves behind a fairly pure metal that needs further refining, as you can see in Figure 1–1.

Metallic oxides may also be separated chemically, but with coke, an industrial fuel made from coal. Coke supplies carbon that combines with the oxygen; this produces carbon dioxide that escapes as a gas, leaving behind the metal. Some metallic oxides, like the iron oxides hematite and magnetite, melt only at very high temperatures. For this reason, lime-

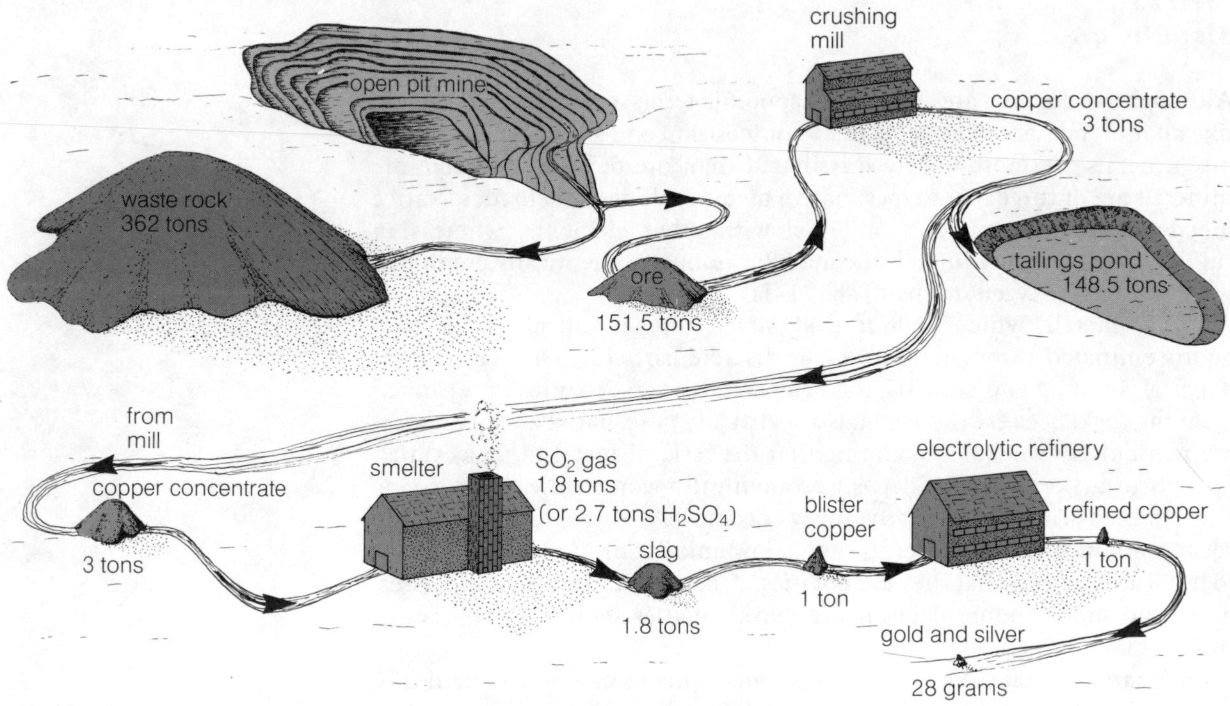

Figure 1–1

Mining and metallurgic flow diagram for copper. Today most copper is mined from open pit mines. Assuming an ore of 0.6 percent recoverable copper, about 362 metric tons of waste rock and 151.5 metric tons of ore have to be removed for each ton of copper produced. The ore is taken to a crushing mill where the metallic minerals are separated from the worthless rock, generating about 3 tons of concentrated ore and 148.5 tons of finely crushed waste. The concentrated ore is smelted with limestone and quartz sand, and the sulfur is oxidized into a gas that can be converted to sulfuric acid. Iron impurities in the ore concentrate form a glassy slag that is also removed. The remaining one ton of blister copper is purified electrolytically, and about an ounce of silver and gold are also recovered.

One of the guano islands off the Peruvian coast; thick deposits of the bird droppings are mined for their nitrate and phosphate content.

stone is added to lower the melting point of the whole mass of iron ore. Thus, when melted and oxidized, the iron ore and some of the rock (which wasn't completely removed in the mechanical separation of ore) produce metallic iron, carbon dioxide, and *slag,* which is a fused calcium silicate solid. Metals removed from sulfide and oxide ore minerals may be further purified by *electrolytic refining,* a process which passes electric current through molten, unpurified metal. Because oppositely charged ions attract, the positively charged metal ions accumulate at the negative electrode and the negatively charged impurities deposit at the positively charged electrode. The final product is a virtually pure metal that can be used in foundries and mills to produce metal ingots, wire, tubing, sheets, and other materials for industry.

Nonmetallics

Although we tend to think of mineral deposits only in terms of their valuable metal content, nonmetallic deposits are at least as important. In fact, nometallic minerals produced in the United States are more than twice the value of metallics. Moreover, each person in the United States annually uses nearly 9 metric tons of rock, sand, and gravel—most of it in construction.

Evaporite minerals like chlorides and sulfates are valuable sources of potassium, sodium, magnesium, sulfur, and chlorine for the chemical industry. Other significant nonmetallics include nitrates and phosphates used for fertilizer. Even though some fertilizers are now synthetic, both organic and inorganic natural sources of nitrogen and phosphorus are still utilized. Large amounts of nitrates are mined from the guano excreted by marine birds on islands off the South American west coast. Phosphates are extracted from marine sedimentary rocks—many of them in Florida—rich in inorganically precipitated phosphorus.

Many ordinary rocks provide other nonmetallic materials and minerals for industry: gypsum for plaster; sand, shale, and limestone for cement; gravel and crushed stone for road beds; clay for ceramics; diamonds and garnets for gems and abrasives; and asbestos for insulation and brake linings. Again, while these substances are widespread, they must exist in localized deposits in sufficient quantity and concentration to have economic value.

Methods of mining and quarrying nonmetallic deposits vary widely. For example, salt deposits below ground may be mined like coal or by digging wells and circulating hot water through them. With the latter method, the brines are pumped to the surface and evaporated to recover the salt. Stone, gravel, and sand are quarried, screened to separate the different size grains, and then washed.

1-2 How They Occur

We should keep in mind several points about how minerals are deposited. First, mineral deposits result from normal geologic processes accompanied by special conditions that concentrate metals and nonmetals. Second, the time required for their formation is almost always very long from the human point of view, and hence such resources are considered *nonrenewable*. Finally, given these special circumstances and the long time needed for formation, economic mineral deposits are relatively uncommon geologic phenomena. For these reasons, such deposits must be viewed as scarce and valuable resources to be conserved carefully for current and future human generations.

Economic mineral deposits result from special conditions accompanying ordinary geologic processes like igneous intrusion, contact metamorphism, sediment deposition, and chemical weathering, as described in Table 1-4. Certain properties of rock allow a higher than average concentration of metals or valuable nonmetals. Primary properties, or those created during rock formation, might include porosity and permeability, which localize ore-bearing fluids from magmas. Secondary properties like joints, faults, and folds—imposed on rocks after their formation—also may control the movement of ore-bearing fluids and concentrate them in narrow zones. Climate, too, can cause special conditions; chemical weathering of rocks after their initial formation may remove worthless metals and concentrate other more valuable ones. Also, climate may evaporate large volumes of seawater in isolated embayments, which leads to the precipitation of valuable salt deposits.

Table 1–4 Modes of Occurrence of Mineral Deposits

Process	Special Circumstances	Examples
Magmatic segregation	By settling of early formed minerals during magma crystallization	Layers of magnetite, chromite, and platinum-rich pyroxenite in the Bushveldt intrusion, South Africa
	By settling of late-crystallizing but dense metalliferous parts of the magma, which either crystallize in the interstices of older silicate minerals, or are injected along faults and fissures of the wall rocks	Copper-nickel deposits of Norway and most of those of the Sudbury district, Canada Injected bodies of magnetite in Sweden and in New York
	By direct magmatic crystallization	Diamond deposits of South Africa
Contact-metamorphic	By replacement of the wall rocks of an intrusive by minerals whose components were derived from the magma	Magnetite deposits of Iron Springs, Utah; some copper deposits of Morenci, Arizona
Hydrothermal deposits	By filling fissures in and replacing both wall rocks and the consolidated outer part of an intrusion by minerals whose components were derived from a cooling magma	Copper deposits of Montana and Utah; lead deposits of Idaho and Missouri; zinc deposits of Missouri, Oklahoma, and Kansas; silver deposits of Nevada; and gold of California, Colorado, and South Dakota
Sedimentary	By evaporation of saline waters, leading to successive precipitation of valuable salts	Salt and potash deposits of Germany, Canada, New Mexico, Utah, Michigan, Ohio, and New York
	By deposition of rocks unusually rich in particular elements	Iron deposits of Alabama, and some in Minnesota and Labrador Phosphate deposits in Florida, Montana, and Wyoming
	By deposition of rocks in which the clastic grains of valuable minerals are concentrated because of superior hardness or density	Gold deposits of Australia, California, Siberia, Alaska; titanium of India and Australia; diamond placers of Southwest Africa
Chemical weathering	By weathering that causes leaching out of valueless minerals, thereby concentrating valuable materials	Iron ores of Cuba, Bilbao, Spain, and some of those of Michigan and Minnesota; bauxite (aluminum) ores of Arkansas, Jamaica, and Surinam

Igneous and metamorphic deposits

Although we should expect the metallic composition of magmas to vary slightly from an average value, we don't know why one magma should be especially rich in nickel, tungsten, or chromium, and another not. What *is* clear is that magmatic activity creates many valuable ore deposits. That is, many metallic ores are found within igneous rock, with special circumstances during magmatic activity leading to concentration of metallic minerals.

Magmas enriched in certain metals produce ore deposits in three ways. First, ore minerals crystallize directly from the magma. Second, they originate from contact metamorphism, when rocks are intruded by the magma. Third, hot, watery magmatic fluids penetrate rocks surrounding the intrusion and travel along joints and fractures, leaving veins of ore minerals.

During crystallization of a magma, some denser ore minerals develop early and settle at the base of the igneous rock mass where they form an ore-rich layer, as you can see in Figure 1–2(a). In other situations, different ore minerals crystallize late, apparently because they fill interstices between earlier-formed minerals, as in Figure 1–2(b). In either case, both kinds of mineral deposits result from separation and concentration of metallic minerals during igneous intrusion, a process called *magmatic segregation* (Table 1–4). Magmatic segregation is merely a special example of the general igneous phenomenon of magmatic differentiation.

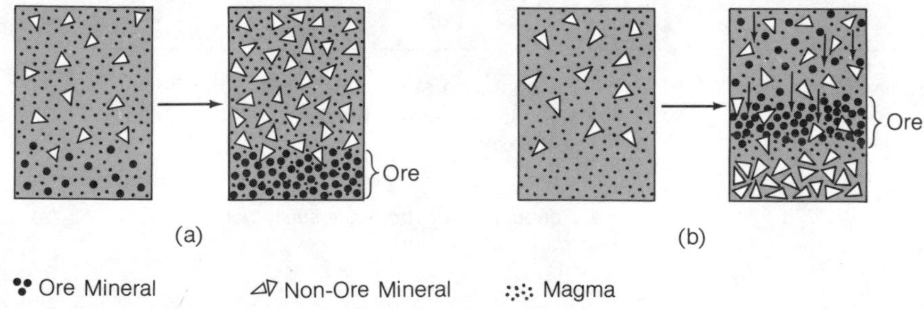

Figure 1–2

Ore deposited by magmatic segregation. (a) Early-formed, denser metallic minerals crystallize and settle toward the base of a magmatic body. (b) Early-formed, nonore crystals settle out, followed by later-crystallizing ore minerals that settle into an ore-rich layer much higher in the magmatic body. Some ore minerals crystallize so late that they remain in the upper part of the cooled magma within the interstices of earlier-formed minerals.

Mineral deposits may also be produced by contact metamorphism, when an intrusive magma reacts chemically with preexisting rocks, as shown in Figure 1–3(a). Magma dissolves rocks at the margin of the intrusion, and immediately replaces them with newly crystallized ore minerals.

Very late in the cooling of a magma hydrothermal mineral deposits may develop. Such deposits are left when hot, watery solutions replace part of the intrusion's outer portion, including some contact metamorphic rocks. Solutions may also be injected beyond the intrusion proper and into surrounding nonmetamorphosed rock, as in Figure 1–3(b). This kind of hydrothermal deposit fills joints and fractures as veins, or unevenly disseminates itself in various sizes and shapes.

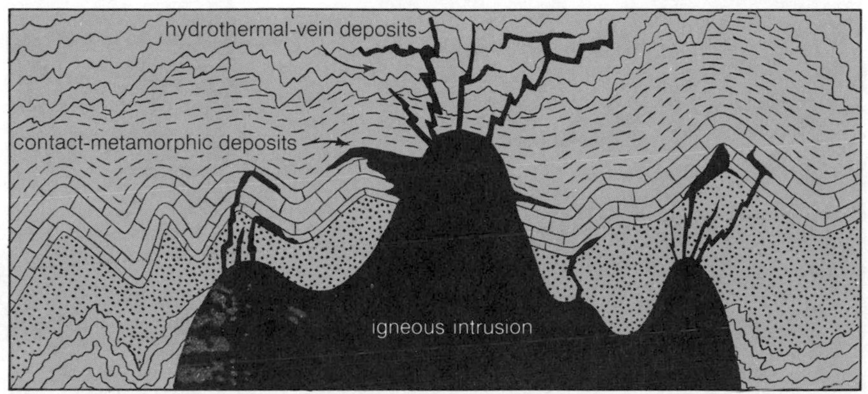

Figure 1–3

Ore deposited by magmatic fluids reacting with the surrounding rock. (a) Intrusive magma reacts with limestone strata in surrounding rock and forms mineral deposits by contact metamorphism. (b) Hydrothermal solutions from the intrusion radiate outward into rock and fill joints and fractures (the latter were present before the intrusion or created by the intrusion), producing vein ore deposits.

Sedimentary deposits

Metals and useful nonmetals concentrate in economic mineral deposits through sedimentary processes like seawater evaporation, selective sorting and transportation of mineral grains, and deposition of sediments unusually rich in certain elements. When seawater evaporates, minerals precipitate in a regular sequence according to their solubility, as depicted in Figure 1–4. In order to produce sufficiently large deposits of these minerals, which would make them economically worth mining, huge quantities of seawater must be evaporated; each 1000 m of sea water yields only 15 m of bedded salts. For this reason, evaporite deposits a few hundred meters thick must represent repeated evaporation of enormous volumes of seawater.

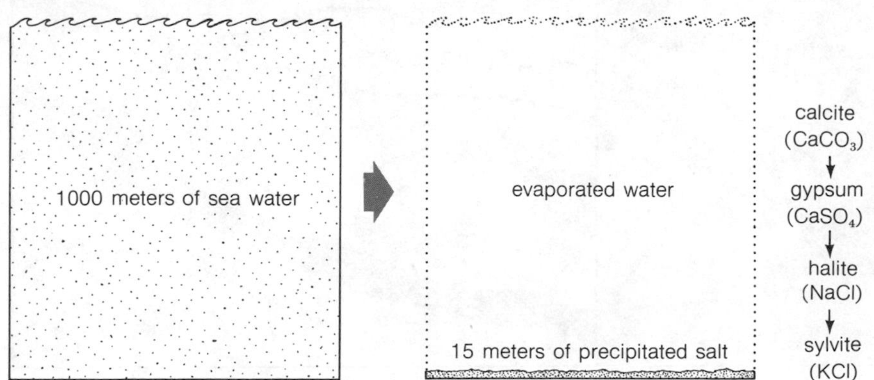

Figure 1–4

Evaporation of seawater to form salt deposits. One thousand meters of seawater will evaporate to 15 meters of salts that precipitate in order: calcite, gypsum, halite, and sylvite. Other minerals also precipitate from the final brines, according to variations in temperature and mixing of the brine with earlier-formed crystals.

Metallic mineral grains eroded from rocks travel along stream beds or beaches where they accumulate in concentrations called *placer deposits.* Formation of placer deposits is illustrated in Figure 1–5. Strong resistance to chemical weathering allows minerals like gold, cassiterite, chromite, and magnetite to be eroded, transported, and deposited without being altered chemically. Metallic mineral grains also concentrate physically

Some placer ore deposits are found offshore on the continental shelf. They formed at times of lowered sea level during a glacial period so that beaches or streams occurred farther seaward than now.

Commercial salt production from seawater evaporation in Israel.

because of their higher density. So heavy, metallic minerals accumulate together, while lighter, nonmetallic ones are dispersed and moved away. Gold in alluvial gravels that cover the lower, western slopes of the Sierras in California exemplify such heavy-metal placer deposits.

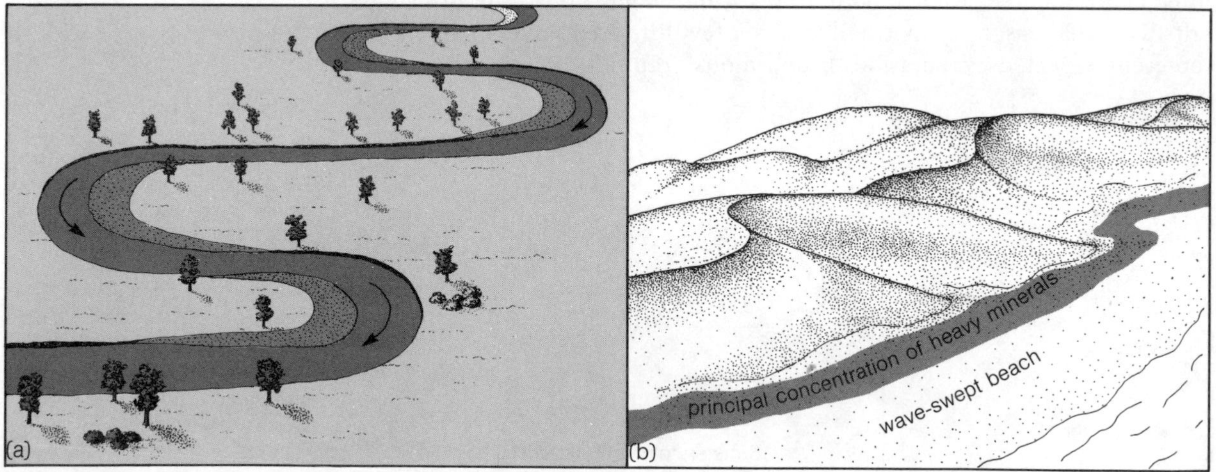

Figure 1–5

Formation of placer deposits. (a) Concentrations of dense, resistant minerals on point bar deposits along the inside bends of a meandering river. (b) Similar concentration of heavier, usually metallic mineral grains along the upper beach slope. Wave swash removes the less dense, lighter minerals, which are mostly low in metal content.

Ordinary sedimentary rocks like sandstones and limestones are significant sources of economic minerals such as quartz for glass and lime for cement. Typical sediment deposition also may yield valuable ore minerals. For example, during Precambrian times—1.8 to 3.3 billion years ago—some particularly interesting and unusual sedimentary rocks of economic value were deposited as *banded iron ores,* like those pictured in Figure 1–6. These ores, which formed as iron oxides in various places around the world, were chemically precipitated by the earliest oxygen-producing organisms around 2 to 3 billion years ago. At that time, the atmosphere and hydrosphere lacked free oxygen. The primitive earth atmosphere was rich in carbon monoxide and dioxide, water vapor, and lesser amounts of methane and ammonia. Iron in seawater was then in the soluble ferrous state (Fe^{2+}). As oxygen-producing plants evolved, the ferrous iron oxidized to the much less soluble ferric state (Fe^{3+}). Consequently, large amounts of insoluble iron oxides were precipitated by the oxygen from plant photosynthesis. Thus the dark, iron-rich layers alternating with light, silica-rich layers that you see in Figure 1–6 record fluctuations in iron precipitation resulting from variations in oxygen production by primitive marine plants. It took about 1.5 billion years for the world's oceans to be swept clear of huge quantities of iron by primitive forms of life. Today, these iron deposits are major resources for civilization.

Figure 1–6

Banded iron ore from Minnesota. Iron-rich layers (dark) alternate with silica-rich layers (light).

Iron deposition of the kind just described was a unique phenomenon in earth history. As the oxidizing atmosphere evolved further, soluble ferrous iron released by rock weathering rapidly oxidized and precipitated. Hence, it is now impossible for soluble iron in the oceans to accumulate and later be precipitated by photosynthesizing plants into such bedded iron ores.

Secondary enrichment

When rocks are weathered, metals of otherwise low abundance may concentrate and form deposits of economic value. This process is called *secondary enrichment* because the rock was not rich in metals at its initial formation, but later chemical weathering made it so. Such weathering is common in the tropics where heavy rainfall, warm temperatures, and abundant soil acids slowly remove the worthless, soluble components of a rock and leave an insoluble residue enriched in metallic oxides. As an example, bauxite, an important aluminum ore, is abundant in present-day tropical areas like the Caribbean, South America, and Africa, as well as in places like Arkansas, where the climate was tropical 50 million years ago.

Some bauxite ores arise from chemical weathering of feldspar, as described in Figure 1–7. Upon weathering, more soluble elements like potassium, sodium, calcium, and magnesium are chemically removed and a residual concentration of hydrous aluminum oxide remains. In a similar

We discuss such chemical leaching some more in Chapter 5.

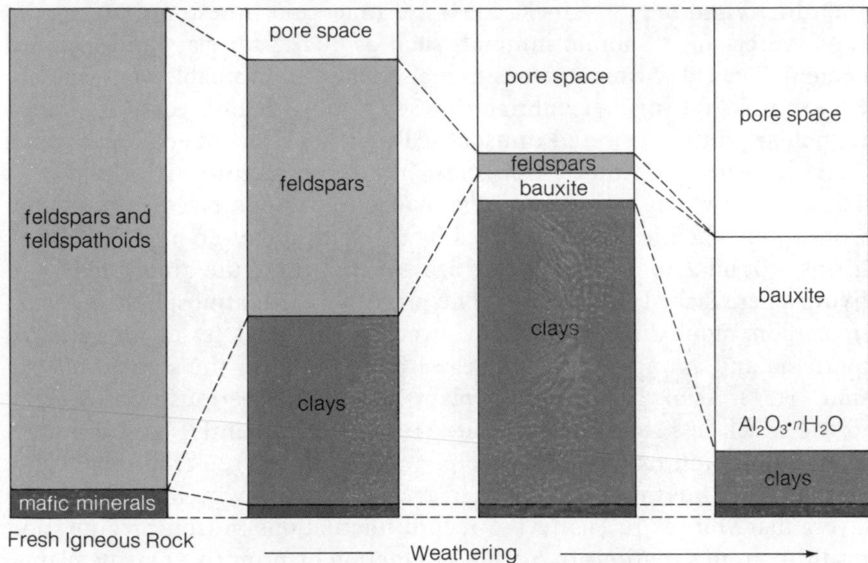

Figure 1–7

Chemical weathering of igneous rock—syenite—to bauxite in Arkansas. Note the changes in volume and mineralogy of syenite with increased weathering. Feldspars and feldsparlike minerals were chemically altered to various clays, mostly kaolinite, and eventually to bauxite.

way, when iron-bearing igneous and metamorphic rocks like gabbro and serpentinite weather chemically, the iron content in the rocks increases to ore quality. Thus, secondary enrichment of low-grade ores with marginal value may upgrade them into valuable ore deposits, which can be recovered economically.

1-3 Distribution of Mineral Deposits

The popular image of a grizzled, old prospector scouring a bleak and rugged landscape for obscure veins of gold or silver corresponds with our general impression of the hit-or-miss distribution of mineral deposits. In a way, this impression is justified because from our ant's-eye view of the planet, mineral deposits are pretty chancy things, being few and far between. But if we can step back a bit and look at the earth from a larger perspective, we see that mineral deposits have regional or even global trends in their distribution. If we know something about how mineral deposits occur, along with geographic distributions of those already discovered, we can significantly improve our chances of uncovering new ones. Such a perspective becomes more necessary as most obvious surface and near-surface deposits are tapped. If we are to find subsurface deposits hidden from view, we must develop a strategy for increasing our prospects of locating them. For this reason, we now examine some known regional trends in mineral deposition and consider contemporary ideas about global patterns of mineral resources.

Regional distribution

Geologic processes work on a reasonably large geographic scale. From this fact, it should be logical to assume that a process responsible for one local mineral deposit may have operated in nearby areas. For instance, placer deposits of gold or tin in one part of a stream channel might point to similar deposits upstream or downstream. In fact, if you explore rock outcrops in the stream's drainage basin, you might find the source where the gold or tin originally eroded. Or perhaps careful searching around the metamorphosed contact of an igneous intrusion might lead to the discovery of additional ore deposits, if you had already found one deposit along the contact.

In a similar way, mineral deposits laid down in an ancient sea can be explored by systematically mapping the sea's former limits and by studying vertical and lateral changes in its accumulated sedimentary strata. Copper-bearing shales of northern Europe, for example, are less than one meter thick but cover thousands of square kilometers: from Britain to the shores of the Baltic Sea, and southward into the Netherlands, Germany, and Poland. The rock is an organic-rich, limy shale that was slowly deposited in a shallow part of a sea during Permian time, some 275 million years ago. Copper sulfides and lesser amounts of lead and zinc sulfides in these shales form ores of several percent metal; these deposits have been mined continuously since the twelfth century. Another example of regionally distributed ores are the banded iron formations mentioned earlier. These have been extremely important sources of iron in many parts of the world, especially the Mesabi Range of Minnesota, and are located within the Precambrian cores of all the continents; see Figure 1–8.

Nonmetallic deposits, too, exhibit similar regional trends in their distribution. The Oriskany Sandstone of the Appalachians, for instance, is a valuable source of pure quartz sand for manufacturing high quality glass. Many quarries have been opened in this sea deposit of Devonian time along the flanks of the Appalachians from New York to Virginia, following the direction of the rock across the countryside.

Global trends

Strategies for developing new mineral prospects were revised lately with the discovery that ore mineralization appears closely associated with plate tectonics. At divergent plate boundaries, ore-bearing fluids from magmas along midocean ridges may deposit metallic sulfides (Figure 1–9); continued plate movement extends these deposits out from the ridge. As the plates travel away from the ridge, the metallic-rich sediments are transported along with them, in much the same way that a conveyor belt carries soda bottles. Some metal-rich solutions also may enter the seawater around the ridge and later be precipitated in the sediments accumulating along

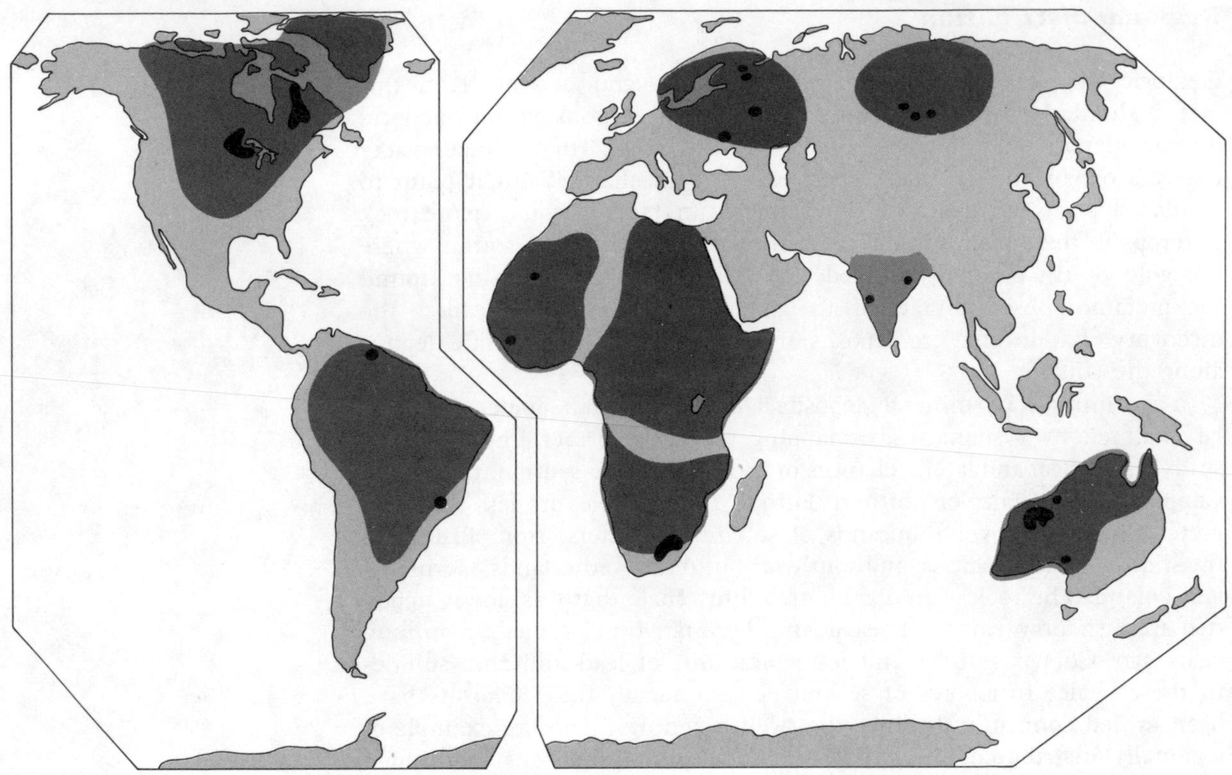

Figure 1–8

Banded iron ore formations (black) located within Precambrian shield areas (shaded) of each of the continents, except Antarctica. These deposits are the major reserves of iron; they formed some 1.8 to 3.3 billion years ago.

We say more about these interesting deposits in Chapter 4.

its flanks. Manganese nodules, which cover hundreds of thousands of square kilometers on the ocean floors, may well have been formed this way.

When plates converge, metal-enriched parts of the ocean plate are conveyed toward the continents, where they plunge downward along a subduction zone. Magmas generated near a subduction zone may be enriched in these metals and further concentrate them in overlying continental rocks which they intrude, as depicted in Figure 1–10. Concepts like these have been proposed to explain the general west-to-east concentration of iron, copper, lead, zinc, and gold across the spine of the Andes Mountains in South America and the Canadian Rockies.

These theories explaining how plate tectonics may have significant control over metallic mineral deposits are still in the development stages,

Figure 1–9

Congealed basaltic lava that erupted 2000 meters below the sea along the Mid-Atlantic Ridge. Such magmatic activity may produce metal-rich solutions at diverging plate boundaries.

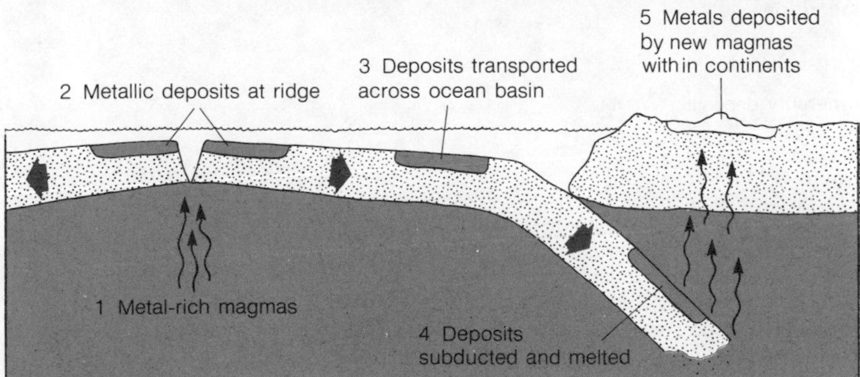

Figure 1–10

One hypothesis for the formation of mineral deposits at converging plate boundaries. Metal-rich magmas concentrate metals at midocean ridges, then seafloor spreading carries these deposits toward continental plates where they plunge downward along subduction zones. Magmas generated in the subduction zone rise, further concentrating the metals and producing ore deposits in overlying rocks which they intrude.

but they do present fascinating possibilities (Figure 1–11). We know that plates have been creeping along for the last 150 million years, and probably for at least 300 million years. In light of these new theories, therefore,

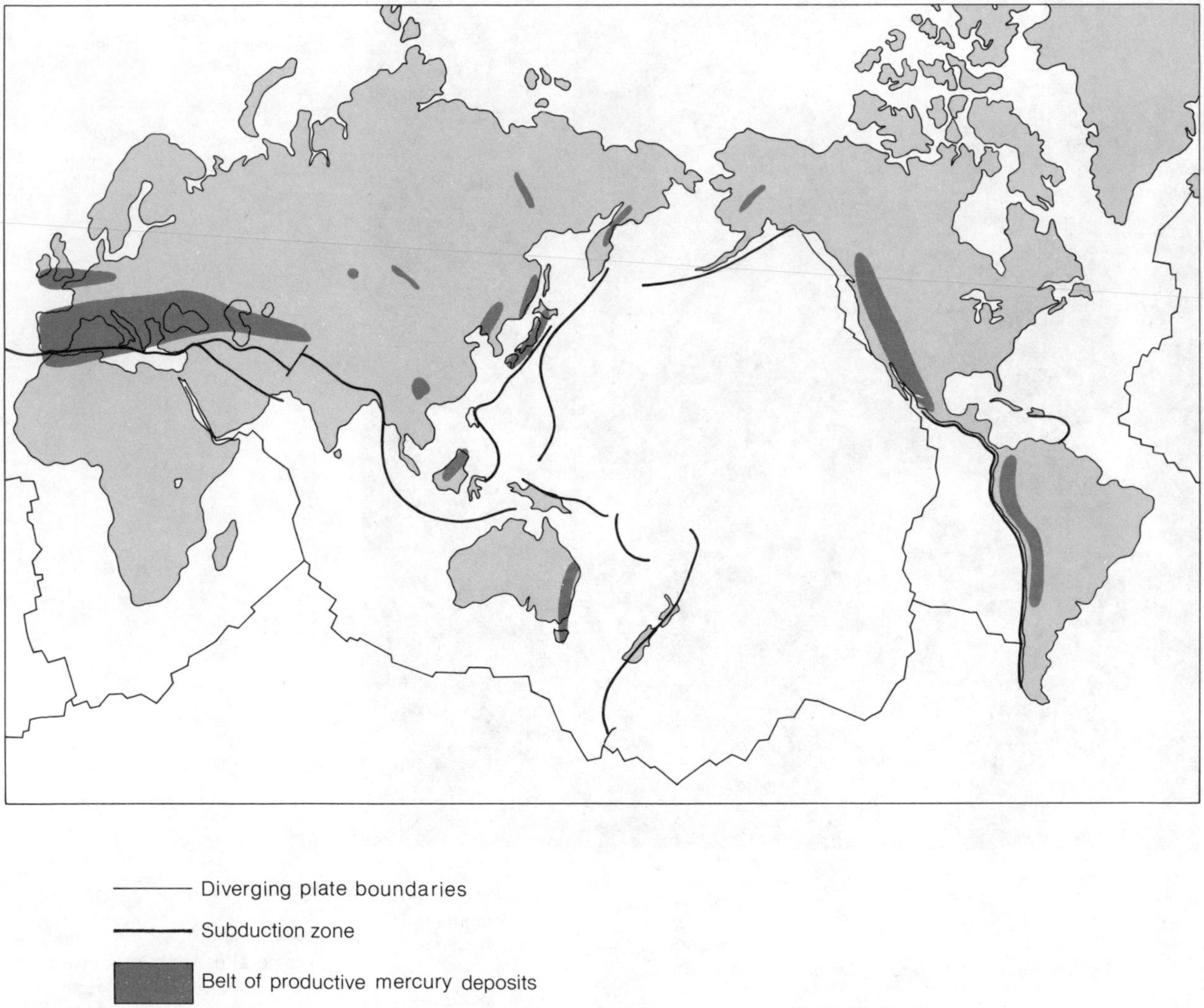

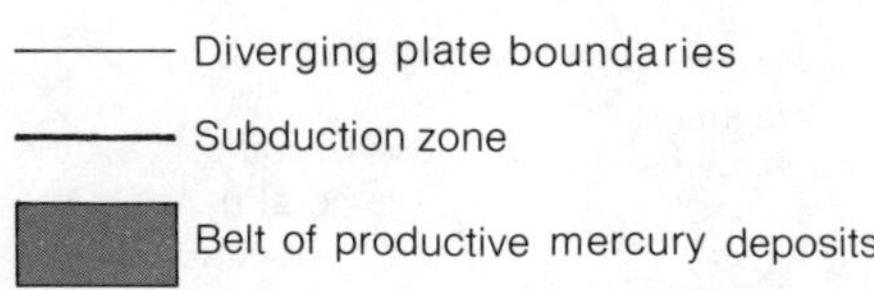

Figure 1–11

Coincidence of mercury deposits (shaded) and subduction zones at converging plate boundaries. Most of the deposits lie on the continent side of subduction zones that have formed in the last 150 million years. Exploration for additional deposits in remote parts of the world near these subduction zones might reveal significant new sources of mercury.

a systematic investigation of known ore mineral provinces might reveal how they formed. With this knowledge, we could try to locate earlier plate boundaries lying within present-day continents. Such old plate boundaries may well contain vast and untapped mineral deposits.

We might pause here for a moment to emphasize that gaining an understanding of fundamental geologic processes, however irrelevant they might seem in solving real, practical problems, may be ultimately the most useful way to approach such problems. Of course, frequently we have to pursue short-term solutions to environmental issues; but in applying scientific know-how, we shouldn't ignore the basic science, which investigates fundamental mechanisms and relationships of earth processes and events. For example, a while back no one would have dared to justify the study of plate tectonics for solving problems of mineral exploration; yet today plate tectonics might be the single most promising concept in developing future mineral resources.

1-4 How Much for How Long?

As world population grows, and as per capita use of minerals increases with living standards, total demand for metals and nonmetals rises proportionally, as you can see in Figure 1–12. Will this future demand be met? If so, how? And with what consequences? In this final section, we review current estimates of the world's reserves of minerals, some implications of meeting rising mineral demands, and methods for uncovering new mineral deposits.

Of the total world consumption of these 18 mineral commodities, what percentage does the U.S. consume?

Current estimates

A summary of the United States' position regarding its minerals resources was published in 1973 by the United States Geological Survey, a federal agency within the Department of the Interior whose job includes identifying and keeping track of national resources like metals, nonmetals, energy, and water. Some pertinent data in this study are summarized in Table 1–5. Domestic resources can supply most mineral commodities required to meet the minimum anticipated demands of the United States for the rest of this century. Domestic supplies for tungsten, asbestos, mercury, and chromium, however, are predicted to be in serious short supply. Potential deficiencies will have to be made up through imports, substitutions, or recycling. Even though sand and gravel might seem to be virtually inexhaustible, their rate of use is so high (over 51 billion metric tons will be required between 1968 and 2000) that, depending on the demand, domestic resources can supply only three-quarters to twice the needed amount during the next few decades.

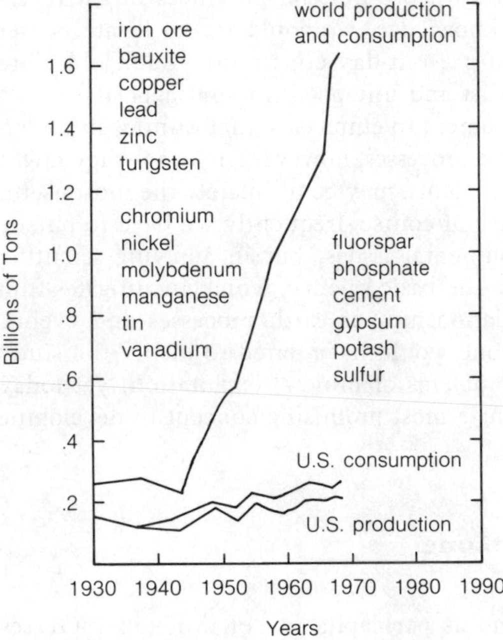

Figure 1–12

Mineral production and consumption curves for the last four decades. Note rapidly increasing world production and consumption since World War II. The gap between U.S. production and consumption has also been increasing, and thus the United States is becoming more and more dependent on foreign sources for its minerals.

McKelvey's Viewpoint at the chapter's conclusion emphasizes this important conservation aspect of mineral resources.

Many commodities listed in Table 1–5 can be recycled: iron, copper, and most of the other metals. And we can use substitutes for some, at least in part; aluminum can often substitute for copper, for instance. As other nations demand more of these commodities, it will be increasingly difficult and costly to import those in short supply. After the year 2000, every nation will have to reclaim and recycle a much larger proportion of these materials. If large-scale recycling develops, the world's great demand for minerals will further increase its already huge demand for energy.

The lead time required to find and develop new resources—not to mention initiating large-scale reclamation and recycling programs—is fairly long, on the order of at least a decade or more. Prudence would suggest that during the remaining years of this century such activities ought to be carried out with imagination and energy to forestall serious world mineral shortages in the early twenty-first century. Our past record in this regard has been poor. The current energy shortages and those predicted for the next decade could have been avoided if appropriate measures had been taken in the last fifteen to twenty years. The world's political and social stability requires an adequate supply of minerals.

Increasing per capita demand

There is a striking correlation between a country's standard of living and its demand for raw materials which makes that standard possible. Two

Table 1–5 Potential U.S. Resources[a]

Commodity	Domestic Resources for Minimum Anticipated Demand, 1968–2000
gypsum sulfur	more than 10 times
aluminum iron molybdenum phosphate titanium zinc	2 to 10 times
clay copper gold lead manganese nickel sand and gravel silver	3/4 to 2 times
tungsten	1/3 to 3/4 times
asbestos mercury	1/10 to 1/3 times
chromium	less than 1/10 times

[a]Includes reserves that are currently of economic value as well as those that might be exploitable in the future under favorable price conditions or improved technology.

examples demonstrate this correlation: the per capita consumption of steel increasing with a rising *gross national product*, a measure of total goods and services produced by a nation, as described in Figure 1–13; and per capita copper consumption of North America and Western Europe compared with that of Eastern Europe, Japan, South America, Africa, and Asia, as indicated in Table 1–6. If world population continues to escalate at its present doubling rate of every thirty-five years, and if rising expectations around the world for a better life are met, then the total global demand for steel and copper will be very large indeed. If the world population doubles to 7 billion by the year 2000, and if each person consumes as much steel as currently used by a U.S. citizen (about 700 kilograms), then the total annual demand for steel will be almost 5 billion metric tons—10 times the current rate of world production!

A recent study suggests that the rate of increase of metal consumption slows down once a nation has become fully industrialized. Until then, however, the rate of consumption is geometric.

Remember that 1 kg equals 1000 grams. Each gram is equivalent to 0.035 ounces; thus, it takes about 28.3 grams to make 1 ounce.

With copper, if we make similar assumptions about population and per capita demand in the United States (6 kilograms), the projected total annual demand will be 42 million metric tons, about seven times the current world production rate. These time estimates are surely wrong, for it is unlikely that the so-called underdeveloped countries will rise to

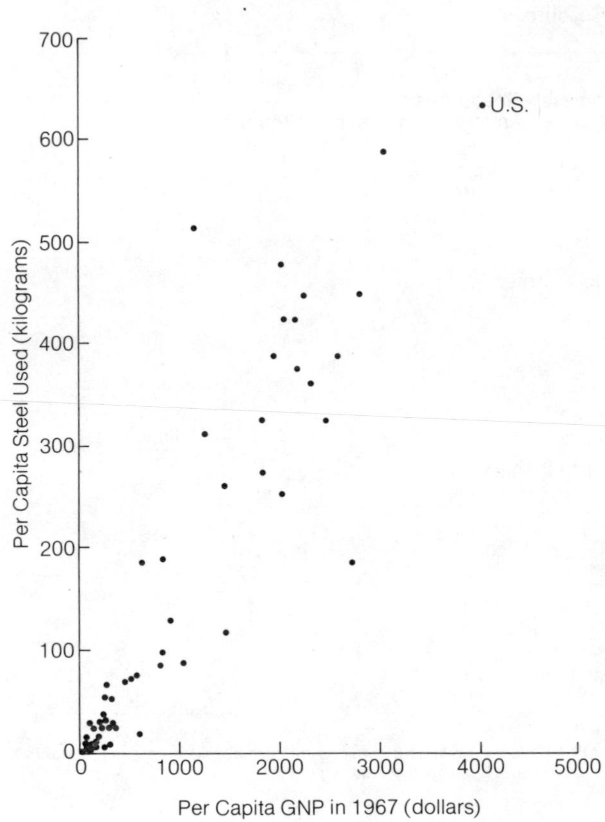

Figure 1–13

Linear increase of steel consumption with growth in the gross national product (GNP). This graph indicates that rising living standards require increasing consumption of mineral deposits.

North American or Western European living standards within a generation or so. But perhaps in the early decades of the twenty-first century these demands will become reality with worldwide increases in living standards.

While demand for mineral deposits will increase, grades of metallic ores will decrease. Past trends verify this relation, and there is nothing to suggest a reversal. Figure 1–14 illustrates, for example, the decline in copper ore quality over the last century. This means that more and more waste rock will be discarded to provide the metals that meet our growing demands. To return to our examples, if we assume that ore grades for iron and copper decrease by half, the amount of rock waste will increase twenty times what it is now for iron, and fourteen times for copper. Presently, the waste rock-to-ore ratio for iron is 3.5 to 1. If we assume the ratio will increase to, say, 5 to 1, almost 25 billion metric tons of waste will be generated annually. Mining ore at 0.25 percent copper to produce 42 million metric tons of copper metal will create another 17 billion metric tons of waste. Correspondingly, more energy will be needed to produce these metals from their lower grade ores, and the problem of disposing of such huge volumes of crushed waste rock will be formidable.

In a general way it has been determined that as ore grade declines arithmetically, the reserves increase geometrically . . . as will the waste rock.

Table 1–6 World Copper Consumption

	Year	Population (millions)	Metric Tons Used (thousands)	Kilograms per Person
Group I	1961	543	3280	6
(Western World)	1969	646	4140	6.4
Group II	1961	403	925	2.5
(Eastern World and Japan)	1969	500	1770	3.5
Group III	1961	2115	267	0.13
(Third World)	1969	2704	359	0.12

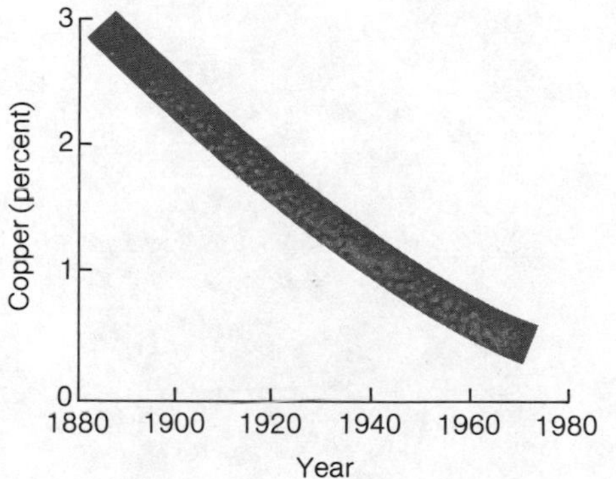

Figure 1–14

Decreasing ore grade of copper during the last century. Current economic feasibility of working low-grade copper ores is made possible by large-scale open pit mining, which uses mechanized equipment of all types.

New prospects

While the total amount of mineral deposits is obviously finite, additional supplies of metals and nonmetals presumably await discovery. Most rich mineral deposits near the earth's surface undoubtedly have been located. To increase our supplies, therefore, we will have to scavenge for those metals deep within the earth, on the sea floor, or in remote corners of the earth. Such discoveries will require careful and complex exploration, including ground and underwater surveys, aided initially by plane, ship, and satellite reconnaissance.

With photographic, infrared, and radar imagery, we can carry out high-altitude aerial and satellite observations of surface land features like faults, folds, igneous structures, and so on. And, with alternative observation methods, features poorly defined by one imagery technique may be clearly seen by another, as shown in Figure 1–15. Such reconnaissance is now carried out by satellites in the Earth Resources Technology Satellite (ERTS)

Figure 1–15

High-altitude radar image of the northwestern coastline of Oregon. A large semicircular structure, about 10 kilometers in diameter, is clearly seen, even though conventional black and white photographs did not reveal it owing to heavy vegetation in the area. The structure is related to past volcanism.

program, which for the first time gives complete coverage of the globe. The three-quarters of the earth's crust covered by water still have to be explored by more tedious and less thorough methods. Sea floor dredging and coring in water depths up to several thousand meters are now possible. And despite the slow and discontinuous rate of reconnaissance, new mineral prospects are being found. Airborne and shipborne instruments that measure unusual variations in gravity or magnetism may locate other metallic mineral deposits, because a deposit's higher density and higher metallic content contrast with those of surrounding rocks.

Geochemical prospecting techniques can also reveal the presence of mineral deposits. Investigations of soils, rocks, surface water, and groundwater have aided in locating ore bodies. For example, chemical sampling of soil, rock, and water may indicate amounts of desirable metals in concentrations that, while low, are above the average. Careful sampling may show that these concentrations increase in a particular direction and eventuallly lead to the source rock from which the metals are being carried.

Plants may thrive or do poorly in soils with certain trace elements, or they may absorb some of the trace elements. So plants are also indicators of mineral deposits. From variations in vegetative cover seen in high altitude photographs or satellite infrared imagery, we can often map the underlying geology, even though the rock outcrops themselves are obscure or hidden.

Viewpoint **V. E. McKelvey**

Vincent E. McKelvey is Director, U.S. Geological Survey, Washington, D.C. Dr. McKelvey's research has been in the fields of mineral economics and seabed resources. In this Viewpoint Dr. McKelvey stresses the need to implement broad policies of mineral conservation if we are to ensure adequate supplies for the future.

Mineral Conservation—A Requirement for the Future

Along with energy and water, minerals are essential components of industrial society's lifeblood. They are the source of metals used for machines and other labor-saving devices and for transportation, illumination, communication, heating, and cooling systems. They are the substance of roads, buildings, chemicals, fertilizers, and pigments—of nearly all of the things we use. Minerals are the basis for most of the comforts and conveniences that characterize life in developed countries. Their increasing use has contributed greatly to the progressive rise in level of living in the United States and many other nations. Modern industrial society would be as crippled by a cutoff in the mineral supply as it would be by a shortage of energy or water. What, then, are the prospects for the future? Is it likely that mineral supplies will continue to be available for future generations?

The answer is complex and involves many contingencies. Before going further, however, we can say unequivocally that resources are not adequate to support consumption if it continues to increase at exponential rates.

Perhaps the simplest way of making this point is to say that a supply of any mineral sufficient to satisfy world requirements for one billion years at present consumption rates would last only about 582 years if consumption were to increase at the rate of only 3 percent per year. If we establish, then, that continued exponential growth is impossible, can we expect to meet future needs at more conservative rates of use?

Minerals are often called nonrenewable resources because their accumulations do not renew themselves in short periods of time as do forests and most surface water supplies. The total amount of each mineral contained in the earth is as finite as the planet itself. What is often ignored, however, is that mineral resources, which consist of substances usable or potentially usable by man, are literally created by human ingenuity and that the availability of minerals can be greatly extended by the same intelligence. Whereas the total amount of the elements in the earth is fixed, it is impossible to say how much of these resources man will find usable and to what extent the elements' availability can be extended by conservative practices. We can be certain, however, that if we work hard to develop and apply creative and conservative processes to the supply problem—and if we are able to prevent continued growth in population—we have a good chance at satisfying our needs far into the future.

What are the creative and conservative processes required? We create resources, not of course as the alchemist hoped to make gold, but by devising ways to use and recover minerals that were not usable or recoverable before. We can also develop methods of finding minerals concealed beneath the surface that could not have been found previously by any economical means. Until now the development and application of such processes for recovering minerals have largely supported our continuing use of minerals. We can therefore expect ongoing creativity in materials science, mineral technology, and geologic science to contribute further to our mineral supply. For example, we have close at hand the technology to mine manganese oxide nodules from the ocean floor. These nodules are also an immense source of copper, nickel, cobalt, and other metals. Tools, methods, and geologic knowledge to support profitable exploration for concealed deposits of this kind are still developing. In the effort to create new resources we must also find ways to substitute abundant for scarce materials.

It is impossible to say how long we could continue to meet mineral needs through such creative processes, but there is much evidence to suggest that it is unwise to rely completely on these methods. While there is not yet a minerals crisis, trends in mineral supply have been developing in a pattern similar to those preceding the energy crisis. This does not suggest that we are running out but rather that we may be straining our ability to meet continually growing demands for particular minerals. Worrisome also is the fact that as we mine and process progressively lower grade ores, we require progressively larger amounts of energy. In addition, progressively larger areas are subjected to environmental risk and strain and possibly to irreparable environmental damage if appropriate precautions are not taken in mining and processing.

We should therefore place much more emphasis on the processes of extending mineral supply. More conservative use and the avoidance of waste are essential, for at some point, as indicated earlier, continued growth in consumption must inevitably cease. Desirable also are increased recycling of materials and increased efficiency in the utilization of these materials. Technological advances that make it possible to accomplish the same function with only half the materials used previously or with twice the life in use add to the supply just as would a new discovery. Steps that lead to conservation in use and recycling can therefore greatly extend the life of a fixed supply.

100% recycling

Another dividend from these conservation practices is that such efforts lessen environmental strain. Environmental damage results from consumption and waste as well as from the production of raw materials. For this reason conservation in use may contribute as much to the maintenance of environmental quality as will the avoidance of waste and recycling. If we recognize that pollution is for the most part waste of potentially usable materials, we can go a long way in helping to solve both supply and environmental problems.

The contingencies referred to earlier in response to the question about the availability of future supplies depend, then, on our ability to control population growth, to continue to improve materials, minerals, and geologic science, and to further develop and adopt conservation practices. The adoption of conservation practices offers perhaps the most difficult challenge. It will necessitate developing an economic system and perhaps a way of life that are very different from those to which we are accustomed. Conservation of use, leading to the creation of market surpluses and curtailment of production, could be almost as disruptive as material shortages. A steady-state economy might also be a stagnant one in which the incentives to creativity are greatly reduced. Controls introduced for conservation of use, avoidance of waste, and recycling might result in the loss of some of the freedoms we value so highly and in other undesirable consequences of a highly regulated life. These are not inevitable results of the extensive adoption of conservation practices, but we will have to exercise social, economic, and political ingenuity to avoid them. Difficult as it may be to bring about mineral conservation in relatively painless ways, such efforts are a prerequisite to the development of continuing mineral supplies for the future.

Summary

Most ore minerals occur either as uncombined native elements or chemically combined with sulfur and oxygen. Nonmetallic mineral deposits include a variety of rocks and minerals like chlorides, carbonates, and sulfates, along with common quartz or rare diamond. A mineral deposit's value is determined by the costs of extracting, processing, refining, and transporting the product. Variations in these costs may make a marginal deposit sometimes worth mining, other times not.

Special circumstances accompanying ordinary geologic processes may concentrate metallic and nonmetallic minerals. Igneous and metamorphic processes include magmatic segregation of crystals developed early or late during cooling, contact metamorphism of surrounding rock by the intruding magma, and later hydrothermal solutions that penetrate the intrusion.

Sedimentary processes include evaporation of seawater and differential transportation and sedimentation of mineral grains, which concentrate valuable minerals and rocks. Chemical weathering can increase minerals in low initial abundance by removing less valuable materials and leaving a residue enriched in valuable ones.

Processes that produce mineral deposits can operate over broad regions. Therefore, one mineral deposit may well indicate that there are others in the area. Theories of plate tectonics provide new insights into possible global trends in mineral deposition, even though the relatively rare occurrence of mineral deposits and the long time required for their generation make them nonrenewable, finite resources. World demand for minerals grows not only with population but also with rising living standards. Consequently, mineral demands are increasing exponentially, requiring that we use poorer grades of ore for many metals; this in turn creates greater energy demands and potential environmental problems arising from disposal of large quantities of rock waste. Although some minerals soon will be in short supply, in general the rising demand for minerals will probably be met. Longer-term demands, however, will require continued mineral exploration; recent advances in high-altitude reconnaissance of the land and deep sea exploration may open up new and significant deposits.

Glossary

contact metamorphism Chemical alteration of preexisting rock at or very near the contact of an intrusive igneous rock.

economic nonmetallics Concentrations of nonmetallic minerals, sediments, or rocks that can be exploited at a profit.

magmatic segregation Particular kind of magmatic differentiation that results in concentration of ore minerals within an igneous rock.

nonrenewable resource Resource exploited by humans at a rate faster than its natural formation.

ore Concentration of metallic minerals that can be exploited at a profit. Ore grade refers to the required proportion of metal in a rock to make it an ore.

placer Sedimentary ore composed of dense, resistant metallic minerals.

secondary enrichment Concentration of ore minerals by weathering that makes a rock of low metallic content into one that can be profitably mined.

Reading Further

Cameron, E.N., ed. 1973. *The Mineral Position of the United States, 1975–2000.* Madison: University of Wisconsin Press. A collection of articles reviewing current and future national demand for minerals.

Rona, P. 1973. "Plate Tectonics and Mineral Resources." *Scientific American,* July, pp. 86–95. How plate tectonics provides clues to the location of mineral deposits.

Skinner, B. 1969. *Earth Resources.* Englewood Cliffs, N.J.: Prentice-Hall. A summary of metallic, nonmetallic, water, and energy resources.

U.S. Geological Survey. 1973. *United State Mineral Resources.* U.S. Geological Survey Professional Paper 820, Washington, D.C. A comprehensive survey of sixty-four mineral and fuel commodities.

Energy 2

The energies of our system will decay, the glory of the sun will be dimmed, and the earth, tideless and inert, will no longer tolerate the race which has for a moment disturbed its solitude.

Arthur J. Balfour, 1895

After the air we breathe, the water we drink, and the food we eat, energy ranks as our next essential resource. When humans discovered the use of fire, we began exploiting the earth's energy resources to support life and raise it above the level of bare subsistence. From fire, we moved on to a dependence on animals to carry loads, plow fields, and transport people. Before long, we were exploiting coal, oil, and gas for our expanding energy needs. And now it appears that nuclear fuels will satisfy more and more of our world's energy demands.

Our reliance on the earth's energy resources has spiraled upward, until today virtually everything we use and do somehow depends on energy. Transportation of food to urban areas, where most of the world's population lives, depends on energy; without it contemporary urban existence would be sharply curtailed. The manufacture of products as diverse as newsprint, plastics, synthetic fabrics, camping gear, surgical instruments, nuts and bolts, and virtually everything else we use in our daily lives relies on one energy resource or another. (Look around you right now and see if you can find any object that has *not* been produced by oil, gas, or coal.) Our life style thus depends heavily on energy resources. Even though we could surely survive without the benefit of many energy resources, most of us would be seriously inconvenienced.

Energy consumption, like that of mineral resources, is closely correlated to a nation's gross national product, as you can see in Figure 2–1. Although we cannot equate GNP with standard of living, they are closely related. Not only are we dependent on energy for our living standard, but in the United States during the early 1970s, total energy consumption was doubling every 14 years, while electrical energy consumption was doubling every 10 years. The sharp rise mainly has been due to the increase in per capita consumption, rather than general population growth, which until recently had been doubling only every 70 years.

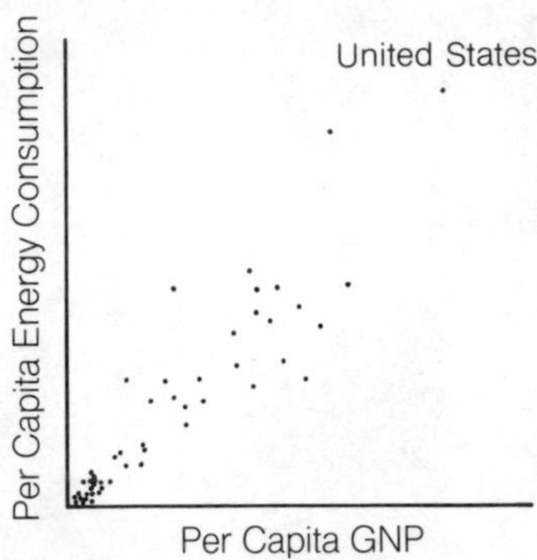

Figure 2–1

Increase in energy consumption per capita GNP for 50 countries. As world population increases—it will double in the next 35 years—and as the global standard of living increases, energy consumption will proportionally increase.

With 6 percent of world population, the United States now consumes about 35 percent of the world's energy. Presumably, as other nations raise their living standards, we can expect rapidly accelerating energy demands throughout the world.

In this chapter we discuss the energy resources of the earth, including fossil fuels of coal, oil, and gas; nuclear and geothermal energy; and solar and water energy. We examine the geologic conditions under which these resources occur, where they are located, and what their current reserves are judged to be.

2-1 Coal, a Long-lived Resource

Coal was an early energy source for humans. Today it is still a dominant fuel, although it has been superseded by oil and gas in the United States since the end of World War II; see Figure 2–2. Reasons for this decline include rising costs of mining and transporting coal as compared with oil and gas, as well as the high sulfur content of many coal deposits. (When high-sulfur coal is burned, the sulfur escapes as sulfur dioxide gas which is toxic to animals and plants.) With decreasing domestic production of oil and gas, coal will undoubtedly regain its position as a principal energy source. The world's coal reserves are much larger than those of oil and gas, and in the next century coal and nuclear power may well supply most of the world's energy.

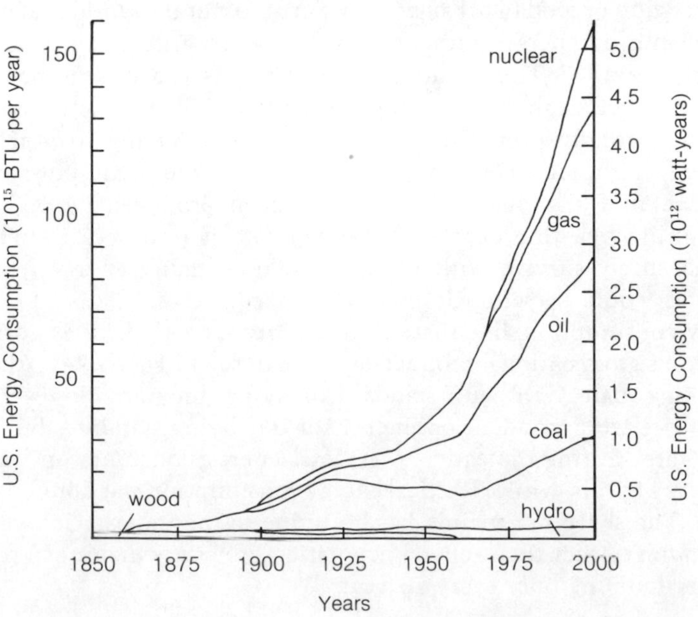

Figure 2–2

The rapid increase of U.S. energy consumption during the last century. Note the changing contribution of wood, coal, oil, and gas in the past, and the increasing reliance on nuclear power and coal in the future.

Origin and distribution

Coal is a sedimentary rock rich in carbon derived from ancient, swamp-dwelling plants. When organic matter preserved from these plants burns, it generates heat and produces carbon dioxide. It also gives off small amounts of sulfur dioxide and mineral ash (mostly from sand and silt buried with the plants in the coal beds).

Coal deposits form in areas of low relief where there is poor surface drainage, for instance, deltas, coastal plains, and broad interior lowlands. In these areas warm temperatures and abundant rainfall support a lush vegetation. Low relief regions permit relatively little erosion and lowered sediment influx, and swampy drainage helps plants to accumulate faster than they can oxidize or be decomposed by microorganisms. The land also subsides to allow thick deposits of dead plant material to accumulate. Periodic intervals of sedimentation by shifting rivers, fluctuating sea levels, or epeirogenic uplift interrupt plant accumulation by burying them in layers of sand or mud. Over time, the pressure of overlying sediments compacts the plant layers and removes much of their water and volatile substances. As these are removed, the plant materials transform into peat, lignite, bituminous, and anthracite coal—as carbon content progressively increases. And, in general, as the carbon content increases, so does the coal's heat value, as seen in Figure 2–3.

Geologic conditions favoring coal deposition are much like those prevalent today in the Florida Everglades. The presence of warm-climate plants in Arctic and Antarctic coals points to past tropical climates in these regions—further evidence for continental drift. It has been estimated that, to produce one meter of coal, it takes several centuries of plant growth and accumulation in such tropical conditions. Because of this slow rate

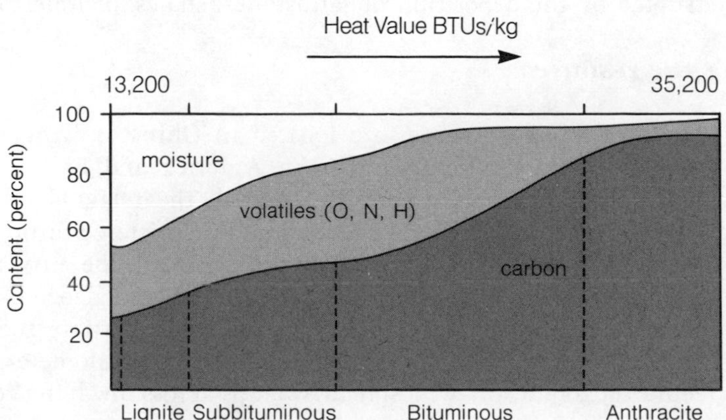

Figure 2–3

Grades of coal defined by content of moisture, volatiles, and carbon. Note that heat value of coal increases with carbon content.

The unit of heat, BTU, stands for British Thermal Unit and is the amount of heat required to raise 1 pound of water (about 1 pint) 1 degree Fahrenheit.

Mechanized underground mining of coal in Pennsylvania. More than 3700 metric tons of coal a day are excavated and carried to the surface on a conveyor belt that lies next to the digging machine.

of formation, coal is virtually a nonrenewable resource.

Sedimentary rocks of diverse ages contain coal deposits. The coal usually occurs in thin seams measuring a meter or less in width. The seams recur at intervals throughout a thick section of sedimentary rocks, like those in Figure 2–4. The coals in Figure 2–4 were deposited in freshwater environments marginal to a late Cretaceous sea that covered much of this area some 100 million years ago. Note that the coal-forming environments migrated eastward with time as the sea gradually withdrew. Coarse alluvial rocks, like conglomerates and sandstones, accumulated on the landward side of the coal swamps, while shallow marine sandstones and offshore shales were deposited seaward of the swamps. The interfingering of these various sedimentary rocks records constant shifting back and forth of their environments. These intervals record periodic episodes of swamp conditions interrupted by the deposition of sandstones, shales, or limestones.

Tapping the resource

Most of the world's coal resources are located in China and the Soviet Union; lesser amounts are found in North America and Europe. The southern hemisphere has only a small fraction of the total, as you can see in Table 2–1. In the United States, coal deposits are scattered throughout the country, with significant resources in thirty-six of the fifty states indicated in Figure 2–5. Much of the coal occurs in late Paleozoic rocks of the eastern United States and in late Mesozoic and Tertiary rocks of the western states. Covering many thousands of square kilometers, the deposits record geographically widespread swamps across low-lying coastal plains which formed tens to hundreds of millions of years ago.

One metric ton of coal yields about 28 million BTUs.

Of the more than 1400 billion metric tons of coal resources in this

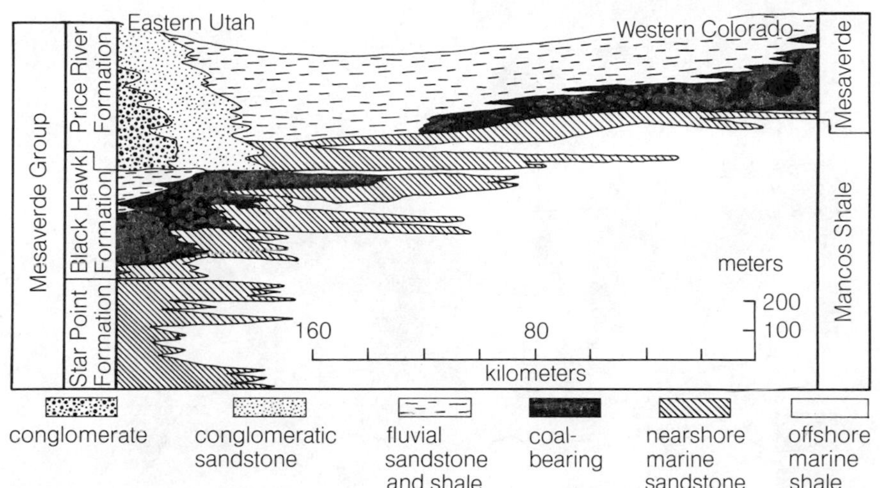

Figure 2–4

Stratigraphic cross section of Upper Cretaceous rocks of eastern Utah and western Colorado showing coal-bearing strata.

country, only about 350 billion metric tons (some 25 percent) are economically recoverable by present strip-mining techniques. Three-quarters of the coal that can be surface-mined is low-sulfur coal, defined as containing less than 1 percent sulfur. The decline in domestic oil and gas production, combined with a need for low-sulfur or "nonpolluting" coal, has led to more intense strip mining. Even more important for the coal industry, the productivity of surface mines, currently averaging more than 18 tons per man-day, is more than twice that of underground mines.

The cost of shipping low sulfur coal by railroad from the West is sufficiently high that East Coast power plants now find it cheaper to import low sulfur coal from Poland by boat.

At present, more than half of the coal mined in the United States comes from *strip mines,* which are becoming more common. But several unfavorable consequences arise from this surface mining. When vegetative soil cover is removed, the exposed loose sediment easily erodes and moves into neighboring streams. The streams, in turn, choke with sediment and upset the natural water drainage. Carbon and sulfur compounds in the surface-mining debris oxidize and produce acids that contaminate natural

Table 2–1 World Coal Resources (10^9 metric tons)

	Identified	Predicted	Estimated Total
Asia	6370	3640	10,010
North America	1565	2621	4186
Europe	564	189	753
Africa	73	146	219
Oceania	55	64	119
South and Central America	18	9	27
Total	8645	6669	15,314

Figure 2–5

Major coal occurrences in the United States. Anthracite is restricted to northeastern Pennsylvania, and most bituminous coal is found in the eastern states. Most of the coal in the western states is subbituminous and lignite.

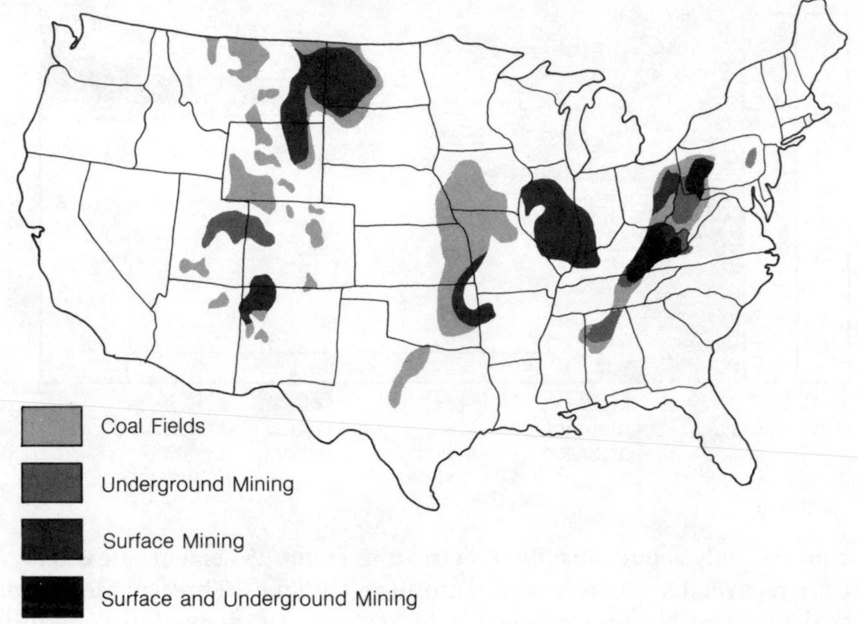

waters and harm the local fauna and flora. These undesirable effects can be reduced significantly, however, if the land is regraded and revegetated after removal of the coal.

2–2 Oil and Gas, Less Predictable Fuels

Oil and gas, like coal, are products of fossil remains buried in sediments. But unlike coal, which is terrestrial in origin, the organic matter that forms oil and gas derives from aquatic plants—usually marine. Some oil shales accumulated in ancient freshwater lakes; these are the exception. Also, the distribution of oil and gas is more irregular and unpredictable than that of coal. Sulfur content in oil also poses an environmental problem; however, the sulfur can be removed during refining.

These liquid and gaseous fluids migrate readily from their source rocks, and may concentrate in porous and permeable rocks from which they are recovered by subsurface drilling. While the trend has been to go from underground to surface mining for coal, gas and oil drilling has penetrated ever deeper as the more obvious, shallow reservoirs have been discovered and used. Estimates of oil and gas resource depletion indicate it will be more rapid than coal. Peak world production of the two fuels will probably come within the next few decades and decline thereafter, while peak world production of coal and its subsequent decline probably won't occur for a few centuries.

Estimates for time of U.S. peak oil production range from the early 1970s to the mid 1980s. Domestic gas production has already peaked.

Origin and accumulation

Oil and gas are organic substances composed mainly of hydrogen and carbon. They also contain minor amounts of nitrogen, oxygen, and sulfur slowly generated from the natural decomposition of plant matter buried in sediments. A small part of abundant life in the seas—especially floating phytoplankton—eventually ends up on the sea floor, where microorganisms and scavengers feed on it or oxygen dissolved in seawater oxidizes it. Usually organic matter is deposited on the sea floor faster than it decomposes, so a portion of it gets buried with the accumulating sediments. Most marine sediments contain only about 1 percent or less of organic matter. Occasionally, though, the sea's bottom waters become depleted in oxygen, thereby eliminating bottom scavengers and microorganisms, and organic matter abounds on the sea floor. Also, under ocean areas where plant production is high, sediments contain unusually large amounts of organic matter.

So as the sea floor subsides, a thick pile of organic-rich sediments accumulates. With continued burial, rising temperature and pressure cause large, complex molecules in the organic matter to break down into simple ones. These simpler ones form crude oil and natural gas, and are called *hydrocarbons.* The breakdown, or natural "cracking" process, begins at depths of 450 meters and continues with burial. It is analogous to the cracking process carried out in oil refineries when heavy crude oils are broken into lighter, more volatile components like gasoline and kerosene.

The sedimentary rocks where hydrocarbons form are the *source rocks;* the concentration of hydrocarbons there is too low for profitable exploitation. Rather, the oil and gas in source rocks must migrate into porous and permeable *reservoir rocks* where they can accumulate in large enough quantities for subsequent recovery by drilling. Because hydrocarbons are less dense than the water also residing in sedimentary rocks, the hydrocarbons rise upward until they reach the earth's surface or some impermeable stratum that obstructs further movement. If the hydrocarbons reach the surface, the gas is lost to the atmosphere, while the oil is oxidized and becomes a sticky tar that eventually may seal off the seepage. Virtually all hydrocarbon deposits, however, are recovered from subsurface geologic structures like anticlines and fossil reefs that have trapped large amounts of migrating oil and gas in the pores of their rocks (Figure 2–6). Not only must the reservoir rocks, like sandstones and limestones, be porous enough to provide ample space for the oil and gas, but the pores must be interconnected. That is, when the reservoir is tapped by drilling, the hydrocarbons must be able to flow freely through the pores toward the well.

A productive gas or oil well requires a source of rock for the hydrocarbons to form, a porous and permeable reservoir rock where they can accumulate, and a geologic structure that traps and concentrates the accumulation so it can build up. As with mineral deposits, economic factors also determine if a well is profitable. Obviously, the market price of oil and gas must be greater than costs of exploration, drilling, recovery, refining, and transportation to market.

Finding the needle in a haystack

Exploration for oil and gas is much more difficult than for coal. Coal is solid and cannot be drawn up a well as a fluid can. Thus exploration

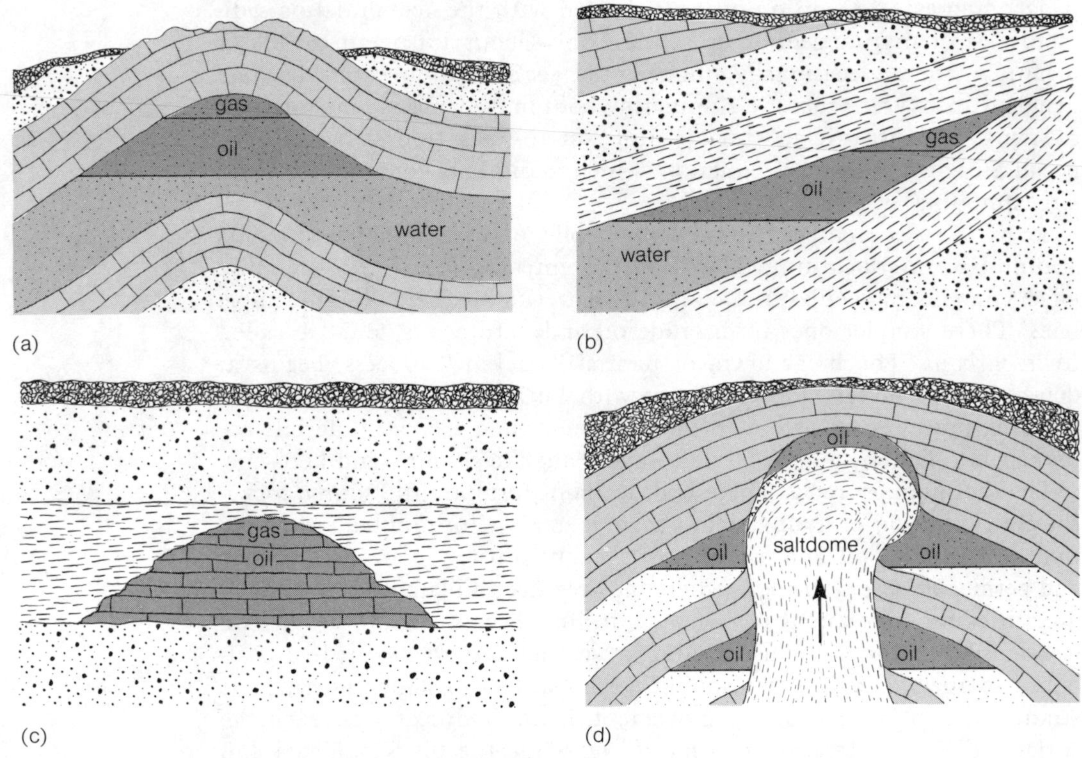

Figure 2–6

Common geologic structures that trap oil and gas in the subsurface. In each case, the oil and gas originated in organic-rich source rocks and migrated to a favorable structure where they accumulated in abundance. (a) Oil and gas in the crest of an anticline; the less dense oil floats on dense salt water within the sandstone. (b) Oil and gas in a sandstone that is overlain unconformably by an impervious shale. (c) Oil in a reef limestone surrounded by impervious shales. (d) Oil in the upturned portions of porous sandstones that have been penetrated by a slowly rising salt dome. The salt is less dense than the overlying rocks, so it rises slowly from a horizontal stratum of salt and deforms the overlying rocks as it moves up.

for coal is necessarily limited to surface or shallow subsurface occurrences, and is guided by knowledge of ground surface geology. Oil and gas, however, can be profitably recovered from depths up to several thousands of meters. Unfortunately, there are many subsurface reservoirs whose existence bears little or no relation to our knowledge of geologic conditions at the surface. Consequently, the effort and time required to find new oil and gas deposits are now very large, and will increase as shallower, easier-to-find deposits diminish in number.

Aerial view of Oil Mountain, an oil-producing anticline in Wyoming.

Exploration techniques include aerial and ground surveys to determine regional geology and drilling to ascertain subsurface geologic conditions. Once a potentially suitable geologic structure is found, the needle-in-a-haystack hunt begins. The search is for *possible* hydrocarbons because the oil and gas pool may occupy only a small part of the structure, or there may not be any hydrocarbons at all. For each successful well, about ten exploratory wells have to be drilled. If a reservoir is found, *production wells* are drilled to recover the hydrocarbons.

To discover a million-barrel oil field, 50 to 100 exploratory wells may have to be drilled.

Both exploratory and production wells are drilled with a rotating bit made of extremely resistant steel. A muddy fluid is circulated down the hole to cool the bit, lubricate the drilling, and clean out the hole by removing small chips of rocks, some of which are used for geologic study. The drilling mud also provides counterpressure to prevent any subsurface fluids from blowing uncontrollably out of the hole. Such fluids are under pressure that increases with depth, and a well that gushes out of control endangers lives, pollutes the environment, wastes a valuable resource, and costs money. So the typical oil gusher scene is a romantic image that survives from early exploration days and, today, one that is to be avoided.

Reaching the supplies

The distribution of hydrocarbon production and proven reserves is limited to areas of unmetamorphosed sedimentary rocks, as shown in Figure 2–7. Sedimentary rocks provide both the source and the reservoir rocks for almost all oil and gas. If the rocks are too deformed and metamorphosed, though, the hydrocarbons are lost. Areas of igneous and metamorphic

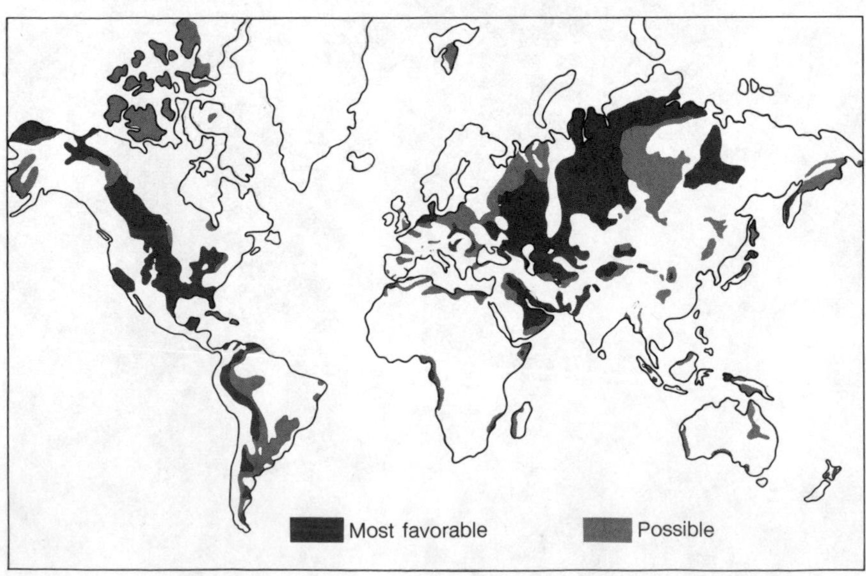

Figure 2–7

Oil map of the world. Most favorable sites for oil and gas are in regions of thick, undeformed marine sedimentary rocks; they lie outside of Precambrian shields of crystalline rocks and highly deformed and metamorphosed parts of mountain systems.

Table 2–2 World Crude Oil Production, January 1974

	Million Barrels per Day	Percent
Western Hemisphere	**15.9**	29
United States	8.9	
Venezuela	3.3	
Canada	1.8	
other	1.9	
Middle East	**20.8**	38
Saudi Arabia	7.5	
Iran	6.1	
Kuwait	2.8	
other	4.4	
Africa	**5.7**	10
Nigeria	2.2	
Libya	2.0	
other	1.5	
Far East	**2.4**	4
Indonesia	1.4	
Malaysia	0.4	
Australia	0.4	
other	0.2	
Europe and Asia	**10.5**	19
USSR	8.9	
China	0.9	
other	0.7	
Total World	55.3	100

rocks are therefore unlikely prospects for oil and gas production. Within the large areas of the earth underlaid with thick deposits of sedimentary rocks, oil and gas fields are irregularly distributed. In part, this irregularity reflects differing degrees of exploration, but apparently it also results from irregular and still unpredictable geologic factors that control the formation and accumulation of hydrocarbons.

The large oil and gas producers today, indicated in Table 2–2, are North America (West Coast, Gulf Coast, and midcontinent regions), Venezuela, the Middle East, the Soviet Union, northern Africa, and Southeast Asia. Since World War II, offshore sedimentary rocks have been good producers. Much present-day exploration is being pursued on the continental shelves, especially those of northwestern Europe, West and Gulf coasts of the United States, and Southeast Asia. Interest in possible continental shelf deposits along the Atlantic Coast of the United States has grown considerably. One expert has noted that the continental shelf area south of Cape Hatteras, North Carolina, has much in common geologically with the oil-rich deposits of Saudi Arabia.

Because of the unpredictable distribution of oil and gas deposits, estimates of future hydrocarbon resources vary widely. The assumptions behind such estimates are not uniformly reliable, and depending on the estimater's viewpoint and experience, estimates come in high and low. Current estimates of future U.S. oil production range from 28 to 56 billion metric tons, or 200 to 400 billion barrels. At present rates of annual oil consumption—more than 6 billion barrels—these yet-to-be-discovered domestic resources would be used up in a generation or two; see Figure 2–8. But with oil consumption doubling every twenty years, these resources would not last much beyond the year 2000.

We discuss the various levels of certainty associated with such estimates in Chapter 6.

One metric ton of crude oil yields about 40 million BTUs; it is equivalent to 7 barrels of oil, with each barrel containing 42 gallons.

Tar sands and oil shales

Hydrocarbons also occur as tar in sandstones that cannot be produced by subsurface wells. Mining and heating these tar sands removes the tar, which is then refined to oil. The Athabasca Sand in Alberta Province, Canada, contains an estimated 600 billion barrels of oil (84 billion metric tons)—an amount equal to the total known and inferred petroleum resources of the world! Current production from the Athabasca Sand yields 45,000 barrels of oil from 90,000 metric tons of sand mined daily.

Oil shale is another organic-rich sedimentary rock of both freshwater and marine origin. Strip mining can extract the shales' widely dispersed hydrocarbons. The Green River Shales of Colorado, Wyoming, and Utah cover an area of hundreds of thousands of square kilometers and lie at or near the ground surface. A yield of 1800 billion barrels of oil (252

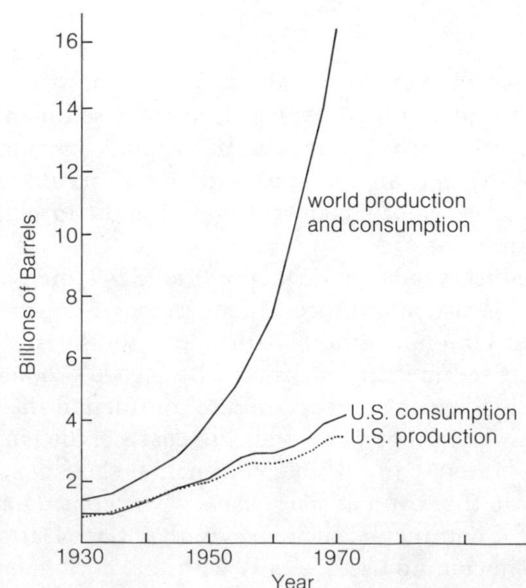

Figure 2–8

World and domestic crude oil production and consumption. Note the sharp rise in world production and consumption following World War II, and the increasing gap in U.S. production and consumption. In 1940, the United States used about half the world's oil; in 1970 this ratio dropped to about one-quarter.

billion metric tons) has been projected from a portion of these shales, which average 150 liters of oil per metric ton of shale. Although these shales have not yet been commercially exploited, booming national energy demands and declining domestic resources of petroleum may make their eventual use inevitable. As with coal, strip mining oil shales can have widespread harmful environmental side effects. In particular, every cubic meter of oil shale that is processed produces 1.3 cubic meters of waste rock. Moreover, for each barrel of oil produced, 1 to 2 barrels of water is consumed and almost another barrel of water would be needed for waste disposal. Consequently, large amounts of water are needed to produce oil from oil shale, but most oil shale deposits occur in arid and semi-arid regions of the United States.

One liter equals 1000 cubic centimeters and is equivalent to 0.264 gallons.

Processing of oil shale results in an expansion of the shale of about 30 percent.

2-3 Nuclear Fuels

In the last several decades, a radically new energy source has been developed from the nuclear interactions of certain radioactive isotopes. In the *fission process* of nuclear energy generation, neutrons bombard uranium-235 atoms and break them down into other isotopes. The breakdown triggers a tremendous energy release which can be used to generate steam to drive turbines that produce electricity. A single gram of U^{235} releases energy equal to 2.7 metric tons of coal, or 13.7 barrels of oil. In the *fusion process* of energy generation, the combination of two hydrogen isotopes, deuterium and tritium, releases a similar large amount of energy. The deuterium derived from a cubic meter of sea water can release energy equal to 269 metric tons of coal or 1360 barrels of oil.

In this section we discuss only the nuclear fuels necessary for fission because energy from fusion is not likely to be produced commercially in the near future. However, when fusion reactors do become practical, the large amount of deuterium available in sea water will be five hundred thousand times the energy available in the world's total supply of fossil fuels—past, present, and future.

Uranium and thorium

Uranium isotopes that power fission reactors are found in such uranium-bearing minerals as *uraninite,* or pitchblende, a uranium oxide; *coffinite,* a hydrous uranium silicate; and *carnotite,* a hydrous vanadium and uranium oxide. Present-day commercial nuclear reactors are *nuclear fuel burners* which use the scarce U^{235} isotope in a controlled fission reaction to generate heat, as explained in Figure 2-9. Because U^{235} is only 0.7 percent of natural uranium—which itself accounts for a mere two parts per million (0.0002 percent) of the earth's crust—scientists are experi-

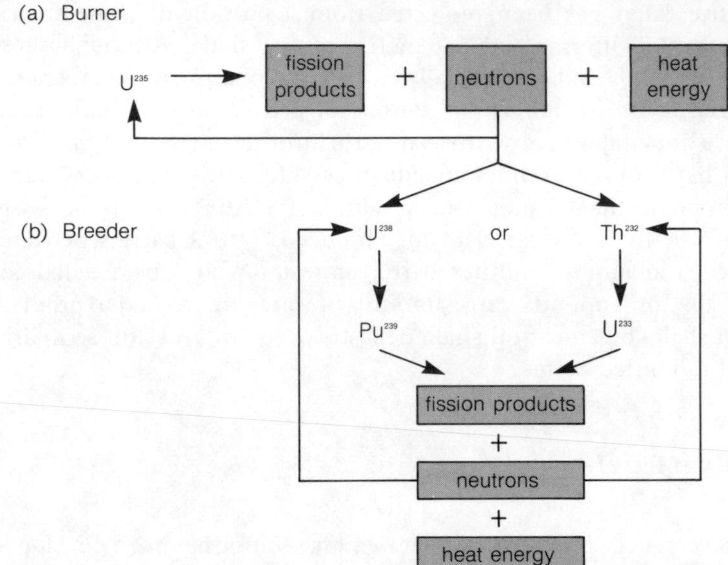

Figure 2–9

Simplified diagram of burner and breeder fission reactions for generating heat that can be converted to electricity. (a) In a burner reactor, the spontaneous fission of U^{235} produces heat and neutrons that maintain the fission process. (b) Uranium-235 can be used as starter fuel in a breeder reactor so that the neutrons bombard either U^{238} or thorium-232, transforming them into plutonium-239 or U^{233}. The latter will then spontaneously undergo fission, producing heat and more neutrons that maintain the breeder reaction.

menting with *breeder reactors* that can use the relatively more abundant isotopes of U^{238} and thorium-232. The latter are not themselves fissionable, but they can be converted by neutron bombardment from U^{235} to fissionable plutonium-239 and uranium-233. Thus, even breeder reactors need initial amounts of U^{235} to start the nuclear reactions subsequently taken over by U^{238} and Th^{232}.

As a result of our growing domestic energy demands, by the year 2000, nuclear-generated power may supply as much as 60 percent of the total electricity in the United States. If this energy is provided by burner reactors alone, the demand for uranium will steadily increase. If, as some experts believe, breeder reactors replace burners in the mid-1980s, then the demand for uranium would return to the relatively low, current level described in Figure 2–10. Only a small amount of uranium is needed to start up the breeders, which use thorium as well as uranium.

Uranium prospects

Current identifiable domestic resources of uranium amount to 250,000 metric tons, enough to supply the U.S. nuclear power industry until the early 1980s. World demand for uranium during this decade is estimated at 600,000 metric tons, while the world's uranium resources are calculated at almost 1.5 million metric tons. If breeder reactors are not in production by the year 2000, clearly, new sources of uranium will have to be developed to meet projected domestic and global demands.

Uranium originates from magmas, crystallizing as a minor mineral like uraninite, or combining with other minerals in igneous rocks. Upon weathering, uranium-bearing igneous rocks release their uranium minerals in two forms. Either they are released as clastic sedimentary grains that may form placer deposits, or else as dissolved uranium ions from chemical weathering that are later precipitated on to clays or organic matter found in sediments. Ore-grade deposits require a uranium enrichment of about one thousand times the average crustal concentration.

Virtually all identifiable and recoverable uranium ores in the United States are in freshwater and marine sandstones, which average 0.2 percent uranium (or the equivalent of 2 kilograms per ton). Uranium minerals occur chiefly as uraninite and coffinite in the pore spaces of the sandstones. Sometimes, however, they actually chemically replace or substitute for atoms of what were originally sand grains or plant fossils. Some fossil logs discovered in Colorado were almost completely replaced by carnotite, and each was worth a small fortune to its discoverer! Most uranium resources are located in New Mexico and Wyoming, with smaller deposits in Texas, Colorado, and Utah. (Figure 2–11 shows a uranium strip mine in Wyoming.) Uranium is also presently recovered as a by-product from the processing of phosphate rocks and copper ores. Although not exploited today, large, low-grade uranium resources are contained in some widespread, marine organic shales and in a few granite intrusions. Strip mining of these shales and granites would produce huge surface excavations and enormous amounts of rock waste.

Because breeder reactors are not yet commercially feasible, the demand for thorium is small. Most thorium is supplied as a by-product of mining titanium and other elements. Consequently, thorium resources are not well known, although thorium-bearing hydrothermal veins in igneous and metamorphic rocks in the western United States may well be a valuable future resource for this element.

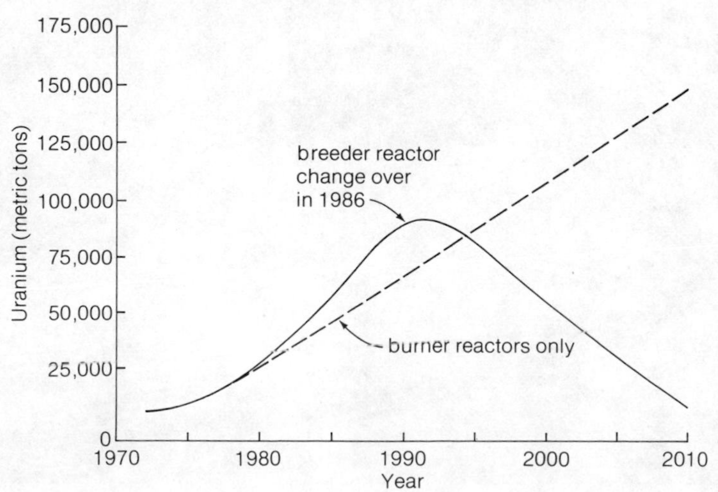

Figure 2–10

Future uranium demand for nuclear reactors. If only burners are used, the demand for uranium will steadily increase. But if there is a change to breeder reactors in 1986 with subsequent phasing out of burners, the demand for uranium will decline to about its present level.

2-4 Geothermal Energy, a Clean but Limited Resource

Heat derived from the earth's interior, referred to as *geothermal energy,* is currently serving on a small scale to generate electricity, heat buildings, run air conditioners, warm greenhouses, and process paper and other industrial products. This heat originates at hot spots in the crust close to magmas, and is transferred to circulating underground water. The hot water and steam rise to the ground surface in hot springs or can be tapped by wells.

Many economic and technical factors as well as geologic ones determine the present and future use of geothermal energy as a resource. Therefore, it is difficult to estimate accurately its magnitude. One informed calculation puts the world's potential geothermal resources at approximately equal to 280 billion metric tons of coal or 1420 billion barrels of oil, with 5 to 10 percent of this energy resource available within the United States. (This domestic supply would last about 100 years at the 1975 U.S. annual rate of energy consumption.)

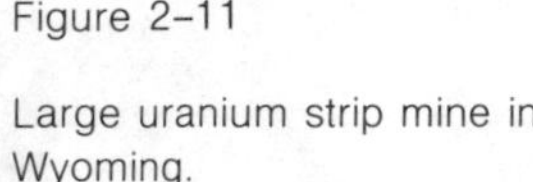

Figure 2–11

Large uranium strip mine in Wyoming.

Origins and distribution

The temperature of the earth's crust increases with depth. This heat comes from the decay of radioactive isotopes in the crust and upper mantle, as well as from the residual heat of planetary formation in the lower mantle and core. Most of this heat cannot be tapped, because wells would have to be drilled to depths of 10 kilometers or more to reach rocks with sufficiently high temperatures. However, hot spots scattered around the world, particularly near plate boundaries, have sufficient heat at shallow depths (3 kilometers or less) to provide economically useful energy. For example, almost 400,000 kilowatts of energy come from the geothermal fields in Geyser, California, enough for about half of San Francisco's needs.

A watt is a measure of power, equivalent to one joule per second.

Geothermal heat sources are rocks heated by magmas that raise the temperature of circulating underground water by several hundred degrees. The heated groundwater rises toward the surface through porous and permeable rocks and is replaced by colder water percolating down from the surface above, which is illustrated in Figure 2–12. The geothermally heated steam and hot water may reach the ground surface through a hot spring or a man-made well. Geothermal sources vary in temperature: some are all steam, some are a mixture of steam and water, and others are

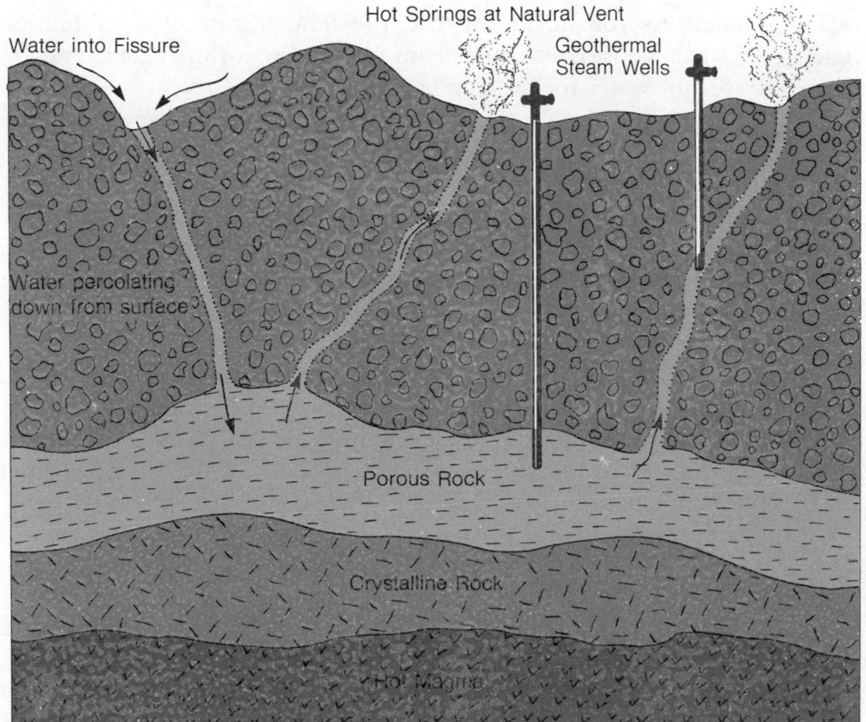

Figure 2–12

Schematic cross section of a geothermal site. Heat from a magma is conducted through crystalline rock to underground water in overlying rocks. Water heated to several hundred degrees is tapped by man-made wells, or may escape through natural vents forming hot springs at the surface. Cooler surface water percolates downward from above and replenishes the underground water supply.

Terraces of calcium carbonate deposits precipitated by hot springs in Yellowstone National Park as seen in the late nineteenth century.

just hot water. As you might suppose, the temperature of a geothermal field determines its uses: whether steam for driving turbines that generate electricity or hot water for heating buildings.

Several experimental geothermal fields are being developed in hot, dry rock; wells are drilled into the rock which is then fractured with explosives and surface water is circulated through it.

In addition to use for electricity or other purposes like space heating and industrial processing, the water that condenses from the steam can provide safe drinking water as well as elements like boron, potassium, lithium, and calcium. The lifetime of a geothermal source is twenty-five to fifty years, depending on how much heat is recovered, how fast the underground water is replenished, and how long the pipes last before they are fouled by minerals precipitated from the water and steam.

Although geothermal power was first harnessed in the United States in Geyser, California in 1960 (see Figure 2–13), it has been an important energy resource in Italy for most of this century. Other countries which have recently tapped geothermal energy include Mexico, Iceland, the Soviet Union, Japan, and New Zealand. Compared with more conventional sources of energy, particularly fossil and nuclear fuels, geothermal energy has minimal environmental impact. It doesn't pollute the air, produce dangerous radioactive wastes, or require large-scale alterations in the landscape. But there are several possible side-effects of geothermal energy use. First, the local surface waters can overheat when hot water is discharged from a geothermal power plant, and salts in the hot water may pollute the waters. Also, the ground surface might subside as a result of massive withdrawals of hot underground water. These undesirable side effects can

Figure 2–13

Steam jets escaping from geothermal wells in Geyser, California.

be eliminated or reduced by returning used water to the subsurface, which also would replenish the supply of underground water.

2-5 Water and Solar Energy

Energy from flowing surface water and direct heat from the sun are also significant energy sources. In some areas, water flowing down rivers and moving in and out with the tides can be harnessed to generate electricity. The disadvantage of such power plants is that they require massive and costly engineering works like dams and hydroelectric stations. And with rivers, these power plants have a lifetime of only a century or two, because streams emptying into the reservoir eventually fill it with sediment.

Solar energy is inexhaustible, and although not yet practical on a major scale for generating electricity, in sunny climates it can heat buildings, run air conditioners, remove salts from seawater, and do many other things. But to generate electricity from solar energy, even on a moderate scale, requires new technology and large expanses of ground or roof surface to collect, store, and transmit the energy.

Water power

Water traveling down stream and river channels can be harnessed to generate power. Before the days of electricity, such energy was widely consumed in textile, saw, and flour mills by diverting the flow through a water wheel. You can still find many examples of these early mills throughout New England and the South. But more recently, water power has been converted to electricity by big dams whose water flows through power-generating turbines.

Estimates place the world's potential water power supplied by rivers at almost 3 million megawatts, of which less than 10 percent is now being utilized; refer to Table 2–3. This potential is three to four times the global electrical power currently consumed. Full development of water resources for power generation would thus provide four times the world's present electricity demand. But as this demand doubles every few decades, water power would be fully consumed in several decades or less. Moreover, such development would require damming virtually every stream and river in the world and would have severe environmental and aesthetic impact. For example, the Aswan Dam in Egypt, while providing irrigation water and electrical power so necessary for that developing country, holds back nutrients and sediments which formerly reached the Nile delta and Mediterranean Sea. As a result, the delta is being seriously eroded, and fishery catches in the eastern Mediterranean have declined drastically. To make matters worse, a water-borne parasite has spread in the reservoir behind the dam, infecting thousands of people living in the region.

A second source of water power is that generated by the rise and fall of tides along coasts. Dams can be built to create holding basins which fill with water at high tide and empty out at low tide. The inflowing and outflowing water drives turbines that generate electricity. Tidal power is harnessed only in embayments and estuaries that can be spanned by a dam, and where the fluctuation in tidal level measures more than 5 to 10 meters. Given these restrictions, less than 25 known sites around the world appear to be practical for harnessing tidal power. Most of them

Table 2–3 World Water Power Capacity (10^3 megawatts)

Region	Potential	Percent of Total	Developed	Percent Developed
Africa	780	27	2	0.4
South America	577	20	5	1
U.S.S.R., China, and Eastern Europe	466	16	16	3
Southeast Asia	455	16	2	0.4
North America	313	11	59	19
Western Europe	158	6	47	30
Australasia	45	2	2	4
Far East	42	1	19	45
Middle East	21	1	—	—
Total	2857	100	152	

(a)

(b)

Hydro and solar energy. (a) Hydroelectric dam in the Swiss Alps. Water trapped behind the dam passes through electricity-generating turbines and then released down the tailrace in lower right. (b) Solar furnace in the French Pyrenees, where research in the economic and efficient conversion of solar energy to electricity is being carried out.

are located in the Bay of Fundy of northeastern North America, and along the northwest coast of France. The potential energy of these sites has been calculated at 13,000 megawatts, a mere one-third of 1 percent of the potential water power available on land.

Solar power

The amount of energy reaching the earth from the sun is enormous and surely will last for many millions of years. Year-round solar energy in sunny climates provides power for heating, air conditioning, and distilling sea water. How practical it is to draw on solar energy to produce large outputs of electricity is still questionable. Even for a medium-sized electrical power plant, the equipment and facilities required for the capture, storage, and transmission of solar energy and its conversion to electricity would span several tens of square kilometers and preclude other uses of the land surface. Some experts believe, nevertheless, that solar energy could be a productive supplement to energy sources already in heavy demand. For instance, solar energy could be exploited more widely for space heating and cooling, for producing artificial fuels from organic wastes and plants grown specifically for fuel production, and for powering solar batteries. These same experts, however, point out that while solar energy is a valuable natural resource, considerable research and development of appropriate technologies must be carried out before this potential is realized.

2-6 The Energy Crisis

In the early 1970s, shortages of home heating oil and gasoline stirred much consternation and discussion about the "energy crisis." Some people charged that the petroleum industry had manipulated the market to raise prices and profits and to generate pressure to build the trans-Alaska oil pipeline. Others claimed that unrealistic demands by environmentalists were severely limiting construction of new fossil and nuclear power plants. Still others asserted that affluent America was simply wasting exorbitant amounts of energy. The public needed more foreign oil, but the controlling governments in the Middle East and North Africa cut back on imports to exert pressure on the United States to settle the conflicts between Israel and its neighbors.

The energy crisis is obviously a complex issue, incorporating all the elements that bear on a nation's use of its natural resources: geologic, technologic, economic, political, and social. For that reason the energy crisis is worth examining, if only briefly, because these nonscientific issues bear on how we exploit resources.

Supply and demand

The Viewpoint by Doell in this chapter considers the problem of energy supply and demand.

Whatever domestic crisis exists in energy obviously results from discrepancies in supply and demand. In absolute terms there are enormous quantities of fossil and nuclear fuels, as well as supplementary forms of energy from geothermal, solar, and water power. On the other side of the coin, there are also enormous demands for the energy provided by these resources. In the early 1970s, the rate of U.S. total energy use rose 5 percent per year, doubling every fourteen years, while the demand for electrical power increased 7 percent per year, doubling every ten years. In the early 1970s, each person in the United States annually consumed more than 400 million BTUs of energy (73 barrels of oil or 16 tons of coal). If these rates of use are maintained by the year 2000, the United States will use *eight* times as much electricity as it did in 1970!

Doubling times can be approximated by dividing the annual rate of increase into 70.

The energy crisis results from this rapidly accelerating rate of demand without an equivalent increase in supply. For instance, in the late 1960s the annual consumption of natural gas was almost twice the annual increase of new domestic reserves. Because natural gas is low in sulfur, and less air-polluting than coal or oil, it is preferred for electrical power generation. But recent shortages in natural gas have forced many power plants to return to coal and oil.

Contrary to popular opinion, electric toothbrushes and electric can openers are not major culprits in this energy demand. Rather, the chief household users of electricity, as measured in kilowatts per year, are: home heating and air conditioning, 25,000; water heating, 4000; freezers, 1700;

frost-free refrigerators, 1700; home lighting, 750; color TV, 500. Radios, toasters and electric toothbrushes account for less than 150 kilowatts per year. But actually, household energy use is responsible for only 14 percent of our total national energy demand. Industry requires 32 percent; utilities, 25 percent; transportation, 24 percent; and other miscellaneous consumption 5 percent. If homes and commercial buildings were properly insulated, if cars were smaller and used less for single-person commuting, if planes flew at capacity rather than half-full as many do now, energy savings might amount to one-third or more.

On the supply side of the energy crisis there is less flexibility than on the demand side. For long-term U.S. energy demands, the supply should be adequate because of the possible availability of breeder nuclear reactors, production of gas from strip-mined coal, and advanced technologies for geothermal and solar power. But until these technical advances are made, and questions of environmental protection and safety are answered, there will be a short-term shortage in oil and gas. For the period from 1970 to 1985, demand for petroleum and natural gas will exceed known domestic reserves, as you can see in Table 2–4. In this table, *known reserves* include proved or explored reserves. *Potential economic resources* include potential unexplored reserves, future potential and inferred reserves that can be reasonably expected to be found and recovered commercially using present technologies. *Submarginal resources* include geologic estimates of known or potential resources not now commercially recoverable with present technology and prices. In the next decade, therefore, unless we significantly curtail energy consumption by more efficient energy use, increasing amounts of oil and gas will have to be imported from abroad. Already in the early 1970s, the United States imported more than one-third of its crude-oil needs.

Table 2–4 United States Fuel Mineral Requirements and Resources, 1970–1985 (Cumulative) (10^{15} BTUs)

Item	Requirement	Known Reserves	Potential Economic Resources	Submarginal Resources
petroleum liquids	650	260	2700	14,000[a]
natural gas	450	300	2100	4500[a]
coal	270	4800	3000	25,000
uranium	200	170	430	475,000
oil shale				80,000
thorium				550,000

[a]Includes U.S. continental slope deposits.

We can predict further that strong economic factors will come into play during this period. The cost of all forms of energy will climb sharply as a consequence of greater demand and fewer supplies. Price hikes will also result from requirements to minimize the environmental impact of obtaining and utilizing our energy resources. In short, the crisis in energy is real, and because its causes are complex and interrelated, solutions will have to be formulated at various levels and within various spheres of our society.

Viewpoint — Richard R. Doell

Richard R. Doell is a research scientist with the U.S. Geological Survey, Menlo Park, California. Dr. Doell was one of the original workers to detect paleomagnetism in ancient rocks; more recently he has turned his attention to national energy needs. In this Viewpoint Dr. Doell emphasizes the importance of examining the demand side of the energy equation, not just the supply of energy.

Our Energy Policy: A Self-Fulfilling Prophecy

The American public was not fully aware of the U.S. "energy crisis" until late in 1973. Yet considerable concern had arisen in professional and governmental circles some years previously. These earlier worries were more of a strategic nature, involving military supplies in case of hostilities, than of an imbalance between supply and demand. But experts turned their attention to overall supply in later years. Let us see how this came about.

Throughout its history, the United States has been a major producer and user of energy in the form of fossil fuels. At the turn of the century coal was the dominant fuel, but the production and use of petroleum, and later natural gas, were growing at such rapid rates that by the end of World War II these liquid and gaseous fuels were a principal resource for energy in this country. Even though U.S. domestic resources were large, in the late 1940s and 1950s, the nation's oil producers found it less expensive and more profitable to explore for and produce petroleum in foreign lands. But U.S. authorities soon recognized the military dangers of the growing reliance on inexpensive foreign supplies and thus took various precautions to ensure that domestic production capabilities were maintained. So long as the nation could, if need be, become self-sufficient, the fact that the percentage of imports continued to rise caused no alarm. And, spurred by abundant cheap energy supplies from both domestic and foreign sources, the nation rapidly increased its energy consumption year after year.

Meanwhile the nation's population was growing, and the gross national product (GNP) was rising so fast that the GNP per capita, that is, per person (which we call the "standard of living"), was increasing exponentially. By and large this economic growth was considered a very desirable feature, and our standard of living was the envy of the world. At the same time, however, both total energy use and energy use per capita were growing exponentially. And we came to believe, rightly or wrongly, that abundant cheap energy was the key to the nation's success and a better way of life. Consequently, over the years the nation has acted on policies that have placed energy prices at artificially low values, and has in this way encouraged greater and greater fuel consumption. Whenever any discrepancy has arisen between projections of future energy "demands" or "needs" and the projections of supplies to meet these demands, we have always increased the supplies since, as an advertisement of the period put it, "a nation that runs on petroleum had better not run short." Moreover, it is easy to encourage greater consumption when you have produced an excess. In fact, it is precisely in this manner that such demand projections became self-fulfilling and led to excess consumption.

In the late 1960s and early 1970s authorities began to realize that this course of action was becoming more and more difficult. Overseas petroleum-producing nations were seriously considering nationalization of their energy industries, often with restrictions on the growth of production rates. The United States' capacity to increase domestic production was gone, that is, the last production-limiting quotas were removed from U.S. wells. In addition, the "environmental movement" began to affect the establishment of new energy production, refining, and use facilities to the extent that these facilities were not ready when planned, and in some cases had to be abandoned.

By 1973 the problems were quite apparent and the political climate was ripe for federal intervention in a more direct manner. In June of 1973, President Nixon asked the Chairman of the Atomic Energy Commission to review the situation and make recommendations for research and development programs that would lead to U.S. energy self-sufficiency by the year 1980. Although the AEC review prompted some consideration of conservation and greater efficiency in energy use, the majority of the recommendations advocated increasing supplies. Indeed, essentially no attention is given in AEC Chairman Dixy Lee Ray's report to the President (*The Nation's Energy Future,* December 1973) to the question of possibly altering the high demands for the future. In fact, the report does not even question whether or not the demand figures are correct or reasonable. The report apparently relies on a projection summary by the Joint Committee on Atomic Energy suggesting that consumption rates by the year 2000 will be two to three times the current rates. The AEC document recommends that, in order to meet the seemingly immutable energy demand, we conduct a massive research and development effort aimed at rapidly increasing production from our remaining oil and gas deposits, vastly expanding coal production, and moving the nation rapidly to dependence on nuclear power, which has yet to be proved a valid long-term energy source. The question remains: how accurate are the demand projections?

Many so-called demand projections are simply projections of past consumption. Others analyze components of demand, such as relative projected price, population levels, income levels, and GNP, but rarely state how these considerations are taken into account. In fact, since as yet we have little data relating exactly how the various components affect demand, it is usually difficult to guess how the projections were actually determined.

Let's consider the projection used by the AEC and others to justify the large research and development proposals. If we are to reach the consumption rates predicted for the year 2000, we will have to increase our consumption at an average growth rate of 3.5 percent per year. Compare this with an average rate of 3.1 percent per year over the past twenty-four-year period, which is itself a significant growth rate and was achieved primarily by a continual reduction of energy prices relative to other commodities. Thus it appears that energy prices will have to decrease even more rapidly in the future if we are to achieve the projected consumption rates. How likely is a continued lowering of prices? It seems to me that almost every known trend is in the opposite direction—that of increasing prices. First, the nation has enacted clean air and clean water legislation to protect the environment from further degradation. In many cases this has raised the costs of producing, refining, and using fossil fuels. Preferential tax treatment for energy companies is currently under attack and certainly there will be no increases in the depletion allowance even if further cuts are not forthcoming in the near future. The removal of tight controls on natural gas price rates for interstate sales and the enactment of health and safety legislation for coal mines are other actions that will substantially raise fuel prices. Finally, because there *are* real shortages, not only of domestic energy resources, but also of other materials necessary for greater energy production, energy is bound to become more expensive. In short, all signs suggest that energy prices will be relatively higher rather than lower in the future.

How much these increased prices will reduce demand in the long run is somewhat uncertain and clearly needs study. Naturally, prices are not the only influence on demand. But it is very difficult to understand how other influences could counteract the price trends sufficiently to lead to the consumption level predicted by the AEC and others.

Authorities are certain that higher energy prices will have many secondary influences and disruptions on American life. The changes envisaged, such as workers moving closer to places of labor, retooling industry to less energy-consuming processes, large-scale adjustment of economic activity away from our present "highway culture" industries, and many others, will all create hardships for many segments of the nation's society. It seems to me that a much greater governmental effort might well be directed toward understanding these and related matters rather than toward the present all-out panic campaign to increase supplies. And one might well ask what we can do for an "encore" when the next energy crisis comes along—as it most probably will.

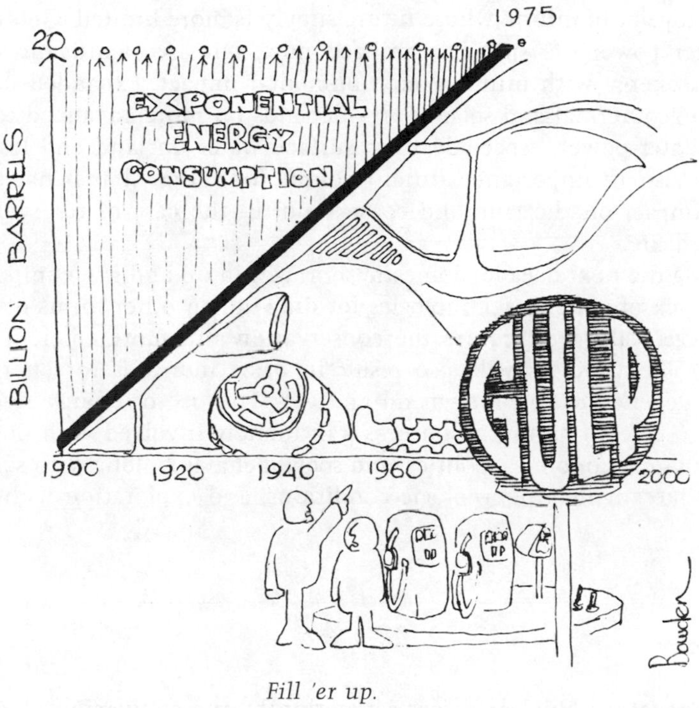

Fill 'er up.

Summary

The fossilized remains of plants may concentrate in solid, liquid, or gaseous accumulations and produce coal, oil, or natural gas. Coal deposits are nonmarine in origin, while those of oil and gas are mostly marine. At an ever-accelerating rate, coal is being strip-mined from the earth's surface, whereas oil and gas must be sought in ever-deeper crustal structures or offshore on the continental shelves. Coal reserves are vast, those of oil and gas much smaller. Peak global production of oil and gas will be reached in the next few decades, but coal will not reach peak production for several centuries. Large, low-grade deposits of fossil fuels also exist in tar sands and oil shales; these resources will undoubtedly be exploited when technologies are developed for utilizing these substances efficiently and economically. As with coal, however, strip mining of tar sands and oil shales will have large-scale environmental impact.

Once breeder reactors become widely available, their nuclear fuels of uranium and thorium will presumably be adequate for many years to come. Present-day burner reactors, on the other hand, use the much scarcer U^{235} isotope of uranium, whose future supply is more limited. Geothermal and solar power are sparingly utilized now, but are significant sources of clean energy with minimal environmental impact. Expanded development of geothermal and solar energy depends on more advanced technologies. Water power, especially from surface water on land and less from tides, is also an important natural resource for energy, but it has considerable impact on the land and coasts, and, in the case of reservoirs, has a limited life.

During the next decade, domestic shortages in oil and gas, compounded by the lack of suitable technologies for drawing on other forms of energy on a large scale, will require the conservation and more efficient use of energy. These factors will also result in price increases for energy and greater dependence on foreign oil and gas. The use of energy resources, therefore, like all natural resources, is intimately involved with nonscientific issues of economics, politics, and social behavior, along with scientific factors like engineering, geologic conditions, and exploration techniques.

Glossary

breeder reactor Nuclear power generation by the conversion of radioactive isotopes like U^{238} and Th^{232} to spontaneously fissionable isotopes like Pu^{239} and U^{233}, which produce heat during their continuing radioactive decay.

burner reactor Nuclear power generation that uses naturally occurring, but rare, U^{235}, which undergoes spontaneous fission to produce heat.

fission Splitting of a large, parent atomic nucleus into smaller, daughter nuclei; the slight mass difference between parent and daughter isotopes is converted into energy.

fusion Joining of two, small atomic nuclei into one larger nucleus; the slight difference in masses is converted to energy.

geothermal energy Energy recovered by humans from the natural heat of subsurface rocks.

hydrocarbons Chemical compound containing only hydrogen and carbon; term usually used for oil and gas, which are natural liquid and gaseous hydrocarbons.

reservoir rock Subsurface sedimentary rock in which oil and gas accumulate.

source rock Subsurface sedimentary rock in which oil or gas originate.

Reading Further

American Association for the Advancement of Science. 1974. "Energy." Special issue of *Science,* vol. 184, no. 4134, April 19. Washington, D.C. Series of collected articles dealing with many energy issues, including people and institutions, public policy, economics, fossil and nuclear fuels, and solar and geothermal energy. Well referenced.

Risser, H. E. 1973. "The U.S. Energy Dilemma." Illinois State Geological Survey, *Environmental Geology Notes,* no. 64. Urbana, Illinois. An excellent summary of the current trends in energy consumption, with carefully derived estimates of future energy supplies from fossil fuels, nuclear and geothermal energy, hydroelectric power, oil shale, and solar energy.

Skinner, B. 1969. *Earth Resources.* Englewood Cliffs, N. J.: Prentice-Hall.

U.S. Department of the Interior. 1972. *United States Energy: A Summary Review.* Washington, D.C. A report on energy situations within the United States, with emphasis on natural energy objectives, requirements, and resource and supply problems.

U.S. Geological Survey. 1973. *United States Mineral Resources.* U.S. Geological Survey Professional Paper 820, Washington, D.C. Up-to-date estimates of U.S. energy resources.

Resources and Man. 1969. San Francisco: W. H. Freeman. Widely quoted chapter on global energy resources by M. K. Hubbert.

Water 3

> *One may not doubt that,*
> *somehow, good*
> *Shall come of water and mud;*
> *And sure, the reverent eye*
> *must see*
> *A purpose in liquidity.*
>
> Rupert Brooke, 1913

Of all natural resources, water is undoubtedly the most critical for supporting life in general and human activities in particular. The volume of water composing the hydrosphere is enormous. If the world's total supply of water were poured upon the fifty United States, the land surface would be submerged to a depth of 145 km (90 miles). Yet only a small fraction of this vital liquid is readily available to us because most of the world's water is bound up in the oceans and glacial ice (Figure 3–1).

Unlike mineral deposits and energy sources, water is a *renewable resource:* the cycle of evaporation, precipitation, and surface flow continually replenishes freshwater supplies in a short time. But, as with mineral deposits and energy sources, our demands for water are booming and even short renewal rates may not keep pace with the demand. Increasingly, there will be a need for water to be better managed and for its natural renewal to be supplemented by technology.

In this chapter we consider the hydrologic cycle, the nature and distribution of surface and underground water, the impact of human intervention on the water supply, and finally the current and future resources of water. As you'll see, there is not much we can do to increase the water naturally available to humans. What we can do, however, is limit the wastes we introduce into natural waters, recycle waste water, and use waters of varying qualities for appropriate functions. More and more, management of our natural waters will be required if we are to meet our rising demand for this essential resource.

3-1 The Hydrologic Cycle

The hydrologic cycle, described in Figure 3–2, includes the fall of snow and rain, the flow of streams and rivers to the seas, and the evaporation from seas and lakes into the atmosphere. Every year, large quantities of

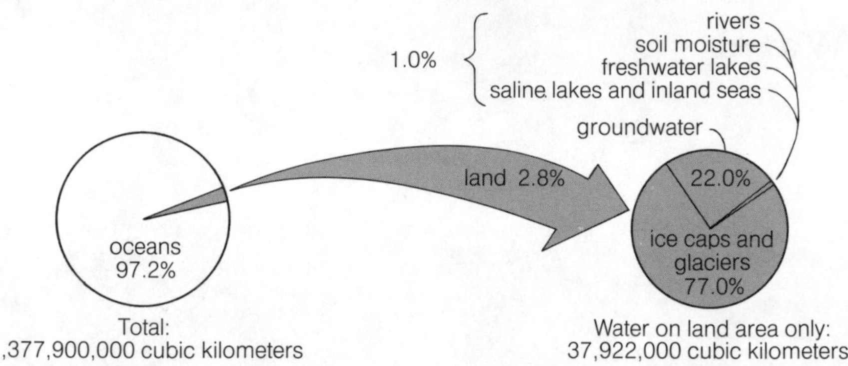

Figure 3–1

Distribution of water in the earth's hydrosphere. Note that most of the earth's water is in the oceans and glacial ice; only a very small amount occurs in freshwater rivers and lakes.

water evaporate from the oceans' surface. Almost 90 percent of this amount returns directly to the sea as snow or rain, while only about 10 percent joins water evaporated over the land. Almost two-thirds of the water that falls on the land is reevaporated; more than one-third travels back to the oceans as runoff from the land. The volume of water in annual circulation is 361,000 cubic kilometers, an amount large enough in itself, but only a little more than one part in four thousand of the total hydrosphere. Of these 361,000 cubic kilometers of water falling annually on the earth, only 99,000 (27 percent) fall on the land; of the latter, only 37,000 (10 percent of the total) are available to humans. Thus only one part in forty thousand is recycled annually and made available to humans.

One cubic mile is equivalent to 4.1 cubic kilometers.

The preponderance of the world's water, locked up in the oceans, glaciers, and underground, recycles at rates of hundreds to thousands of years. Residence times of the earth's water resources are shown in Table 3–1. Only the moisture in the atmosphere, soil, and rivers recycles in a matter of a few tens to hundreds of days.

Note how residence time is calculated in Table 3–1.

Precipitation and evaporation

The numbers cited above for the world's water supply are average global statistics and do not account for local and regional variations in precipitation and evaporation. In any given place, precipitation can vary widely during a year or over several years, and of course it varies greatly from place to place. Precipitation occurs when large masses of moisture-laden air rise vertically in the atmosphere. As moisture evaporates, it takes the form of water vapor, a gas more soluble in warm air than in cold air. But an air mass cools as it rises, because air temperature usually drops at higher elevations. Eventually, water vapor in the air mass condenses into liquid and returns to the ground as rain or, if frozen into small particles of solid ice, as hail or snow.

When air masses thousands of kilometers across and hundreds of meters thick heat up, they become less dense and rise up mountain slopes or collide with and force themselves over other cooler air masses. The resulting precipitation is described in Figure 3–3. For instance, a midwestern thunderstorm happens as an air mass, warmed and moistened near the ground, rapidly rises upward. Different circumstances accompany the heavy winter rains along the West Coast. These rains fall when warm, wet air masses roll in from the eastern Pacific and ascend the western slopes of the Coast Ranges and Sierra Nevada Mountains. Consequently, the mountains' western slopes are well watered, whereas the eastern slopes and valleys beyond the area of rainfall, lying in the area called the *rain shadow*, are much drier. The western parts of the Coast Ranges may be drenched with 50–100 cm of rain each year, while the Central Valley of California receives only 25–35 cm. The high Sierras are soaked with 125–175 cm, whereas the valleys of western Nevada get a scant 25 cm. Storms along the East Coast are commonly generated by wet and warm air masses from the Gulf Coast that collide with cooler and drier ones from Canada. The cooler air, being denser than the warmer air, is forced under the warmer air. As the air masses collide and the warm air is pushed up, moisture in the warmer mass cools, condenses, and precipitates. The average daily precipitation in the United States is shown in Figure 3–4.

Moisture evaporates when plants grow, when air masses move down mountain slopes, or when warm, dry air flows across the land. Plants draw up soil moisture with their roots and use it to transport nutrients throughout the stem and leaves; much of this circulating water evaporates from the leaf surfaces. Plant evaporation, called *transpiration*, keeps plant fluids moving against the force of gravity. Air masses warm up when pulled down a mountain slope by gravity; having lost their initial moisture on

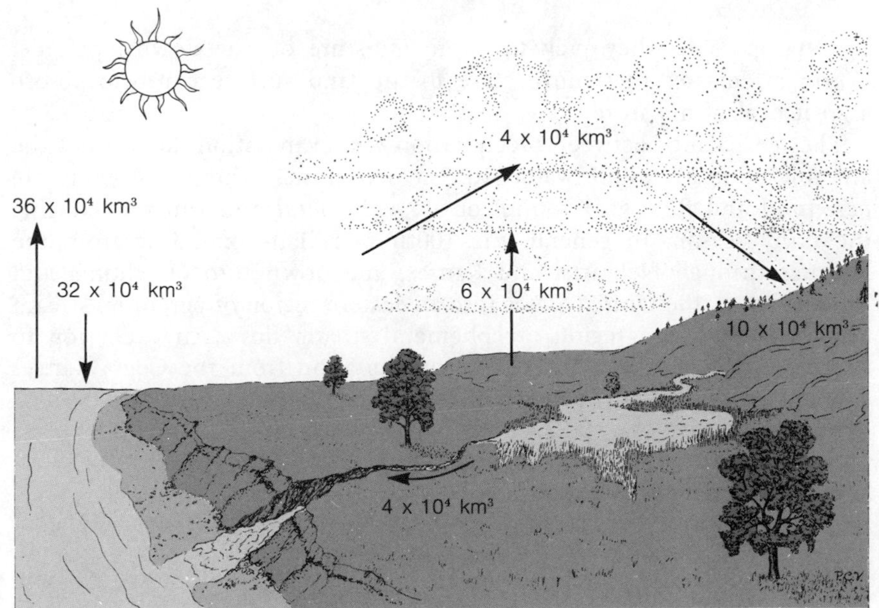

Figure 3–2

The hydrologic cycle showing the annual exchange of water among its different parts. Note that most of the precipitation that falls on the earth is reevaporated into the atmosphere; only a small fraction results as surface runoff on land. The amount of shallow groundwater (less than 800 meters) is more than 100 times that of the annual surface runoff, but its rate of renewal is comparably longer, about 150 years.

Table 3–1 Hydrosphere Residence Times[a]

Resource	Volume (*W*) (thousands of cu km)	Annual Rate of Removal (*Q*) (thousands of cu km) and Process	Residence Time (*T*) $\left(T = \frac{W}{Q}\right)$
total water on Earth	1,460,000	520 evaporation	2800 years
total water in the oceans	1,370,000	449 evaporation	3100 years
		37 difference between precipitation and evaporation	37,000 years
free gravitational waters in the earth's crust (to a depth of 5 km)	60,000	13 underground runoff	4600 years
(of which, in the zone of active water exchange)	4000	13 underground runoff	300 years
lakes	750		
glaciers and permanent snow	29,000	1.8 runoff	16,000 years
soil and subsoil moisture	65	85 evaporation and underground runoff	280 days
atmospheric moisture	14	520 precipitation	9 days
river waters	1.2	36 runoff	12 to 20 days

[a]Minor discrepancies between this table and Figure 3–1 are due to slightly different assumptions and calculations by different authors.

the upslope side, they pick up more moisture on the downslope side. Warm air masses that move close to the land surface can also absorb a great deal of moisture.

The net balance between precipitation and evaporation determines the amount of local runoff water. It also determines whether streams are *perennial* and flow year round, or are *ephemeral* and run only during the rainy season. In general, the 100th meridian—extending from the Dakotas through Nebraska and Kansas, and down into Oklahoma and Texas—bisects the United States into an eastern region of perennial stream flow and a western region of ephemeral stream flow. An exception to this pattern is the far West, where precipitation from the Coast Ranges and the Sierras sustains perennial streams, as seen in Figure 3–5.

3–2 How Much Water?

Some precipitation reaching the earth's land surface percolates down into soil and rocks, where it accumulates as groundwater. Precipitation also falls on the surface where it flows as streams and rivers, in places making ponds and lakes. The amount of local surface water and depth of groundwater depend on precipitation and evaporation rates, kinds of rocks at and below the ground surface, and topography—as well as how fast people withdraw it from rivers, lakes, and wells. The quality of surface and groundwater is determined mainly by its temperature, dissolved salt and oxygen content, and acidity or alkalinity, and all of these factors influence how people use the water.

Groundwater

The mantle of soil and rock debris at the earth's surface is filled with pores interspersed between mineral grains and rock fragments. In the pores, water from rain and melting snow accumulates. Even dense, crystalline rocks are often sufficiently fractured and jointed that they also provide internal pore space for water. This subsurface water contained in pore space is referred to as *groundwater,* and the boundary between overlying, unsaturated and underlying, saturated soil and rock materials is called the *water table.* Water table depth depends on precipitation and evaporation, as well as porosity and permeability of the soil and rocks. In some places the water table lies at ground surface, as with swamps, ponds, lakes, streams, and rivers. In other areas, like deserts, the water table may be tens or even hundreds of meters deep.

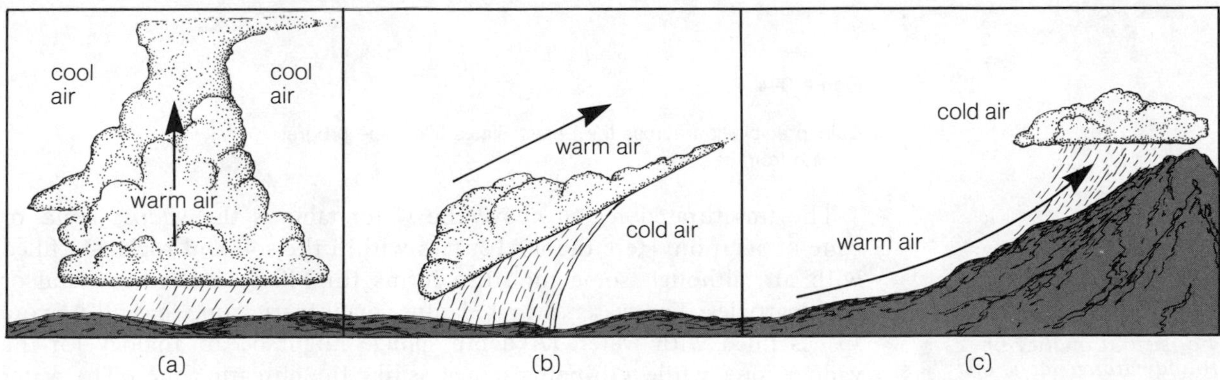

Figure 3–3

Three common causes of precipitation over the land. (a) Thermal convection of warm, moist air into a cooler air mass causes condensation and precipitation of moisture, often as a thunderstorm. (b) Warm, less dense air mass collides with and is pushed over a cold, denser air mass; precipitation occurs along the colliding front of the two air masses. (c) Warm air mass moving up a mountain slope cools, and moisture precipitates.

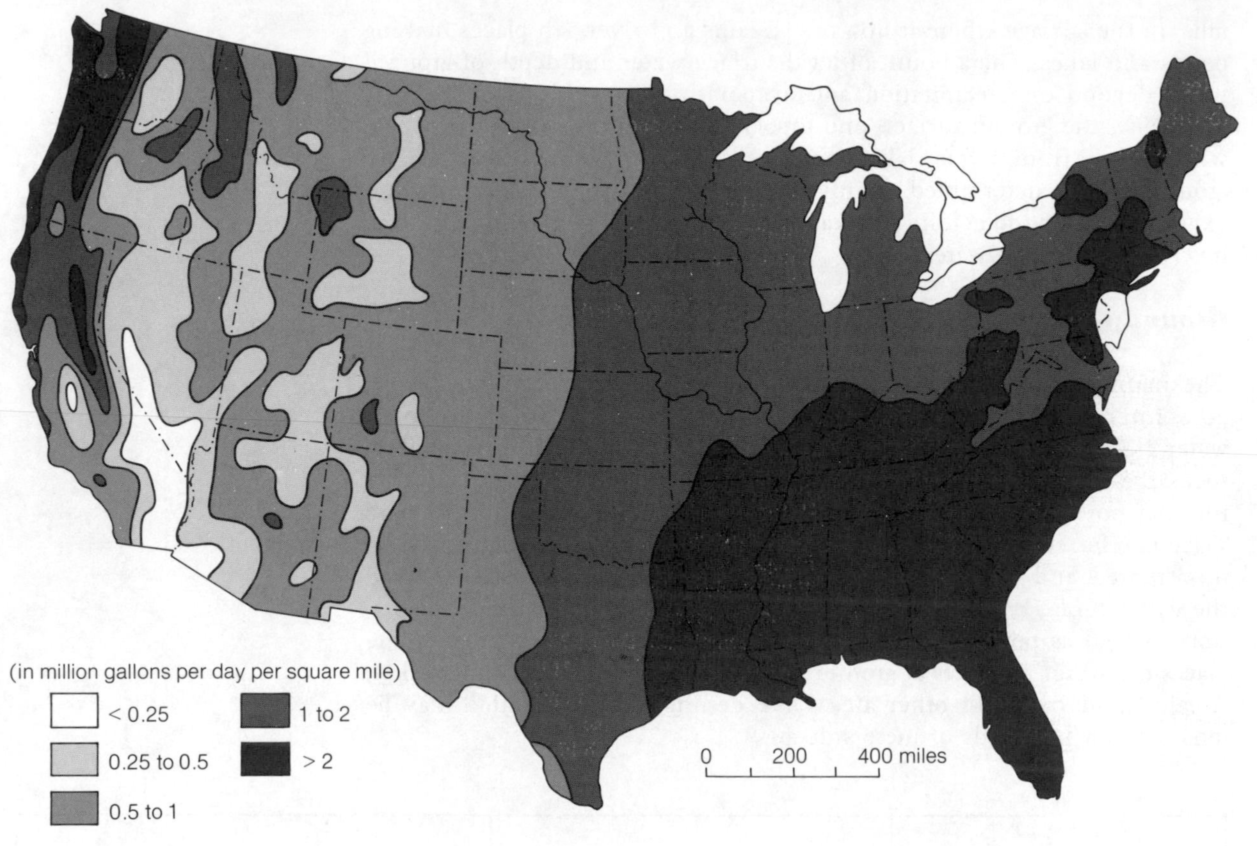

Figure 3-4

Daily precipitation across the United States. Note the progressive decline from east to west.

The natural quality of groundwater reflects, of course, the materials through which it flows in the vadose and phreatic zone.

The unsaturated region above the water table is the *vadose zone*, or zone of aeration. Here the void spaces within the soil and rocks are filled with air, although some moisture forms thin films around mineral or rock particles. The water-saturated zone, or *phreatic zone*, has all its pore spaces filled with water. (A damp sponge might be an analogy for the vadose zone, while a dripping sponge is like the phreatic zone.) The water table is not a level surface, but instead mimics in a subdued way the topography of the ground surface, rising with hills and dipping down under valleys. Wherever the water table intersects the ground surface, a spring, stream, or lake occurs, as in Figure 3-6. In some places a zone of saturated rock lies within the vadose zone, above the main water table, and thus makes a *perched water table*.

Groundwater is not level, and gravity forces it to flow downward and seaward, eventually to meet the saline groundwater of the ocean. Rock strata like sandstones and limestones, which are especially porous and permeable, may serve as conduits for groundwater flow. Conducting rock strata are called *aquifers* (*aqua*, water; *fero*, bear—Latin). Other strata like mudstones and shales are usually quite impermeable and resist groundwater flow; these are referred to as *aquicludes* or *aquitards*. These features of groundwater flow are illustrated in Figure 3-6.

The speed of groundwater flow between two points depends on how permeable the intervening sediment or rock is and how great the difference in elevation between the two points. The difference in water height from one place to another generates *hydraulic pressure* at the lower point. This

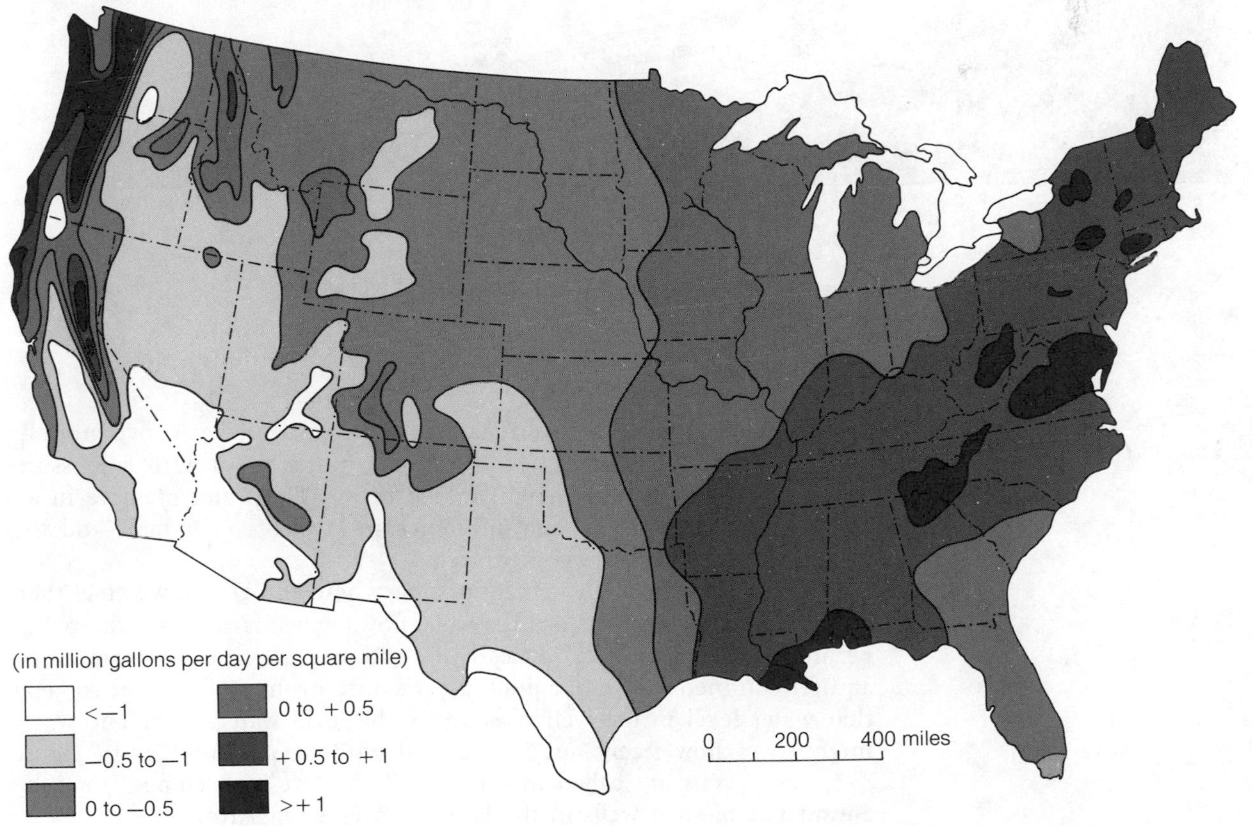

Figure 3-5

Balance between surface evaporation and plant transpiration and precipitation. Perennial streams flow where precipitation exceeds surface evaporation and plant transpiration. Except for the Pacific Northwest and some portions of California, the area west of the 100th meridian is water deficient, having mostly ephemeral streams that flow part of the year.

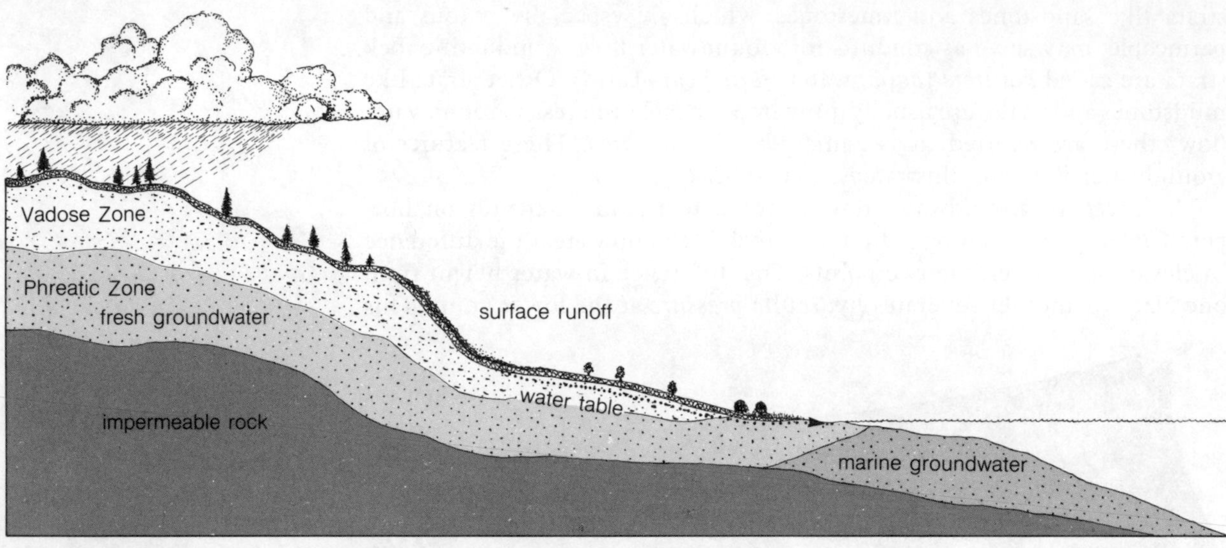

Figure 3–6

Schematic cross section showing relations among precipitation, surface flow, and groundwater. Water table marks boundary between upper, unsaturated vadose zone and lower, water-saturated phreatic zone.

pressure is analogous to that generated by a water tower above ground. When you turn on the tap in the house, water flows with a pressure proportional to the water height in the tower. The water pressure in an aquifer is proportional to the difference in level of water table and the place where the pressure is measured.

Wells are drilled to the phreatic zone where the groundwater is then pumped. How fast water in these wells flows depends again on the rocks' permeability and the local area's hydraulic pressure. If a well reaches an aquifer confined below an aquiclude, pressure in the well may be so great that water level in the well rises above the local water table. The water might even flow freely out of the well without pumping, as in Figure 3–7; such wells are called *artesian wells.* ("Artesian" comes from the abundance of such wells in the French province of Artois.)

As indicated in Figure 3–1, the volume of groundwater is about twenty-two times greater than in lakes and rivers; obviously, then, groundwater is a major source of water.

Surface water

Surface water flows over the ground in stream and river channels, and also forms standing water bodies like ponds and lakes. It is water left over from local precipitation after evaporation and also comes from groundwater that reaches the surface. Thus a perennial stream or lake in an arid region may be springfed by water from below the surface. The rivers and streams of the world would stop flowing in two or three weeks if they weren't continually replenished by the large volume of groundwater, as indicated in Table 3–1. However, this flow is also reversible: a stream or river may lose some water to the subsurface if the water table is low.

Large geographic variations in the volume of surface waters reflect regional differences in precipitation and evaporation rates. About two-thirds of U.S. streamflow is found in the area east of the Mississippi River; of the remaining one-third, most is in the Pacific Northwest. One important aspect of streamflow variation is that in the eastern United States surface water is generated in valleys, where most people live, as well as in mountains. By contrast, in the western United States most streamflow is generated in mountainous areas where population is sparse. So in the West, water management (dams, irrigation canals, and so on) must be carried out relatively far from population centers. As an example, managed rivers like the Sacramento and San Joaquin, which irrigate the Central Valley of California, flow in areas that are dry about half of the year. They can flow perennially because their source areas lie in neighboring mountains where precipitation is sufficient to keep them replenished.

One classic device for regulating streamflow to stabilize variations in seasonal water supply is the construction of dams. Those like the Hoover Dam, near the Arizona and Nevada border, hold back excess river flow during wet seasons for use in dry seasons. These dams also help to check

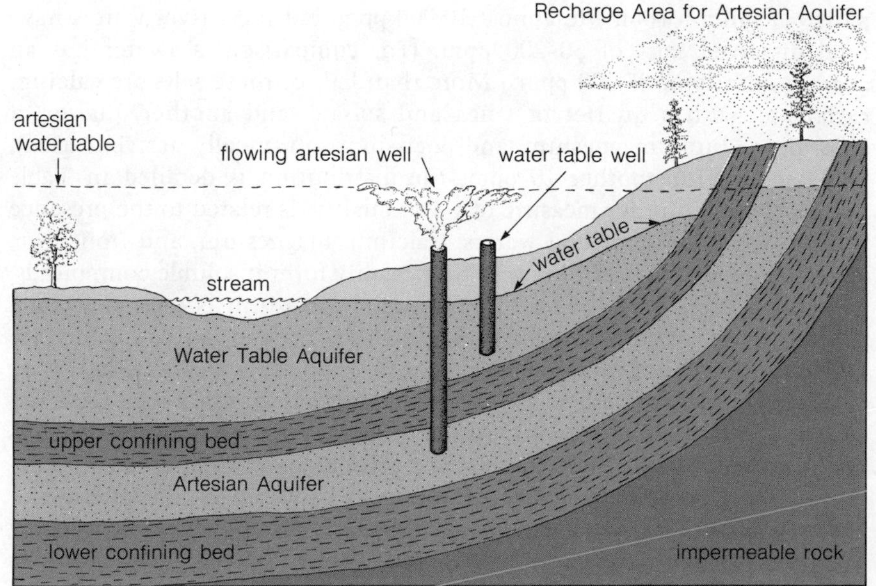

Figure 3–7

Flowing artesian well from a confined aquifer. Two aquifers are separated by strata with little or no water—aquicludes. The artesian well flows freely, since the level of the well lies below the water table within the artesian aquifer shown by the dotted line. The water flows because pressure is generated by the difference in water height between the water table at the artesian recharge area and the well hole.

floods in low-lying valleys downstream when there is exceptionally heavy runoff.

3-3 Water Quality

As we have noted, surface and groundwater vary in quality according to content of dissolved salts, dissolved gases like oxygen and carbon dioxide, acidity, and temperature. These characteristics reflect the natural environment where the water is located. The use of surface and groundwater for all kinds of purposes—manufacturing, diluting sewage, irrigation, power generation, and recreation—alters the natural physical, chemical, and biological properties of terrestrial water. In the next section we discuss some of the substances put into surface and groundwater, and how their quality is consequently affected. Here we want to consider the natural state of terrestrial waters *before* they are altered by human activities.

Dissolved salts

Chemical weathering of the earth's crust introduces several different dissolved substances into terrestrial waters. Moreover, small, wind-borne salt particles blown off the sea surface contribute to the salt content of surface waters. In any part of the world, the total amount and variety of dissolved substances in the water are determined by the composition of underlying rocks and the nature and degree of chemical weathering.

The concentration of total dissolved salts in rivers can range from 10 parts per million (ppm) to almost 10,000 ppm, but most river waters have total dissolved salts of 50–200 ppm. (For comparison, seawater has an average salinity of 35,000 ppm.) More than half of these salts are calcium carbonate, with a quarter of silica and sulfate, and another quarter of chloride, sodium, magnesium, and potassium; organically derived carbon may account for another 10 ppm—the distribution is detailed in Table 3-2. Hardness, another measure of water quality, is related to the presence of dissolved salts in natural waters. Calcium, magnesium, and iron, especially, make water "hard" because they readily form insoluble compounds, particularly with soap. (The ring around the bathtub is one such compound.) Scales that coat teakettles, steam irons, and water heaters are precipitated calcium carbonate, left behind when the water is boiled away.

Water in areas underlain by igneous and metamorphic rocks generally contains dissolved salts totaling less than 50 ppm. The reason is that igneous and metamorphic rock minerals are less soluble than minerals in sedimentary rocks. The latter generally contain soluble minerals like calcite and various sulfides and sulfates and produce waters with dissolved salts ranging from 50–200 ppm. Geothermal waters have still higher salt concentrations because their hotter temperatures permit them to dissolve substances more readily. Deposits of silica and calcium carbonate around hot springs are evidence of these higher salt concentrations. Surface waters in arid and semi-arid regions also have abundant dissolved salts because their rapid evaporation rates readily concentrate the salts; Great Salt Lake in Utah has a salinity of 250,000 ppm. Most state and federal authorities recommend less than 500 ppm dissolved salts in terrestrial waters used for drinking.

Temperature, oxygen, and acidity

Temperatures in most natural waters range about 40 degrees Celsius: from ice at 0 or less, to tropical lakes at 35 to 40 or more, depending on the season and the local climate. Temperature, in turn, controls the content of dissolved gases, notably oxygen and carbon dioxide. Like all gases, oxygen and carbon dioxide are most soluble at low temperatures; high temperatures drive the gases from the solution in which they are dissolved.

One degree Celsius is equivalent to 1.8 degrees Fahrenheit. To convert Fahrenheit to Celsius, subtract 32 and multiply by 5/9. Thus, 68° F equals 20° C (68 − 32 = 36 × 5/9 = 20).

Dissolved oxygen supports organisms living in natural waters, some of which decompose organic matter that collects in streams, rivers, ponds, and lakes. Surface waters should contain at least several parts per million of oxygen to support their living inhabitants. As for carbon dioxide, it forms a weak acid in solution with water, and thus regulates the acidity of natural waters. Acidity is measured in *pH*, a scale that records the hydrogen ion activity of a solution. The pH scale ranges from 0, most acidic, to 14, most alkaline. The number 7 is neutral—neither acidic nor alkaline (pH below 7 is acidic, above 7 alkaline). Each unit increase in pH indicates a tenfold decrease in hydrogen ion activity. The pH of natural waters usually ranges from 6.5 (slightly acidic) to 8.5 (slightly alkaline).

To help visualize pH values, here are the pH's of some common liquids: vinegar, 2.5; orange juice, 4.5; rainwater, 6.0; milk, almost 7; blood, slightly more than 7; sea water, 8.2; detergent, 9.5; ammonia, 11.5; and bleach, 12.5.

Waters with a pH less than 7 are acidic enough to dissolve calcium

Table 3–2 Average Salt Content of River Water

Constituent	Parts per Million	Percent
bicarbonate (HCO_3^-)	58	45
calcium (Ca^{2+})	15	12
silica (SiO_2)	13	10
sulfate (SO_4^{2-})	11	8.5
chloride (Cl^-)	8	6
sodium (Na^+)	6	5
magnesium (Mg^{2+})	4	3
potassium (K^+)	2	1.5
nitrate (NO_3^-)	1	0.8
iron (Fe^{2+})	0.67	0.5
organic carbon	10	7.7
Total	128.67	100.0

carbonate-bearing minerals. Waters with either a high or a low pH will remove silica in solution. Thus the amount and composition of salts in solution in natural waters is partly determined by the acidity and alkalinity of the waters, because pH influences the dissolving power of the waters.

3-4 Withdrawals and Consumption

About 71 percent of precipitation in the United States is lost to surface evaporation and plant transpiration, as shown in Figure 3-8. More than half of this *evapotranspiration* occurs in agricultural and forested lands, while the remainder is lost on unused lands. Twenty-nine percent of yearly precipitation reaches streams, rivers, ponds, lakes, and subsurface groundwater. Although regions differ considerably, on a nationwide scale we currently withdraw 9 percent of this surface and groundwater. Except for some hydroelectric power generation, the remaining 20 percent returns to the oceans unused.

Figure 3-8

Distribution of daily precipitation falling in the United States. Note that about 2 percent of the surface flow is lost by evaporation before it reaches the ocean.

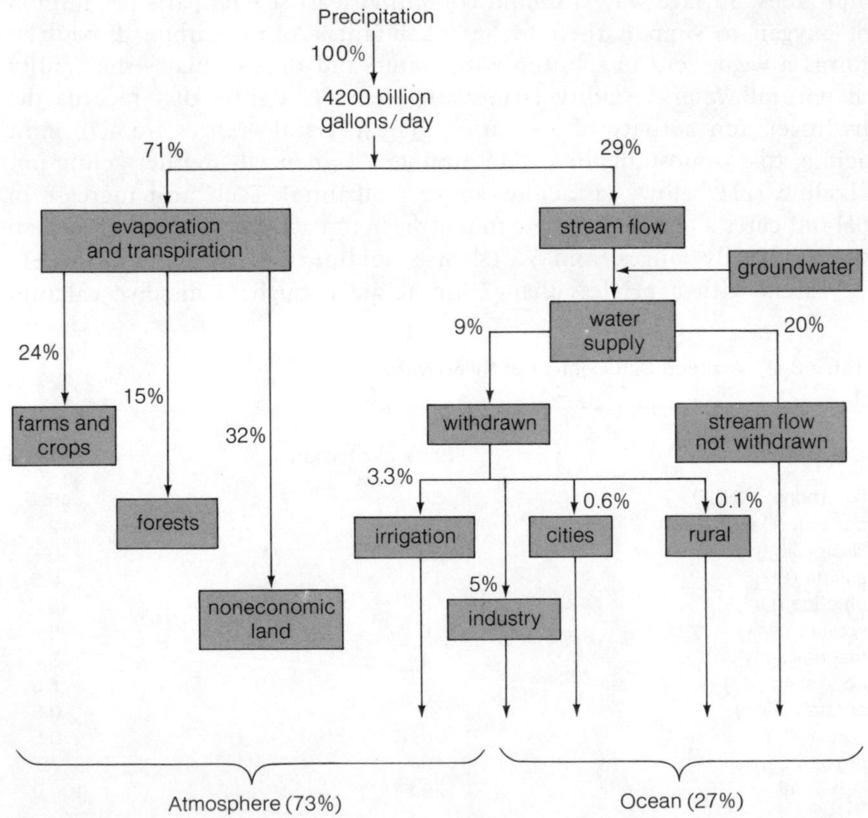

About three-quarters of the withdrawn water comes from surface supplies and one-quarter from groundwater supplies. The chief users of withdrawn water are agriculture, industry, municipalities, commercial establishments, and households. Almost three-quarters of the withdrawn water is merely *used* and returned to the surface or groundwater. Of course, the way water is used may prevent its immediate reuse for something else. Water for diluting sewage cannot be used for drinking (unless subsequently treated), but it may be safe enough to irrigate certain crops. One-quarter of the withdrawn water is actually *consumed;* it is either evaporated, transpired, incorporated into livestock or crops, or otherwise removed temporarily from the supply of surface and subsurface waters.

Agriculture, the big water consumer

In agriculture, most water goes for crop irrigation, and a much smaller proportion is used for watering livestock. In fact, of all major water uses, irrigation consumes the greatest percent. Ninety-five percent of our irrigation water is withdrawn west of the Mississippi River, an area deficient in precipitation and runoff, as shown in Figure 3–9. This regional shortage of surface water for irrigation also explains the rising withdrawal of groundwater during the last few decades. In 1970, 36 percent of irrigation water came from groundwater, compared with 19 percent in 1950—a doubling time of about twenty years. About two-thirds of the water withdrawn for irrigation is lost by seepage from pipes and evapotranspiration in storage ponds, irrigation ditches, and fields. Only about one-third is returned to surface or groundwater supplies.

Similar evaporation losses occur in surface water stored in open reservoirs.

Demand for irrigation water is highly seasonal, occurring three to six months during the growing season, when rainfall in most of the West is virtually nil. Areas where irrigation is important are the same regions where evaporation rates are high. As a result, in irrigated fields salts accumulate in the soil's surface layers. Some of the salts come from the irrigation water itself; others are drawn up with soil moisture from deep in the soil. Fields irrigated for many years often require more than normal irrigation to flush out salts before and during crop raising, because most plants cannot survive in soils with abundant salts. Consequently, the return flow of water from these fields has at least three times as much salt since two-thirds of the initial water volume evaporates, not to mention salts washing from the soil. Besides higher salinity, the return flow is also high in nitrates and phosphates from fertilizers applied to fields. Sediment content increases, too, as irrigation water flows through loose, granular soils and transports finer grained sand and silt downslope.

Industry, the big water user

Industry withdraws the largest share of water—more than one-half of the total—and uses it for hydroelectric power, cooling and washing operations,

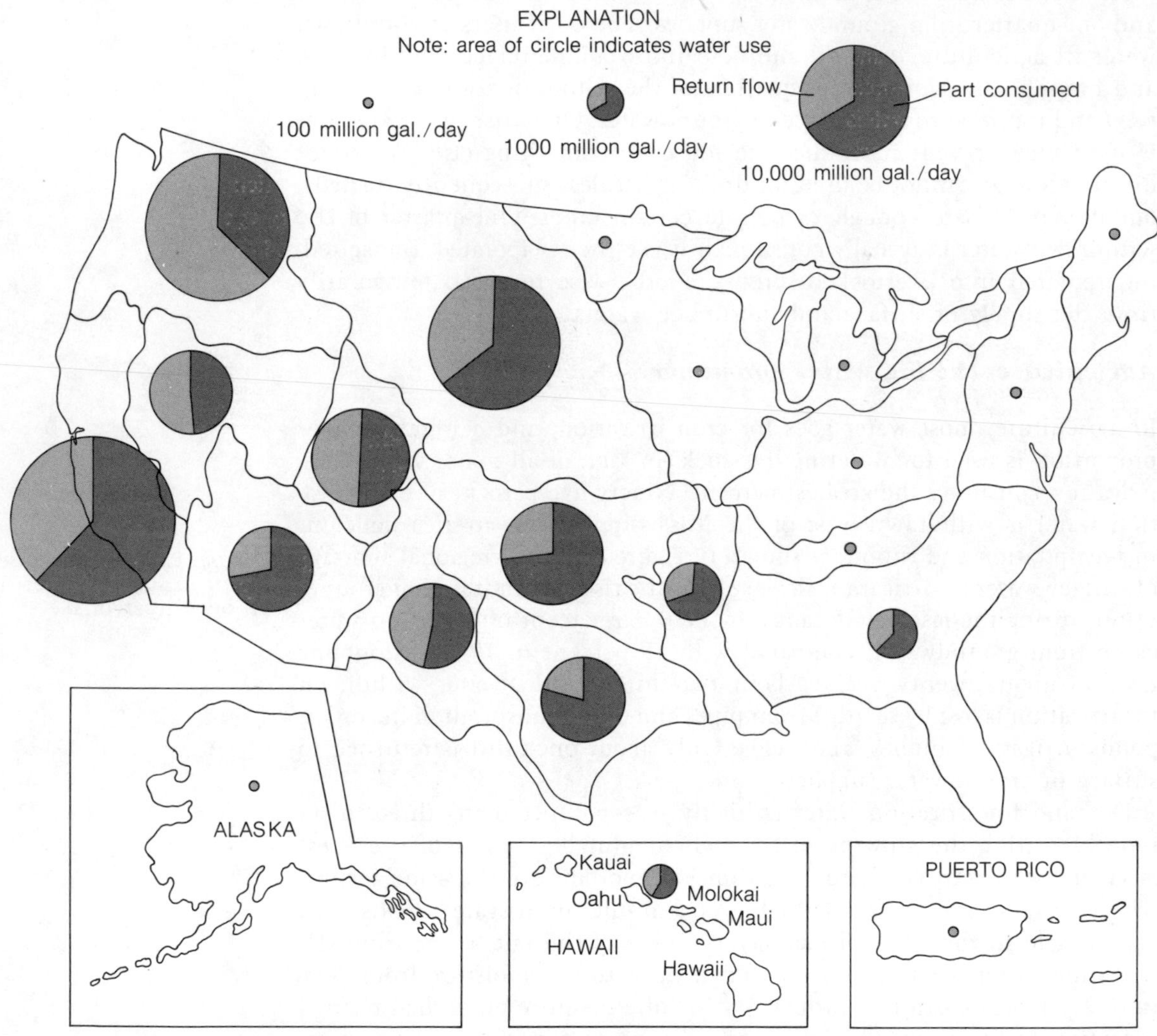

Figure 3–9

Distribution of United States irrigation water withdrawal and consumption for 1970. Ninety-five percent of irrigation water is used west of the Mississippi River, an area of deficient precipitation and surface runoff. Note the high portion consumed by evaporation and plant transpiration.

and thousands of other purposes. Even though a great deal of water is involved, most is returned to surface waters or recycled. Table 3–3 presents some typical water requirements for various industrial products.

Table 3–3 Water Used in the Production of Various Goods

Item Produced	Water Used (liters)
Sunday newspaper	760
wheat for a loaf of bread	1140
tankful of gasoline	1520
1 pound of beef	15,200
automobile	190,000
1 ton of alfalfa	760,000
1 ton of synthetic rubber	2,280,000

About three-quarters of water for industry goes toward generating electricity. In some power plants, dammed water is directed through turbines that generate electricity, and water quality is little altered. In other power plants, water is pumped into the facility, then filtered and heated to produce steam for driving electricity-generating turbines. Later, the steam is condensed with the help of more water and both leave the power plant, entering local waters.

Some fish and other aquatic organisms, particularly small larvae, are killed when water is brought into the plant. Chlorine is usually added to the intake water to prevent these organisms from fouling the plant's pipes and condensers. Chlorine also raises the water's acidity, so any calcium carbonate that might have formed as scale is dissolved. Although about 98 percent of the water withdrawn by a steam-generating power plant is returned, its quality is inevitably altered. The return flow is warmer and more acidic and, in the case of nuclear power plants, contains very small amounts of low-level radioactive substances.

Other industrial uses of water include metal processing and refining —especially in the steel and aluminum industries, food processing and canning, paper production, and petroleum refining. Although these industries also return most of the water withdrawn, its quality is modified. In addition to usually being significantly warmer, the water may contain a variety of toxic industrial chemicals or considerable amounts of organic matter that consume dissolved oxygen. All these conditions may put heavy stresses on organisms living in the receiving waters.

Sources of industrial water are both fresh and saline, in a ratio of about four to one. Most of this water comes from surface supplies (95 percent), while only a small fraction is groundwater (4 percent) and reclaimed sewage water (1 percent). About 80 percent of industrial water is withdrawn in the eastern United States, as shown in Figure 3–10. Water use by Eastern industry is fairly constant throughout the year, whereas demand for irrigation water in the West is predominantly seasonal. Furthermore, heavy irrigation in 17 western states accounts for disproportionate water con-

(a) Alfalfa irrigation in Montana. (b) Orchard blooming in Israeli desert owing to irrigation. (c) Salt accumulation in heavily irrigated fields in California.

(a)

(b)

(c)

sumption compared to 31 eastern states, where most water that is withdrawn is returned to surface flow.

Public and domestic demand

In 1970, water use in the United States amounted to 6840 liters (1800 gallons) per day per person. The greatest portion of this water was claimed by agriculture and industry; only 621 liters (166 gallons) went for urban or rural purposes. And of this 621 liters, a still smaller fraction actually went toward drinking, bathing, flushing toilets, and cooking.

Remember, there are 3.8 liters to 1 gallon.

In cities and towns, water functions in diverse roles like fire fighting, washing streets, heating and air conditioning, watering lawns and golf courses, and filling swimming pools. On farms, in addition to personal uses, water is given to livestock and poultry. Some farms and industries purchase public water supplies for limited irrigation and manufacturing, but when demands grow, they generate their own supplies from rivers or wells. About one-third of the water supplying cities, towns, and farms comes from groundwater; the remainder is drawn from surface waters. Approximately 80 percent of public-supplied water returns to surface and subsurface waters, usually after treatment at a sewage disposal plant.

What is the impact of all these uses on the water itself? There are several major changes in water quality after industrial, commercial, municipal, and residential use: growth in organic content, particularly microorganisms—some disease-causing; addition of toxic chemicals, like oil and gasoline washed from city streets; rise in temperature; and increases in sediment and salt content. Only a few of the substances added are removed by water treatment plants, and the treatment itself often adds still other materials. For example, adding chlorine to waste water kills microorganisms, but unless the amount of chlorine is carefully controlled, it may enter natural waters and kill aquatic organisms living there. Figure 3–11 summarizes water withdrawal and consumption by major users.

3–5 Future Demand

Like the demand for virtually all earth resources, that for water is growing faster than the population. Daily per capita water use in the United States rose from 4940 liters (1300 gallons) in 1950 to 6840 liters (1800 gallons) in 1970, an average annual increase of 2 percent and a doubling time of 35 years. Today we use 31 percent of our available water, and if the current trends continue, early in the twenty-first century we'll be using twice that. But these are average nationwide statistics that do not take into account the particularly heavy demand for water in drier parts of the country. Nor do such data indicate changing water quality resulting

Bergstrom's Viewpoint looks at the national impact of future water demand.

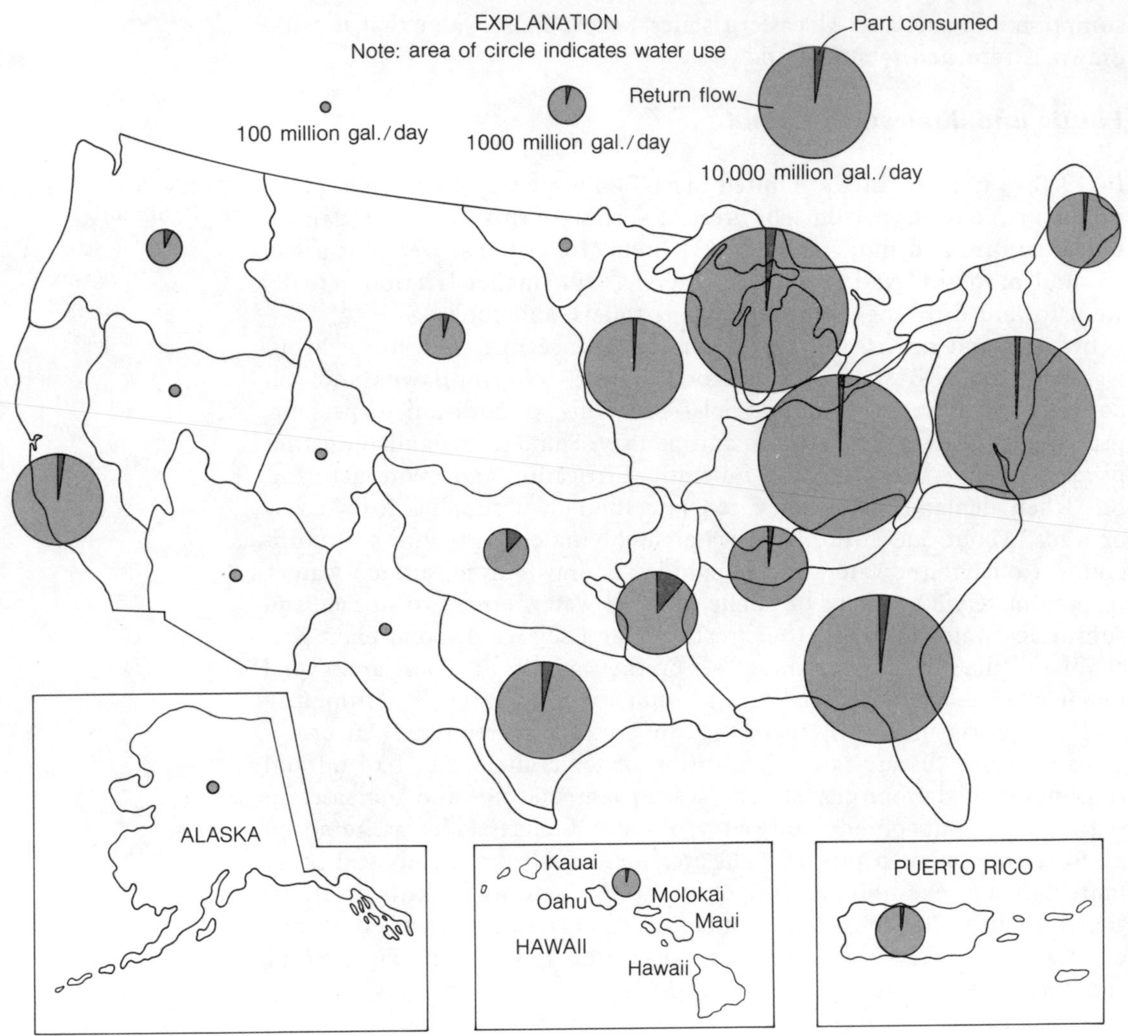

Figure 3–10

Distribution of United States industrial water withdrawal and consumption for 1970. Eighty percent of industrial water is used east of the Mississippi River; note the small amount that is consumed, with most being returned to surface waters. This map does not include water supplied by public utilities—only the amount supplied by the industries themselves.

from expanded water usage. Furthermore, heavy use of natural waters, particularly groundwater, can have other environmental side effects not evident in the statistics. For instance, local land may subside from excessive withdrawal and fresh underground water may become saline upon intrusion of seawater in coastal regions.

Recent trends

Water use statistics for the last two decades reveal regular trends in water demand that provide a reasonable basis for predicting future demand. The fastest growing water user is industry, which withdraws most of its water from surface streamflow. Because the greatest part of industrial water is used for generating electricity, most water withdrawn in the future will be returned at higher temperatures. And additional low-level radioactivity is likely, as more nuclear power plants are built.

There has also been increasing reliance on groundwater for irrigation. Unlike industrial water use, irrigation consumes a large fraction of the water withdrawn and increases its salinity several times.

As we pointed out, two additional problems are associated with heavy groundwater use: local subsidence of the land surface and salinization of subsurface fresh water. When groundwater is removed from porous subsurface sediments and rocks, these materials tend to compact because of the loss of water pressure that held them apart. As an example of the consequences of groundwater removal, in the Santa Clara Valley area of central California, heavy groundwater withdrawal has significantly lowered the water table and has caused the ground surface to subside several meters, as seen in Figure 3–12. Such subsidence can crack and weaken building and highway foundations, as well as disrupt underground utility lines like sewers and water mains.

In coastal regions, the fresh groundwater under the land extends seaward, passing into saline, marine groundwater. Figure 3–13 illustrates what can

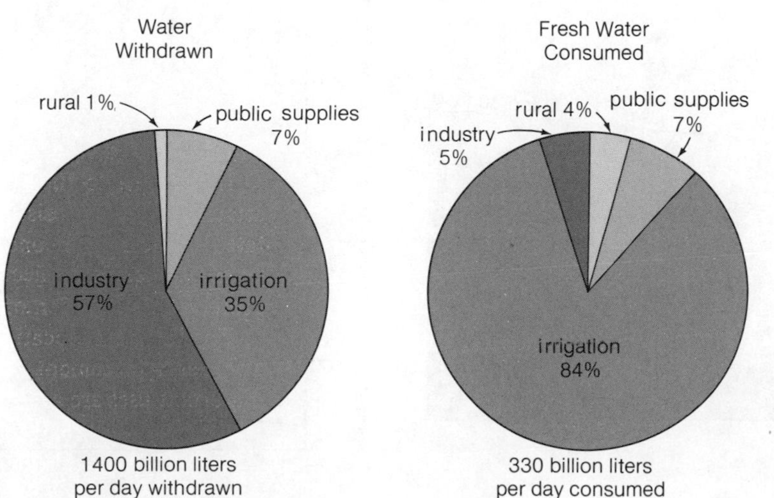

Figure 3–11

Water withdrawal and consumption in the United States by major user. Most water consumption is from evapotranspiration losses associated with irrigation.

happen when fresh water is pumped from wells along the coast. Sea water may replace the fresh water in the underground porous rock formations, and as more and more sea water mixes with the fresh water, the well water deteriorates in quality, becoming more saline. In many areas, such as Long Island, the New Jersey coast, Florida, and Southern California, salt water invasions of fresh groundwater already pose serious water management problems. Inland regions, too, can experience salinization of fresh groundwater; groundwater often becomes more saline with depth. As supplies of fresh water are withdrawn, deeper saline water migrates upward, contaminating the overlying fresh water.

One remedy for land subsidence and salinization of fresh water is to recharge local groundwater with waste water. The waste water percolates downward, gradually purifying itself, and refills the groundwater reservoir. In parts of the country where groundwater enjoys extensive use, *recharge basins* are constructed to store waste water and allow it to seep down into the ground. Further subsidence in the Santa Clara area, for instance, is being checked with the help of recharge basins.

In the year 2000

For most of the country, water demand in the year 2000 will significantly exceed supply. Such projections are based on assumptions that may change from now to then, but even so, they allow us to concentrate on the kinds of water problems we most likely will face.

Water withdrawals can be divided into three categories: In-channel use, on-site consumption, and off-channel consumption. *In-channel use* refers

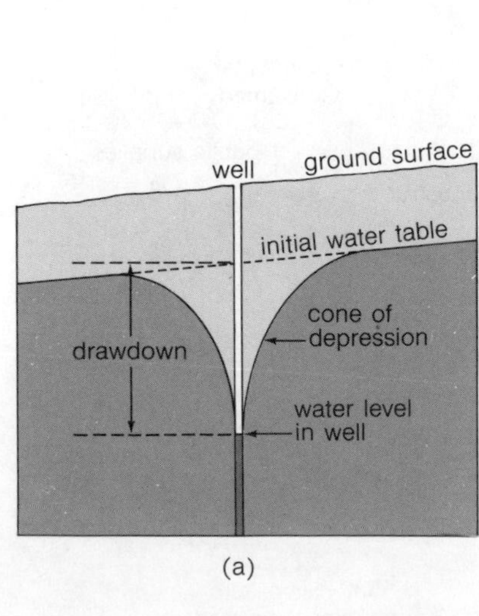

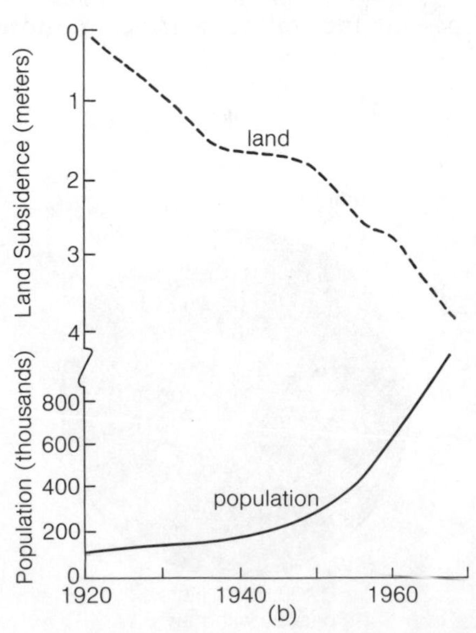

Figure 3–12

Side effects of excessive groundwater withdrawal. (a) Heavy withdrawal of groundwater from a well causes the local water table to drop, forming a cone of depression around the well. Consequently, the water level in the well falls too. A cone of depression is always created when the well pumping rate is faster than the rate of water flow within the phreatic zone or the aquifer. Hence, the water is removed more rapidly than it is replaced, thereby making the water table deep. (b) Graphs showing the increase in population in the Santa Clara valley area of central California and the corresponding subsidence in ground surface, because of increased groundwater withdrawal to serve the various water needs of the population.

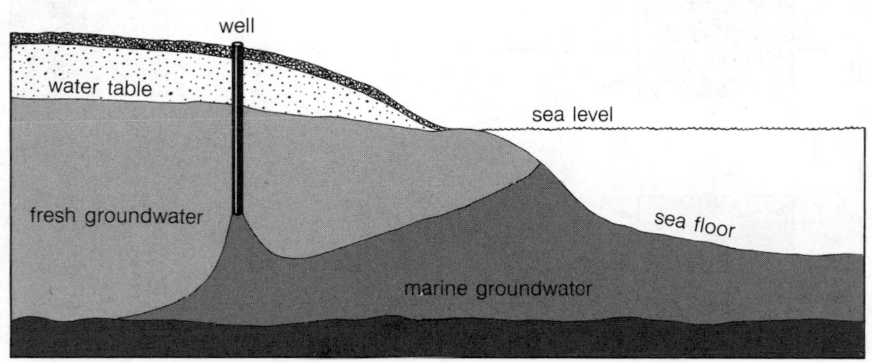

Figure 3–13

Salt water intrusion in a coastal well. Excessive pumping causes the denser, saline marine groundwater on which the fresh groundwater floats to migrate upward and contaminate the well water.

to water used in the stream channel and returned immediately to it. This use includes power generation, transportation, waste dilution, fish and wildlife habitats, and recreation. *Off-channel consumption* takes water away from streams or rivers, as with irrigation by surface water and water transported to cities and towns for industrial, commercial, and residential use. *On-site consumption* refers to water consumed before precipitation and runoff reach a perennial stream (where it is used in-channel or consumed off-channel). Examples are swamps, marshes, reservoirs, fish hatcheries, and vegetated lands where precipitation collects and evaporates. Setting aside water for on-site consumption for wildlife preserves, flood control, agriculture, and lumbering means that streamflow is depleted by evapotranspiration losses, even though water is not actually withdrawn from streams.

Of the major drainage basins within the 48 states, only three—regions in the Northeast, Southeast, and Ohio Valley—will have an assured supply of water in the year 2000 if current trends of water use and consumption continue. In other regions—Mid-Atlantic, Midwest, and Northwest—supply will be greater than consumption, but in-channel water will be in short supply unless we change certain laws and encourage multiple use of water. In the remainder—mostly the West—projected future demand grossly exceeds the total supply. There are two reasons for this predicted shortage: either future consumption will be greater than streamflow, as in the arid and semi-arid Southwest, or there will be increased power generation, as in the eastern Great Lakes and eastern Gulf Coast.

Each water region is a major watershed and drainage basin.

Projected future demands clearly suggest that, although water is a renewable resource, its growing rate of use and consumption is fast approaching its rate of renewal. One solution to water supply problems is heavier reliance on groundwater. But this is only a short-term solution because groundwater furnishes part of the perennial streamflow and also renews itself more slowly than surface water, as shown in Table 3–1. For instance, the estimated residence time of shallow groundwater (less than 800 meters depth) is 150 years. In areas where groundwater is drawn upon extensively,

Figure 3–14

Complementary and conflicting uses of water resources. Water used for irrigation cannot be made available for drinking, recreation, or waste dilution, since these are conflicting uses. However, water held back in reservoirs behind hydroelectric dams can provide an artificial lake for water recreation, act as a storage site for flood waters, and after passing through the hydroelectric plant, be used to dilute waste water. Plans to regulate and control water use must take these complementary and conflicting demands into account.

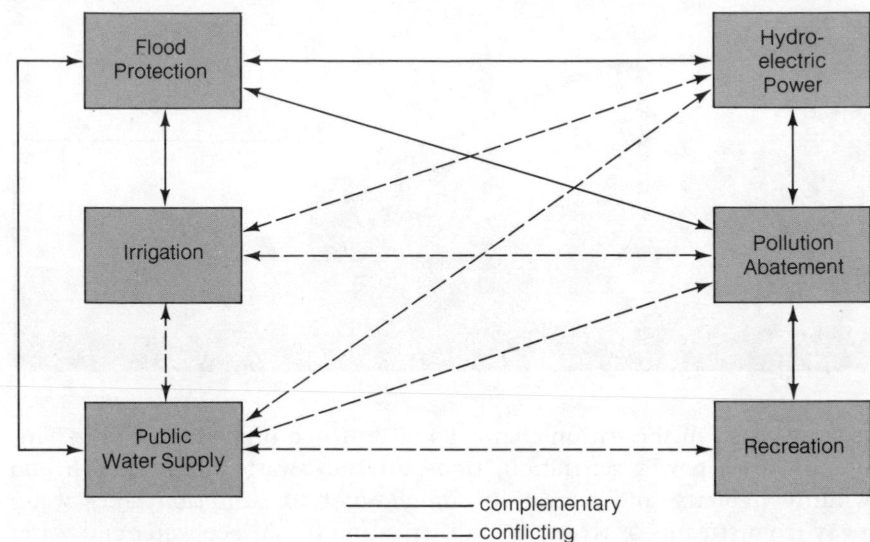

like Arizona, the water table is dropping steadily. Such a drop indicates that the groundwater is essentially being mined like a nonrenewable resource. Without careful management with techniques like surface recharge with waste water, this resource will be depleted, too.

More careful water management is obviously necessary. Yet even the most enlightened management cannot solve all water problems, because it involves both conflicting and complementary demands, as you can see in Figure 3–14. The water supply problems that the United States confronts also face the rest of the world (Table 3–4). By the year 2000, global water use will withdraw about one-half of the surface supplies available on land: 18,700 km^3 out of 37,000 km^3 annual runoff from the land. Given this future high demand, and uneven distribution of water geographically and over time, many parts of the world will have serious water problems before the end of this century.

Table 3–4 Annual Global Water Needs in 2000

Usage	Withdrawals (cubic kilometers)	Consumption (cubic kilometers)
irrigation	7000	4800
domestic	600	100
industrial	1700	170
effluent and waste dilution	9000	0
other	400	400
Total	18,700	5470

Viewpoint **Robert E. Bergstrom**

Robert E. Bergstrom is head geologist of the groundwater section of the Illinois State Geological Survey. Among Dr. Bergstrom's chief research interests is the impact of subsurface solid waste disposal on groundwater quality. In this Viewpoint Dr. Bergstrom considers some of the complex questions that arise from future large-scale water management.

Preparing to Face the Water Shortage

A key point raised in this chapter is that broad management of water resources will be necessary as our demands for water increase to critical levels in the next 25 years. By the year 2000 water supplies in many regions of the United States will be inadequate and some uses of water will be curtailed. Americans who gamely accepted shortages of a few commodities during wartime and who experienced, with some annoyance, fairly widespread shortages of fuels beginning in 1973, will doubtless be dismayed when they are confronted by limited supplies and, probably, government regulation of water.

The reaction to water shortage and regulation will be strong. In the past, Americans have regarded water as a birthright independent of property or economic status and a privilege linked to life itself. In the humid eastern portion of the United States water is essentially taken for granted; it is an accessory of property because it is commonly available beside or beneath the land. An individual has the right to use water from a body of surface water if he owns the land next to the water. This right to use water by virtue of ownership of land contiguous to the water is called the Riparian Doctrine of water law. All states east of the 98th meridian, except Mississippi and Florida, follow the Riparian Doctrine exclusively.

The western states—west of the tier of states from North Dakota to Texas—plus Mississippi and Florida, recognize the Appropriation Doctrine, under which a water right is based upon the beneficial *use* of water. The first individual to appropriate, or claim, *and use* a body of surface water has a right superior to the rights of later appropriators. An appropriation right does not depend on the land's location with respect to the surface water. It is based exclusively on actual use of water and on the maxim of first in time, first in right. In deserts of the West, a water right is commonly the key factor in land use; mere title to land may be valueless without a water right.

Thus, when we consider how to direct the future management of water resources, we must remember that there are complexities in water law that must be resolved. We will also have to consider water demand, physical limitations on our water supply, our technological and engineering capabilities for obtaining water, and the priorities that society may assign to the various uses of water.

One factor in the increasing demand for water is related to energy production. As we move toward making the United States more self-sufficient in energy by developing the oil shale of the West and by converting coal to synthetic gas and oil, we will need vast quantities of water. It appears that oil-shale and coal-conversion industries will be consuming large amounts of water by the year 2000.

Plants that produce synthetic oil and gas will require a tremendous volume of water for cooling and processing. More than 90 percent of this water is used for cooling and can be recycled; but up to 10 percent is actually consumed and must be replaced by makeup water. Some of the consumed water provides hydrogen for the production of hydrocarbons, and some water evaporates. The total water demands and the makeup-water requirements of such plants are comparable to the water supplies required by large cities.

For example, a shale-oil plant will consume 3.4 barrels of water (143 gallons) for each barrel of oil it produces. A plant that produces 50,000 barrels of synthetic crude oil per day would consume more than 7 million gallons of water in the same period. A coal-gasification plant that produces 250 million cubic feet of synthetic natural gas per day would consume from 6 to 30 million gallons of water per day, depending upon the gasification process used. The plant would require a total water supply of over 100 million gallons of water per day. This amount would reach a billion gallons per day if the water for cooling is used only once and not recycled. By comparison, water use in the 100 largest cities of the United States in 1962 ranged from 13 million gallons per day for Greensboro, North Carolina (population 124 thousand) to 1.19 billion gallons per day for New York City (population 8.3 million). The water pumped for municipal supplies represents use, but little consumption of water; most of the used water is discharged as sewage effluent.

The large quantities of water needed by oil-shale and coal-gasification plants pose difficulties in gaining access to natural supply and raise conflicts between water users. Many of these plants will be built in the relatively arid West where the oil shale and thick, shallow coal seams, many of which have low sulfur content, are located. In some areas of the West containing coal and oil shale, water resources are inadequate for synthetic fuel plants. This means that water will have to be transported from distant surface reservoirs. Substantial water supplies will also be needed for the reclamation of mined land. A recent report by the National Petroleum Council concludes that if a maximum effort to develop domestic fuel sources is undertaken, a billion-dollar program to construct dams and aqueducts near oil-shale and coal lands must be initiated almost immediately to assure sufficient water to meet energy needs.

Federal funding will be required to construct reservoirs and aqueducts of the magnitude necessary for fuel plants. This may well bring about conflict between federal agencies who have different responsibilities in construction and in water management, between water users, such as farmers and fuel plants, and between conservationists and developers. The fuel and energy industries will face a number of legal constraints in their efforts to procure the necessary water supplies. They will have to obtain from the state a right to appropriate water or else they will have to secure an existing appropriation. In the case of water stored by federal projects the industries will have to execute contracts with the U.S. government or its designated contracting agencies. Diversion of water for use in energy production may also be subject to interstate compacts and the Mexican Water Treaty, which govern flow in the large river basins of the West. Thus, legal restrictions present an imposing barrier to the efficient deployment of water from water-rich to water-deficient areas.

Even in the eastern states, where water abounds, the large water demands of the coal-conversion industries will conflict with other users' needs, particularly with those of the cities. Such competition will probably result in some form of water allocation. This is because a coal-gasification plant with capacity of 250 million cubic feet of gas per day would use the same amount of makeup-water as would a city with a population of more than 100,000. Such a city would not *consume* so much water, however; it would only use it. In the eastern states that have coal resources, the water supplies for coal conversion must be withdrawn mainly from the major streams or from large reservoirs. This will be necessary because few groundwater reservoirs near the coal fields are capable of providing the makeup-water needed for coal conversion and probably none can meet the total water demand. Attempts to develop groundwater supplies for such purposes would probably lead to intervention by municipalities and agricultural groups.

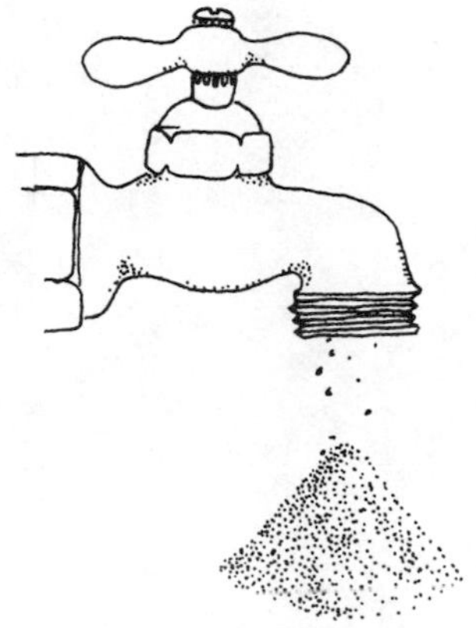

The role of groundwater in meeting escalating water demands in the next few decades is a matter for hard scrutiny. Groundwater is a resource of inestimable value to the smaller water user—the farm, the village, the light industry—that cannot economically treat surface water or bring it from distant points. An important decision water managers will have to make is whether to mine groundwater, that is, to pump it at a rate greater than the rate at which precipitation will replenish the supply. Groundwater is being extracted in this way to support irrigation in some arid regions of the western United States, the Middle East, and North Africa. In these areas, the mining of groundwater is an irrevocable act; there will be no second crop of groundwater under existing climates. It seems imprudent to deplete a groundwater reservoir in an arid region for a short-term economic gain, inasmuch as the development of groundwater is commonly the only feasible means of making such a region habitable.

Summary

Water is a resource continually renewed by the hydrologic cycle of precipitation, surface and underground accumulation, runoff, and evaporation. But only a small portion of the global hydrosphere is actually available at any one time to humans. And as rates of use and consumption rise, approaching the rate of annual renewal, water is fast becoming a scarce resource. Regional variations in precipitation, evaporation, and runoff further complicate the problem. At present, most of the eastern United States has a water surplus, but most of the western United States is water deficient and meets its needs by exploiting groundwater and transporting surface water over long distances.

Groundwater accumulates in the pores of soils, sediments, and rocks, and is replenished by surface seepage and runoff. Surface water itself represents the net balance between precipitation and evaporation, and forms streams, rivers, ponds, and lakes. Some surface flow is maintained by groundwater. The character of natural waters—especially dissolved salt and gas content, temperature, and acidity—is determined by physical, chemical, and biologic conditions where surface and subsurface waters accumulate and flow. Our own alterations of water determine its character as well.

Currently, people use about one-third of the water available on land; by the end of the century they will use about one-half. The chief water users are industry, particularly for power generation, and agriculture, especially for irrigation. Eighty percent of industrial water is used east of the Mississippi River, and 95 percent of the irrigation water is used west of the Mississippi. Besides geographic differences in water use, there are differences in sources of water and its quality after use. Most industrial water comes from surface supplies, whereas most irrigation water is drawn from groundwater sources. Industry makes water warmer, more acidic, and more toxic and returns most of it to the surface. Water for irrigation is altered mainly by added salt and sediment. Only about one-third the amount used returns to natural water bodies; the rest is consumed by surface evaporation and plant transpiration.

Glossary

aquitard A rock layer that impedes or prevents the flow of groundwater; also called an aquiclude.

ephemeral stream Stream (or river) that flows only during part of the year.

groundwater Underground water that occurs within the phreatic zone, or zone of water saturation.

perennial stream Stream (or river) that flows continuously throughout the year.

phreatic zone Subsurface zone of soil, sediment, or rock that is water saturated.

renewable resource Resource used by humans at a rate less than its natural formation.

transpiration Process by which water is lost to the atmosphere by plants.

vadose zone Subsurface zone of soil, sediment, or rock that is not water saturated.

water table Upper surface of groundwater; boundary between vadose and phreatic zones.

Reading Further

Kalinin, G. P., and V. D. Bykov. 1969. "The World's Water Resources, Present and Future." In *Impact of Science and Society,* vol. 19, no. 2, April–June. Paris, France: UNESCO.

Leopold, L. B. 1974. *Water: A Primer.* San Francisco: W. H. Freeman. An extremely readable short text by a leading authority that discusses virtually all aspects of surface and groundwaters.

Murray, C., and E. Reeves. 1972. *Estimated Use of Water in the United States.* U.S. Geological Survey Circular 676. Washington, D.C. Statistical data of water use in 1970 in the United States. Every five years the U.S. Geological Survey publishes such a summary of national water use, providing an interpretation of recent trends.

Piper, A. 1965. *Has the United States Enough Water?* U.S. Geological Survey Water-Supply Paper 1797. Washington, D.C. Analysis of current water use in the United States and predictions of future national needs. Useful tables, graphs and maps.

Skinner, B. 1969. *Earth Resources.* Englewood Cliffs, N.J.: Prentice-Hall. Contains a short, clear chapter on water resources.

Portuguese fishermen.

The Oceans 4

It is awesome to consider that three-quarters of the earth's surface lies beneath ocean water whose average depth is almost 4000 meters. As we might expect, the ocean bottom, like the land surface, is a panorama of broad plains, submarine mountain ranges that tower a few thousand meters above the plains, and trenches that plunge several thousand meters below. Within the water itself is a vast storehouse of dissolved salts, gases, heat, and nutrients. As ocean heat circulates, it influences the world's climate, and as ocean nutrients diffuse, they support a tremendous variety of living things. Beneath the water, under the ocean floor, lie even more valuable resources—deposits of oil and gas, and metals and nonmetals.

A body of water occupying about two-thirds of a world made for man—who has no gills.

Ambrose Bierce, 1906

As resources on land begin to reach the straining point, people look seaward, hoping to find ways of exploiting this marine wealth. Some view the oceans as a gigantic cornucopia, continually bulging with fresh water, energy, minerals, and food—if only we knew how to recover them. Others warn us that these marine resources are either grossly overestimated, too widely scattered and thus inaccessible, or so costly to exploit that we cannot rely on the sea's bounty. Furthermore, the oceans are the final resting place for large amounts of human refuse, so whatever benefits the oceans have to offer may be diminished by the time we arrive to harvest them.

Gross considers some of the problems resulting from dumping wastes into the ocean in his Viewpoint at the end of this chapter.

In this chapter, we want to understand the nature, origin, and distribution of marine resources and to evaluate their future potential. We explore the topography and sediments of the ocean floor, the resources of the sea, and the potential harvests of food from the sea.

4-1 Exploring the Ocean Floor

Until the middle part of this century, our knowledge of the ocean floor was limited by our inability to plumb its great depths and to sample its sediments and rocks. After World War II, scientific exploration of the seas boomed. Echo sounding permitted more detailed mapping of submarine contours, and rocks and sediments were sampled by dredging and coring. Direct observations were made possible with deep sea photography, television, and research submarines.

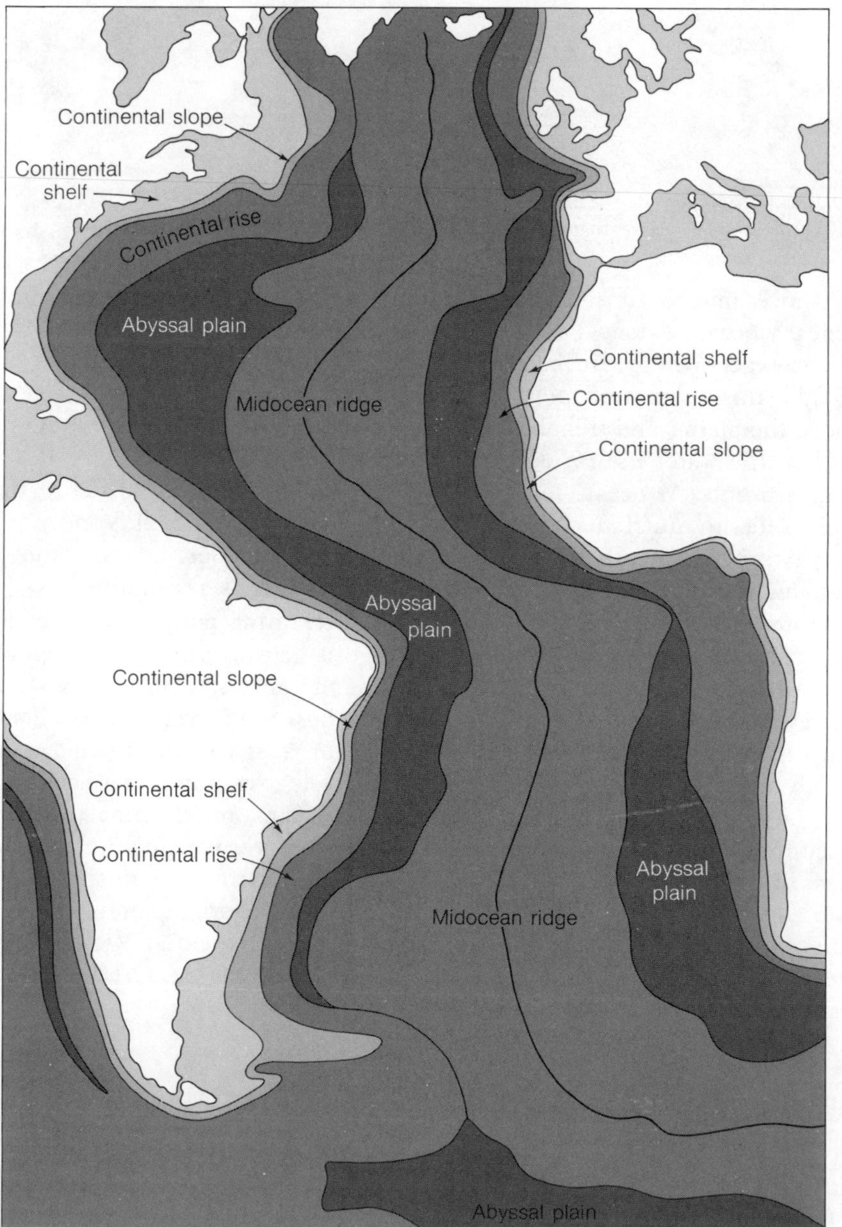

(a)

Figure 4–1

Generalized submarine topography. (a) Map of the Atlantic Ocean showing the narrow continental shelves passing seaward into the continental slope and abyssal plain. The Atlantic, like all the ocean basins, has a broad midoceanic ridge that marks diverging plate boundaries. (b) Cross section of an idealized ocean basin indicating water depths from the continents to the trenches. The Atlantic Ocean lacks well-developed trenches along continental margins because eastern North and South America and western Europe and Africa are on the trailing edges of diverging plates. Notice that the maximum relief between the highest and lowest points of the earth's surface is almost 20,000 meters. Note, too, that only a very thin surface layer of the oceans is lighted by the sun.

Although much remains to be learned, for the first time in history we have a reasonable understanding of sea floor topography and geology. Our ancestors believed that ocean basins were smooth, bowl-shaped depressions that were tectonically stable, blanketed with thick, evenly distributed sediment, and inhabited by huge sea monsters. Today we know that ocean basins differ vastly in topographic relief, are tectonically active, have sediments and rocks of varying composition and thickness, and do contain large sea animals—though none of the kinds described by the ancient mariners.

The first major oceanographic expedition was undertaken in 1872 by the British navy corvette, HMS Challenger.

Submarine topography

Although each of the ocean basins has its own unique characteristics, numerous similarities allow us to generalize about their topography. Proceeding seaward from the edge of a continent to the center of an ocean basin, the sea floor slopes gently across the continental shelf, then drops slightly down the continental slope, and finally reaches a broad, level abyssal plain. This is illustrated for the Atlantic Ocean in Figure 4–1. Along some convergent plate margins, at the foot of the continental slope, lies a trench several kilometers deep. In the middle of the ocean basins, along diverging plates, lies a broad ridge some 2000 kilometers wide and almost 4000 meters high.

The *continental shelf,* whose seaward dip is less than one degree, is the submarine extension of the continental landmass. The width of the shelf averages 65 kilometers. It is usually narrower on the leading edge and wider on the trailing edge of a continental plate, depending on whether it is moving toward or away from another plate.

It's claimed that the shelf is so flat that if you were out of sight of land, you wouldn't know in which direction the deep ocean lay.

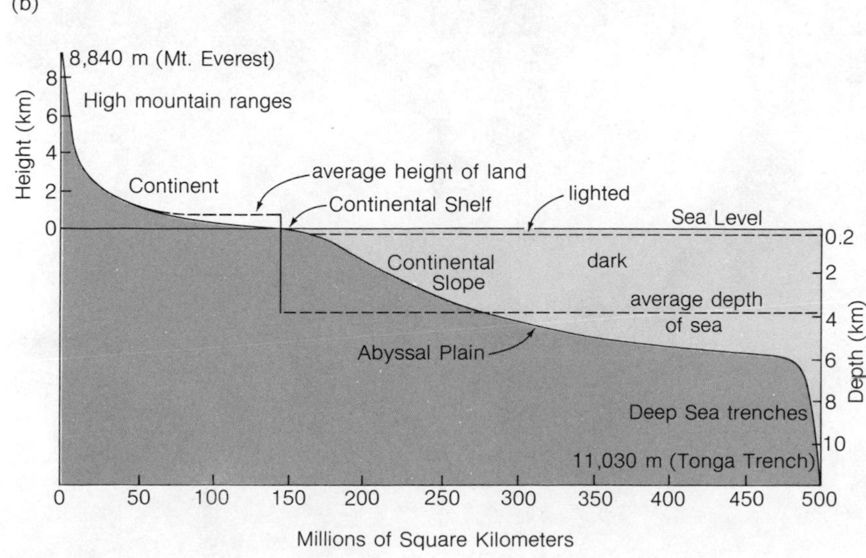

The *continental slope* drops off a little more steeply than the shelf, and traces the boundary between the highly elevated continent and the low-lying abyssal plain under several thousands of meters of water. The continental slope is regularly cut by transverse submarine canyons, and sediments are transported down these canyons to the deep ocean floor below, as pictured in Figure 4–2.

Large portions of the deep sea are floored by abyssal plains—generally featureless, flat-lying surfaces that collect sediments. The sediments are eroded from the continents, washed across the shelves, and carried down the slopes. Relieving the topographic monotony of the abyssal plains are scattered volcanoes, some whose tops have been planed down by wave action before subsiding into the depths. Such inactive, truncated volcanoes are called *seamounts* and often provide the foundations for upward-growing coral reefs.

The midoceanic ridges divide the abyssal plains. They form a broad spine of volcanic rock erupted during periodic magmatic activity along divergent midoceanic plate boundaries. A narrow *rift valley*, created by the intermittent pulling apart of diverging plates, lies along the axis of many midoceanic ridges.

Marine sediments and rocks

Sediments and rocks lying on the sea floor are related to the nature and origin of its topography. Rock formations and structures on continental margins continue out onto the continental shelves; the shelves are veneered

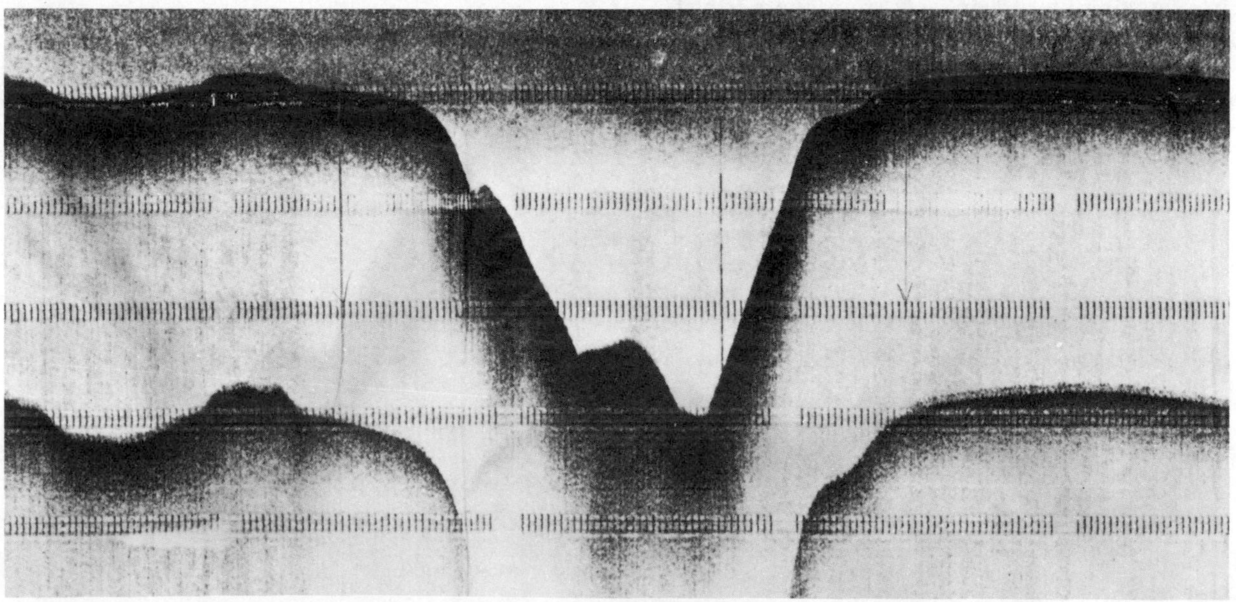

Figure 4–2

Echo sounding profile showing a branch of Hatteras Submarine Canyon on the upper continental shelf off North Carolina. Black trace below sea floor is multiple reflection.

by a thin mantle of sediments eroded from continents, accumulated at river mouths, and distributed by waves and currents.

Shelves lie under relatively shallow water whose average depth is 130 meters. Thus the shelves are periodically exposed when sea level drops during worldwide continental glaciation. In the Pleistocene epoch, glacial ice accumulated and removed water from the oceans. Later, as glaciers melted, they returned the water, and this led to sea level changes ranging from 140 meters (462 feet) below to 60 meters (198 feet) above present-day sea levels. As glacial and interglacial shorelines migrated back and forth across continental shelves, sediments were deposited, eroded, and redistributed.

At least four major advances and retreats of sea level occurred over the last million years or so during the Pleistocene glaciations and interglaciations.

Sediments now lying in deep water on the outer shelves are mainly composed of these older Pleistocene materials. Most sediments eroded from continents today are deposited along the inner portions of shelves. Preglacial sedimentary rocks lie beneath the Pleistocene and Holocene shelf sediments; these sandstones, shales, and limestones were laid down near the former shore in shallow marine environments like beaches, lagoons, and deltas. They were also deposited inland from shore in nonmarine environments like swamps, rivers, and lakes.

Continental slopes are composed of fine-grained, muddy marine sediments that were washed off the shelves or deposited at lower sea levels. Submarine canyons with V-shaped valleys radiate outward from the shelf edge and cut into the continental slopes. At times of lower sea level, large rivers flow across the shelves and down the upper continental slope, eroding some of the upper canyons. Sediment-laden currents farther down the

Small submarine fault scarp, in the floor of the Atlantic near Gibraltar.

slope have continued the erosion, digging out the lower canyons all the way to the abyssal plains. This submarine erosion is accomplished by the downslope movement of *turbidity currents,* sediment-laden flows whose greater density moves them downward by gravity. Recently, some marine geologists have suggested that circular patterns of water and sediment called *sedimentation cells* generate and maintain turbidity currents along coastal margins, as depicted in Figure 4–3 . They theorize that onshore winds push surface water toward the land, while the deeper water below moves seaward. Thus sand and silt transported by rivers to the coast are carried along the shore and across the shelf to the head of a submarine canyon, where turbidity currents carry them seaward. Submarine canyons form boundaries between two adjacent cells and conduct continental margin sediments to the ocean deep. The narrower the shelf, the better developed the cell. (It isn't clear yet if this theory explains Atlantic Coast submarine canyons as well as it does the Pacific Coast ones.)

An early clue to the existence of turbidity currents was the progressive severing of transatlantic telephone cables in 1929 as an earthquake-triggered turbidity current moved across the Grand Banks, south of Newfoundland.

Blanketing the abyssal plains of the world's oceans are coarser grained sediments deposited by turbidity currents. These sediments are mixed with finer grained materials that have settled out of suspension from ocean water. Some of the latter are inorganic, representing the finer fraction of sediments eroded from the continents and carried out to sea by wind or water. Varying proportions of these abyssal plain sediments also may be organic in origin. Many come from the billions of small skeletons secreted by planktonic animals and plants living in the sea's surface waters.

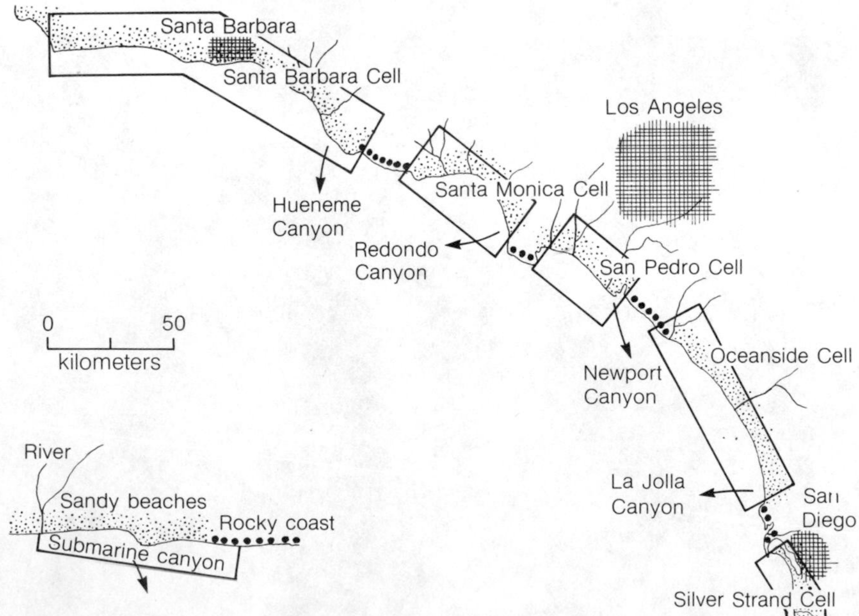

Figure 4–3

Five coastal sedimentation cells along the Southern California shelf. Each cell circulates sediment from the coast to the deep water basins offshore, and is bounded by a submarine canyon.

Inorganic deep sea muds are composed of several kinds of material: wind-blown and water-borne clays from continents, volcanic minerals and rock fragments, and minerals like manganese-rich nodules that precipitate directly on the sea floor. (We'll say more about these nodules in the next section because of their potential value as new sources of metal deposits.) Organically derived muds are rich in skeletons secreted by single-celled plankton living in the upper waters. These muds may be calcareous or siliceous, depending on the relative abundance of lime-secreting organisms like foraminiferans (animals) and coccolithophorids (plants), or silica-secreting radiolarians (animals) and diatoms (plants).

The geographic distribution of these different kinds of deep sea sediments depends on factors like biological productivity of plankton, water depth, rates of sedimentation, and volcanic activity. For example, sediments in water deeper than approximately 4000 meters are silica-rich and lime-poor because at such depths the colder water contains more dissolved carbon dioxide gas. This means that the water is somewhat acidic, and whatever calcium carbonate reaches these depths is soon dissolved, if it hasn't already been removed on its way down (leaving behind the less soluble siliceous sediments). Distribution of abyssal plain sediments is presented in Figure 4–4.

4–2 Seabed Resources

Since many geologic processes in the ocean are similar to those on land, it is logical to assume that terrestrial resources like metallic ores, sand, gravel, oil, and gas also lie on the ocean floor. Exploration and exploitation of land-based resources have been pursued more vigorously because of their accessibility and more obvious presence. But as continental resources dwindle and become harder to exploit, seabed resources are gaining importance and it is now becoming economically feasible to develop them.

Metals and nonmetals

Large portions of the abyssal plains are carpeted by manganese-rich nodules sized and shaped like potatoes, as seen in Figure 4–5. The nodules also contain relatively abundant concentrations of other metals like iron, copper, nickel, and cobalt. The formation of these metal-rich nodules is not yet completely understood, but apparently they accumulate in areas of extremely slow sedimentation. There, metals in seawater solution precipitate concentrically around small fragments of shell, fish bone, or volcanic rock. Lately, the source of the metals has been attributed to magmatic activity along midoceanic ridges: submarine volcanism puts the metals into seawater, from which they later slowly precipitate as nodular ac-

We discussed the probable association of these nodules with diverging plate boundaries in Chapter 1.

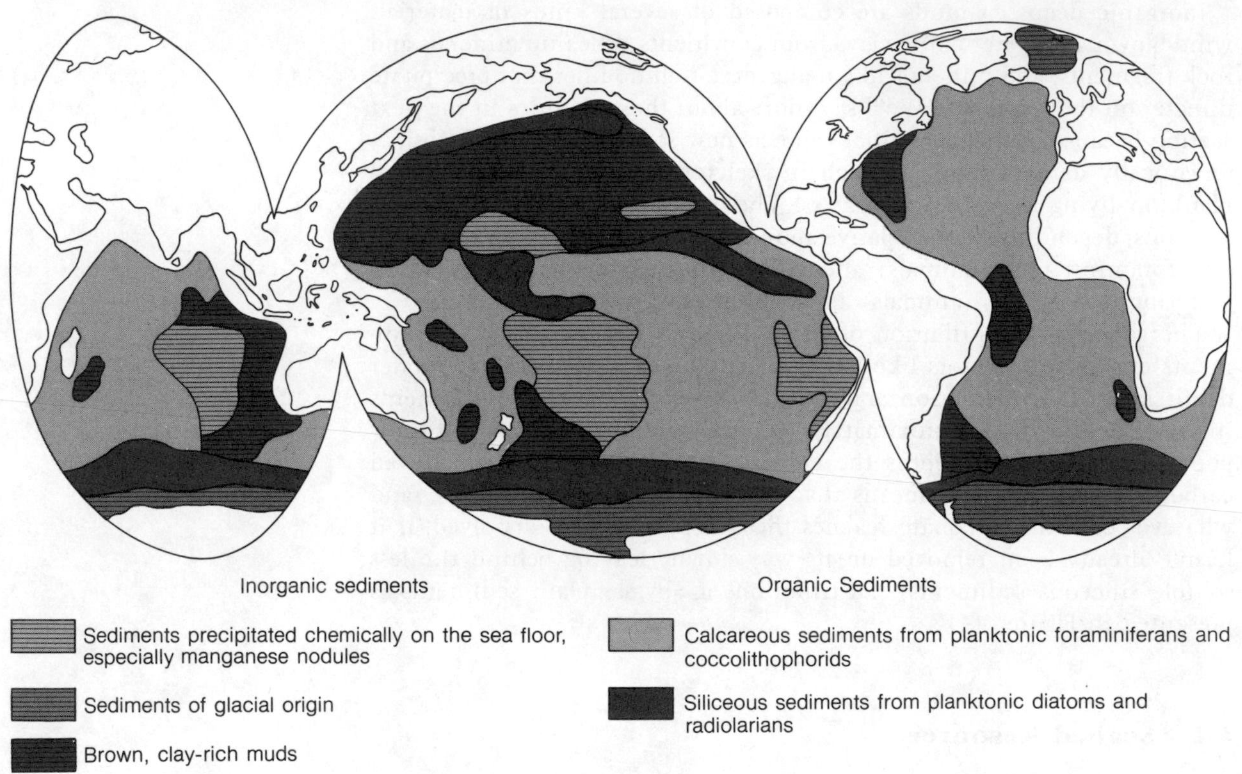

Figure 4–4

Distribution of various types of deep sea sediments.

cumulations. They accrete at a rate of a few millimeters per thousands to hundreds of thousands of years. Therefore, the slow-forming nodules can grow only where sedimentation rates are slower still; otherwise, the incipient nodules would be buried before they had a chance to take shape. For this reason, manganese nodules are common on abyssal plains where sediments gather very slowly. However, abundant nodules are found in some areas of relatively high sedimentation rates—a puzzle yet to be explained.

Regions favorable for nodule formation, especially on abyssal plains in the Pacific Ocean, lie under such deep water that their recovery is difficult. But because they are so rich in metals, mining companies are developing several techniques for mining them. These include dredging with a continuous string of bucket-like devices, vacuuming with a long hose, and sinking a huge barge to be filled with nodules by remote control and later refloated. Thorny issues of international politics come into play in this type of mining, because no one knows who owns resources lying well beyond the territorial waters of any single country. One African nation, Zäire, has even expressed concern that mining manganese nodules, which have a relatively high cobalt content, would seriously threaten its national economy. Unsurprisingly, Zäire's economy is based largely on cobalt exports.

The volume of these nodules in the Pacific Ocean is estimated at more than 1.5 billion metric tons. In places, the Pacific holds more than 10,000 metric tons per square kilometer. Although the nodules contain more manganese than any other metal, their relatively high concentration of nickel, copper, and cobalt generates the most interest. These three metals are as abundant in the nodules as in land-based ores; see Table 4–1.

Other metallic ores in the sea are placer deposits of gold, platinum,

Table 4–1 Metal Concentrations in Manganese Nodules Compared with Land-based Ores

Element	Pacific Ocean, Manganese Nodules (percent)	Minimum Land-based Ores (percent)
manganese	24.2	25
iron	14.0	20
nickel	1.0	1
copper	0.5	0.5
cobalt	0.4	0.01

Figure 4–5

Manganese nodules lying on the deep ocean floor in the North Pacific.

cassiterite, magnetite, chromite, and other metals of high density and chemical stability. Placer concentrations, which are mined in shallow water by dredging, were formed in one of two ways. Either they were recently laid down in nearshore sediments, or they were deposited long ago in stream and river beds which later were covered by postglacial flooding of the continental shelves. Other minerals, like diamond and zircon, are also found in these deposits.

In a few places along diverging plate boundaries—particularly the Red Sea and Gulf of California—hot, metal-rich brines have emerged from the mixing of extensive magmatic solutions and seawater. The brines have precipitated ores of zinc, copper, and lead sulfides within the sea floor sediments. Even though these deposits have not yet been exploited, they do have considerable future potential as a source of copper and possibly zinc (Table 4–2).

Among the nonmetals, loose sediments rich in sand, gravel, or lime have been most valuable to date. The costs of dredging these sediments from shallow water and transporting them by barge are relatively inexpensive. Thus they can compete economically with land-based nonmetals in regions where demand is high and transportation costs great.

Oil and gas

Subsurface geologic structures that trap oil and gas on land may continue offshore onto the continental shelves. As offshore drilling technology has improved—wells drilled in water deeper than 100 meters are now common—petroleum production has correspondingly increased. In the early 1970s, 13 percent of the oil and gas produced in the United States came from the sea floor. Similar amounts were recovered from offshore areas across the rest of the globe: 12 percent of the world's oil and 9 percent of its gas. Estimates of proved, recoverable reserves that can be exploited in the future do not differ much from current recovery percentages. Recoverable oil from the world's offshore areas is somewhat higher than present-day figures—16 percent compared with 12 percent—but future offshore gas prospects are about the same; see Table 4–3.

Table 4–2 Metal Concentrations in Red Sea Mud Compared with Land-based Ores

Element	Red Sea Mud (percent)	Minimum Land-based Ore (percent)
zinc	2.1	2.5
copper	0.7	0.5
lead	0.2	4
manganese	0.1	25

Table 4–3 Proved Recoverable Reserves

	Oil (percent of world total) Onshore/Offshore	Gas (percent of world total) Onshore/Offshore
North America		
Canada	2/not available	4/not available
United States	6/1	15/3
South America	5/trace	3/trace
Europe	1/2	10/3
Asia (includes USSR)	62/12	47/1
Africa	8/1	11/1
Oceania	trace/trace	1/1
	84/16	91/9
Total for 120 Nations	83 billion metric tons	44 trillion cubic meters

Areas most promising for future offshore petroleum production are adjacent to productive onshore areas. In addition, shelves that are broad and possess a thick sedimentary cover hold promise. In the United States, most offshore production has come from salt domes in the Gulf of Mexico and anticlinal traps along the West Coast, where the difficulties of drilling are compounded by the challenge of the sea. Although production has been trivial along the Atlantic Coast, future petroleum prospects are judged favorable because the shelves are wide and the sedimentary rocks are thick. Seaward extension of rich oil and gas deposits along the north coast of Alaska into the Arctic Ocean has been predicted, and some wells already have been tapped. Abroad, oil and gas exploration and production have been carried out predominantly in the North Sea area of northwestern Europe and in the extensive shallow seas bordering Malaysia, Indonesia, and Southeast Asia (Figure 4–6).

Beyond the continental shelves, prospects for oil and gas are much less certain. Not only is the subsurface geology poorly known, but the cost of recovering these fossil fuels is prohibitive. No doubt, continental slope exploration will proceed only when the oil and gas deposits on the continental shelves have been more fully exploited. However, as in Table 2–4, some initial estimates of these resources have been made.

4–3 Ocean Water

As we noted in the preceding chapter, more than 97 percent of the hydrosphere is comprised of oceans. This tremendous volume of water, about 1.4 billion cubic kilometers, accordingly holds a wealth of dissolved salts, gases, and nutrients, as well as heat from the sun. Ocean water, like fresh

Figure 4–6

Oil drilling platform in water 80 meters deep off the south coast of Australia.

terrestrial water, varies in its physical, chemical, and biological properties, but unlike fresh water, these properties vary within a narrower range because the oceans' constant circulation tends to average them. In addition, natural terrestrial waters are more isolated from each other and only remotely interconnected. Even so, the oceans are not one homogeneous body; instead, they are subdivided into specific water masses, each defined chiefly in terms of its temperature and salinity. The subdivisions have names like the Gulf Stream, Deep Atlantic Bottom Water, and the Humboldt Current. These water masses stem from global differences in solar heating, runoff, precipitation, evaporation, and oxygen consumption and production.

Salinity and temperature

Substances dissolved in seawater include virtually all natural elements, numerous organic materials, and myriad man-made chemicals. Dissolved inorganic salts in seawater constitute its average salinity of 3.5 percent, or thirty-five parts per thousand. (Fresh water on land averages less than two-tenths of a part per thousand.) Of these salts, only six—chlorine, sodium, sulfate, magnesium, calcium, and potassium—account for more than 99 percent of the total salinity, as you can see in Figure 4–7. These major seawater components have been dubbed *conservative elements* because their relative abundances remain the same despite local variations

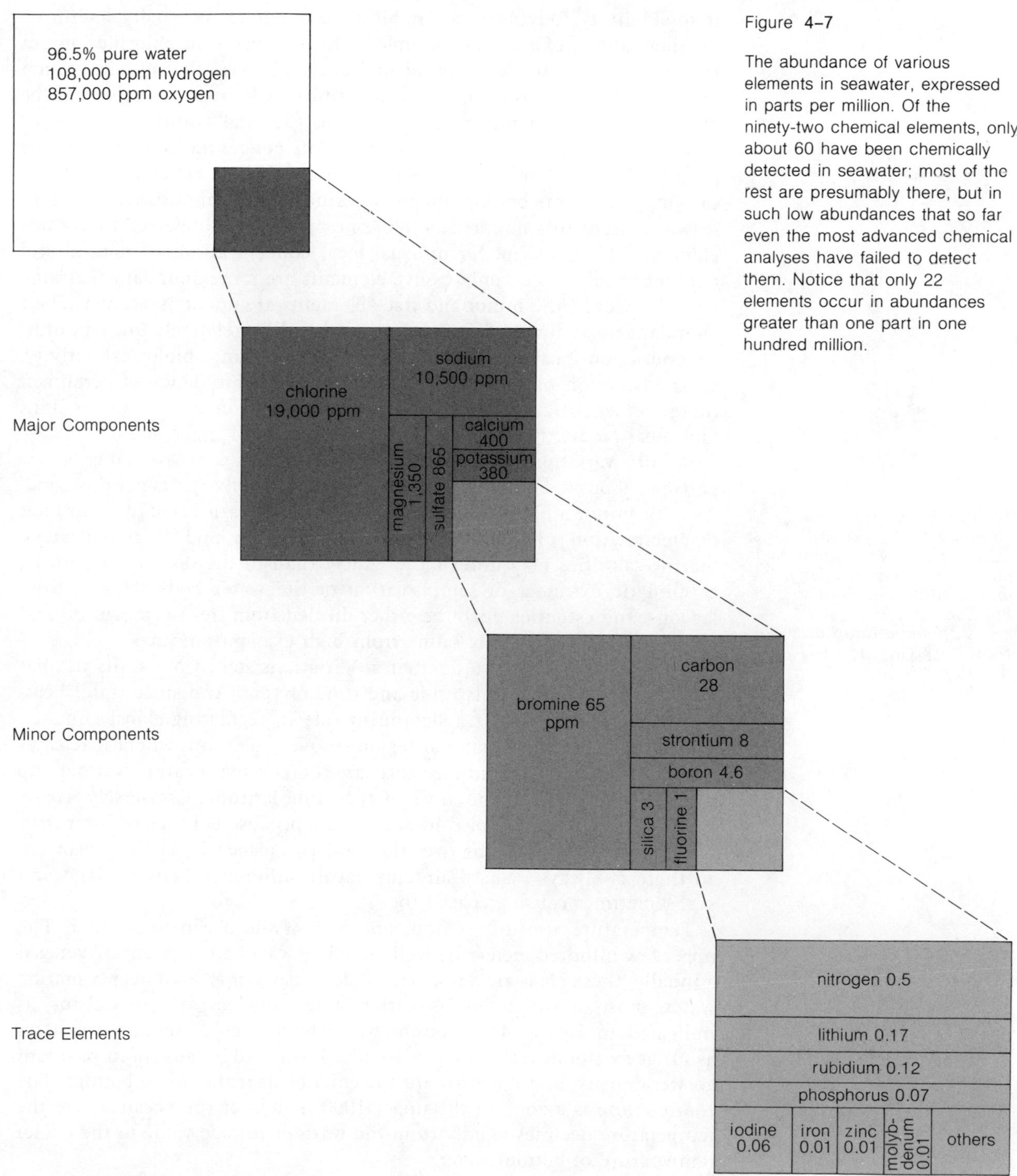

Figure 4–7

The abundance of various elements in seawater, expressed in parts per million. Of the ninety-two chemical elements, only about 60 have been chemically detected in seawater; most of the rest are presumably there, but in such low abundances that so far even the most advanced chemical analyses have failed to detect them. Notice that only 22 elements occur in abundances greater than one part in one hundred million.

in total salinity. Relying on this stability, oceanographers usually determine the total salinity of a seawater sample by measuring just its chloride content rather than every single dissolved substance, a process that requires much more complex analysis. Once the chlorinity is known, its value can be plugged into an equation that easily yields the total salinity.

Minor elements in seawater are those in concentrations of 1 to 100 parts per million (ppm), and this includes another six elements: bromine, carbon, strontium, boron, silicon, fluorine. All other dissolved salts in seawater occur in amounts less than one ppm and are referred to as *trace elements.* Thus, except for unusual local concentrations of natural and man-made substances, only twelve elements are more abundant than one ppm. Moreover, the minor and trace elements are nonconservative. Their abundance may fluctuate widely, although still in relatively low amounts, depending on local conditions like runoff from land, biological activity, their adsorption on sediments, and so on. The abundance of certain of these elements like nitrogen, phosphorus, or silicon may foster or limit biological productivity because they are critical for organisms.

To understand how small a quantity 1 part per million is, think of it as equivalent to 1 minute in 2 years, 1 large mouthful of food in a lifetime, or a hop-skip-and-a-jump between New York City and Los Angeles.

Salinity variations in surface waters of the open oceans range a few parts per thousand either side of the average thirty-five parts per thousand. As with minor and trace elements, total salinity varies according to rates of precipitation, evaporation, and runoff from the land. In coastal areas, marine salinities may differ more widely than in the open ocean, owing to climatic extremes or semi-isolation of the water body. Hence, bays, lagoons, and estuaries might be either diluted from freshwater runoff and precipitation or extremely saline from high evaporation rates.

Ocean temperature also fluctuates. Variations stem from shifts in solar heating with changes in latitude and time of year. And since water heats and cools slowly, it plays a significant role in regulating global climates. Water heated in the equatorial regions moves poleward, where it releases some of its heat. High-latitude coasts are thereby significantly warmer—up to 5° Celsius—than inland areas of the same latitude. Conversely, coasts in lower latitudes are cooled by sea breezes because land heats faster than water; the warm air rising over the land is replaced by cooler ocean air. So there is always a sharp air-temperature difference between land and sea, sometimes causing coastal fog.

Temperature also differs from one part of the ocean to another. The upper few hundred meters are well mixed by waves and currents. Averaged annually, these areas are a few tens of degrees warmer than deeper marine water, most of which hovers within a few degrees of zero Celsius, as indicated in Figure 4–8. Bottom water is very cold since it originates as surface water near the two poles, sinks downward because of its resultant greater density, and flows toward the equator near the ocean bottom. The *thermocline* is a zone in the upper 1000 meters of the ocean where the temperature declines rapidly from the warmer surface value to the colder temperature of bottom water.

Moving masses of water

Temperature and salinity of seawater are two key factors controlling its density. Colder, more saline water is denser than warmer, less saline water. Even the small variations in temperature and salinity experienced by the oceans cause density differences sufficient to propel circulation. For, the same physical conditions that make surface waters denser also make them sink, bringing about vertical and horizontal mixing. For example, Arctic and Antarctic surface waters cool and freeze; since ice cannot hold salt, the freezing waters leave behind a dense brine that sinks and spreads toward the equator.

This circulation is analogous to that of the earth's other fluid shell, the atmosphere, whose density varies with temperature and water vapor content.

When surface waters in the Mediterranean Sea evaporate, they grow more saline and thus more dense. As a result, they sink and flow out through the Gibraltar Straits at several hundred meters' depth. Surface water above this saline tongue flows eastward through the Straits from the Atlantic to the Mediterranean, to replace the deeper, westward-flowing water. In *estuaries,* which are coastal embayments where the sea penetrates the lower part of a river, a similar vertical and horizontal circulation may operate. If evaporation rates are great enough, surface waters in the estuary sink and travel seaward, letting less saline and dense water move up the estuary along the surface. If the river's freshwater runoff exceeds surface evaporation, then the diluted, less saline water simply flows seaward over the denser marine water below.

Water masses within the world's oceans are thus characterized by their density which is, in turn, determined primarily by temperature and salinity, as described in Figure 4–9. Because of the oceans' fluid nature, density differences force water masses to circulate, with denser ones moving below

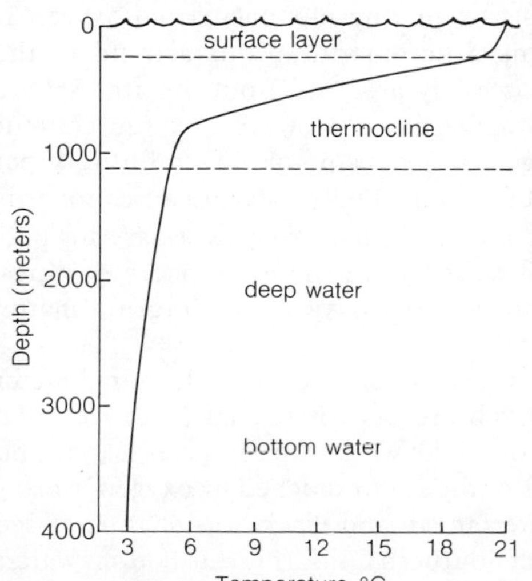

Figure 4–8

Decrease in temperature with increase in depth in the oceans. The average temperature in the earth's temperate zones is 21°C, and surface waters are heated to this value. Mixing by waves and currents keeps the upper several hundred meters near this value.

Figure 4–9

Oceanic water masses defined by temperature and salinity at 200 meters' depth. Density increases from the upper left to lower right of the diagram. Notice how the high-salinity waters of the Red and Mediterranean seas that form in regions of high evaporation influence the water masses of the two oceans into which they flow. Antarctic bottom water, because of its low temperature, is the densest ocean water of all; since it flows into all the oceans, each oceanic water mass contains a very dense, cold portion.

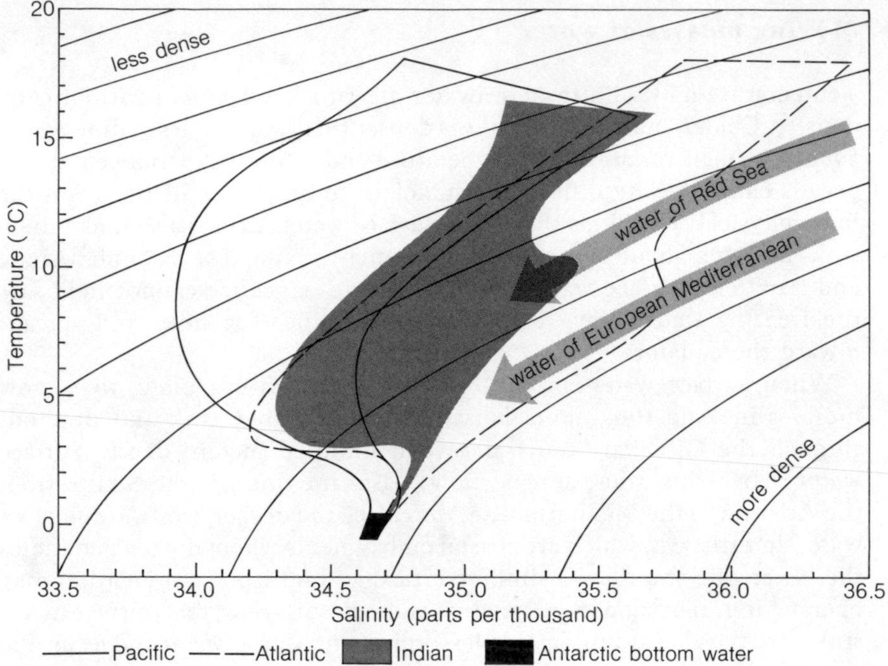

less dense ones. Before density stratification can be fully achieved, new water masses originate and continually maintain the density-generated circulation, which is seen in Figure 4–10.

Oxygen and carbon dioxide

Remember that oxygen and carbon dioxide are found as dissolved gases in seawater. During photosynthesis by marine phytoplankton, oxygen is produced and added to the oceans. Since marine plants abound in the upper surface waters and oxygen is easily absorbed from the atmosphere at this level, these waters are well oxygenated. However, oxygen content steadily declines from an average surface value of 4–5 milliliters per liter to 2 or less at several hundred meters. The principal causes for this decline, indicated in Figure 4–11, are several: sunlight necessary for photosynthesis diminishes; oxygen absorbed from the atmosphere declines; animal and plant respiration removes more oxygen; and organic matter oxidizes in the water.

This vertical decline in oxygen reverses itself at several-hundred-meter depths and begins to climb again. The reversal is caused by oxygen-rich bottom waters which formed in the cold waters of the poles, sank, and moved toward the equator. In parts of the sea untouched by oxygen-bearing polar waters, such as in the Mediterranean and Black Seas or in enclosed submarine depressions like those off Southern California, the bottom waters are low in oxygen and sometimes even stagnant.

Carbon dioxide also enters the sea by absorption from the atmosphere, by animal and plant respiration, and by oxidation of organic matter. Some carbon dioxide is removed from seawater by plants during photosynthesis or by organisms that build their shells with calcium carbonate. As we noted earlier, ocean water deeper than approximately 4000 meters contains relatively large amounts of carbon dioxide because of the water's low temperature. Moreover, the gas makes the seawater sufficiently acidic so that any calcium carbonate that reaches these depths is readily dissolved.

Seawater nutrients

The chief constituents of organic matter are carbon, hydrogen, oxygen, nitrogen, and phosphorus. The latter two elements are often so scarce in seawater that their low abundance limits biological productivity in the oceans. In fact, in the upper surface waters, phytoplankton consume nitrates and phosphates almost completely. But in deeper water, the poor sunlight causes plant activity to decline sharply. Nitrates and phosphates are correspondingly more abundant there, as indicated in Figure 4–12, since decay organisms decompose the accumulating organic matter and release these biologically essential substances. Because the oceans' vertical circulation returns nitrogen and phosphorus from deeper waters to the surface, the rate of biological productivity largely depends on the speed of vertical circulation. Areas of the world's oceans where biological productivity is high are places where water rich in nitrogen and phosphorus regularly comes to the surface. This movement supports the high productivity of phytoplankton which, in turn, maintains considerable productivity throughout the food chain.

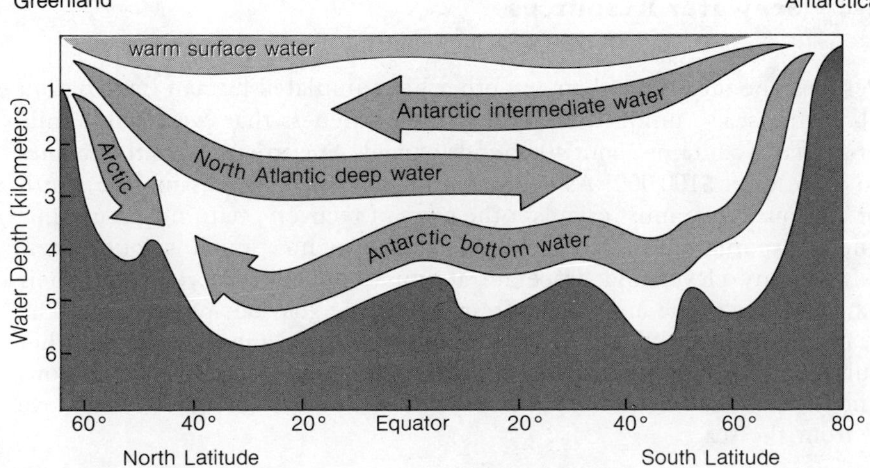

Figure 4–10

Movement of water masses within the Atlantic Ocean generated by density differences related to temperature and salinity. The central portion of the North Atlantic is composed of five water masses, four of which originate in polar regions and flow at various depths toward the equator. The fifth water mass is a relatively warm surface layer.

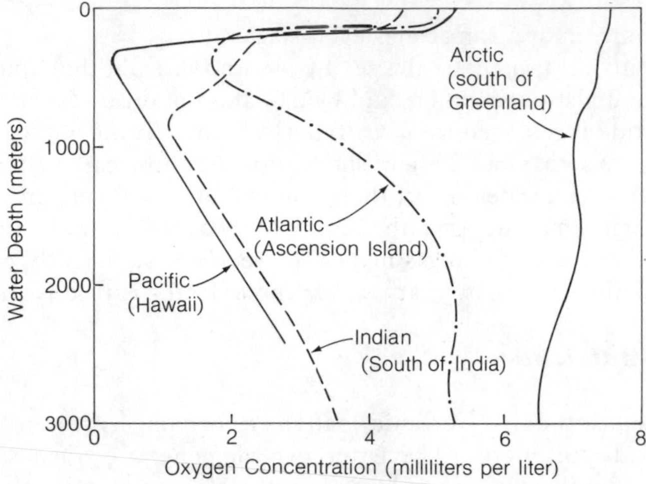

Figure 4-11

Vertical variation in oxygen content of the ocean. Surface waters are rich in oxygen from absorbing this gas from the atmosphere and from photosynthesizing marine plants in shallow, sunlit waters. A sharp decline in oxygen within a few hundred meters reflects oxygen consumption by animal respiration and decomposition of organic matter. Higher oxygen values in deep water reflect bottom-flowing waters that originate near the poles (see Figure 4-10) and account for generally high values throughout the water column in the Arctic.

Seawater nutrients come from the land as well as from the ocean depths. Rivers drain the continents and add nutrients to the surface water; terrestrial organic matter rich in nitrates and phosphates sweeps downstream to the ocean. Coastal marshes, too, with their abundant vegetation and variety of marine invertebrates, fish, and birds contribute generous amounts of nitrogen and phosphorus to the ocean's nearshore areas.

About 50 percent of the world's commercial fishes spend some part of their lives in coastal marshes.

Since nitrogen and phosphorus are so critical in supporting biological productivity, areas lacking vertical seawater circulation or runoff from the land are areas of relatively poor biological activity. Thus continental margins support much more marine life than do the central portions of the ocean far from river mouths and vertical upwelling. And it is these coastal areas that provide the world's great fisheries.

4-4 Seawater Resources

Perhaps one idea more than any other has stimulated human imagination about the sea's "unlimited" bounty: the awareness that every cubic mile of seawater contains about 40 pounds of gold. At current prices that comes to more than $100,000! As is always the case when discussing the worth of a resource, we must calculate the costs of recovery, refining, processing, and transportation, as well as simply calculating how much is "out there." After many clever and desperate attempts, no one has yet made their expenses—let alone any profit—from extracting gold out of seawater. The reasons for difficulty in economic recovery of gold (and almost all other substances in seawater) are low concentration (about ten parts per trillion) and the elaborate technology and costly energy demands required to remove it from the sea.

Salts and water

Seawater is a dilute saline solution of astronomical dimensions: 1.4 billion cubic kilometers of water enveloping 50 quadrillion metric tons of dissolved inorganic elements. Paradoxically, the sea is too salty to drink and too dilute to mine for its precious materials. The only substances recovered from seawater that have significant economic value arc three of its six major components—chlorine, sodium, and magnesium—and one of its minor constituents—bromine. Worldwide, about 30 percent of table salt (NaCl), 60 percent of bromine, and 70 percent of magnesium comes from the ocean. Except for a few other elements, like potassium and iodine, seawater is too dilute to be a major source of metals and nonmetals.

Because most ocean salts exist in such low concentrations, one ppm or less, great volumes of seawater must be processed to obtain sufficient quantities. But such processing requires an enormous amount of energy, whose cost outweighs the value of the materials recovered. When cheap sources of nuclear power have been fully developed, the extraction costs may fall low enough to make the "mining" of seawater worthwhile. But even then, processing ordinary rock for its metal content still might be cheaper. Common granite, for instance, contains 1000 times more uranium, 1500 times more copper, 2000 times more nickel, 3000 times more zinc, and 3500 times more maganese than seawater. Perhaps the problems of rock waste disposal in mining granite would outweigh the lower concentration in seawater which, after processing, could be returned to the oceans. But "mining" ocean water on the required scale might have its own environmental problems.

Can you think of some?

Extraction of fresh water from the seas has been more successful to date than large-scale recovery of most of its valuable minerals. Fresh water

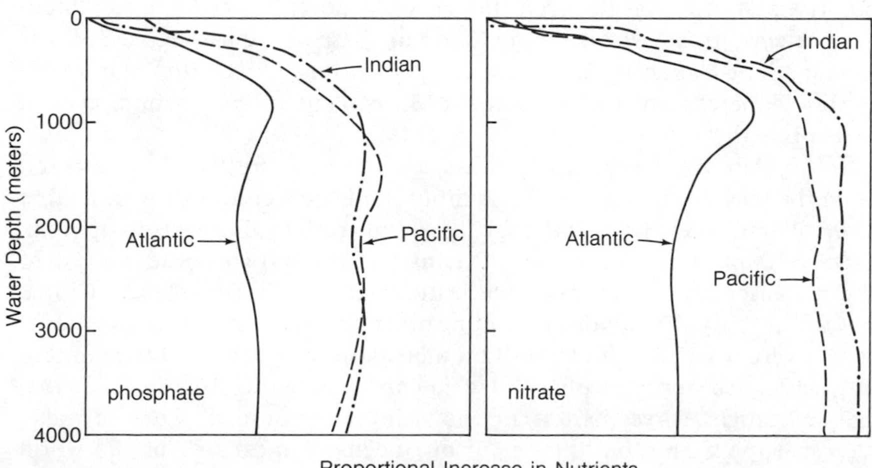

Figure 4–12

Differences in amounts of nutrients, phosphates, and nitrates, with depth. Phytoplankton productivity in upper surface waters deplete the phosphate and nitrate content. With depth, however, bacterial decomposition releases them from organic matter and makes these nutrient elements more abundant.

is usually defined as having less than 1000 ppm dissolved salts, although the U.S. Public Health Service and UN World Health Organization recommend less than 500 ppm for drinking. Desalinization of seawater for potable, or drinking, water thus requires removing almost 99 percent of its salts. This proportion equals the percentage composition of the ocean's six major elements, three of which are now commercially produced from seawater.

Methods for desalinizing seawater include distillation, freezing, ion exchange (similar to a water-softening process), and electrodialysis (whereby an electric current separates and concentrates positively and negatively charged atoms, leaving behind fresh water). All these methods require an energy source and presently burn several hundred kilowatt hours for every 3800 liters (1000 gallons) of fresh water. In most regions, the price of electricity for desalinization runs to approximately $1 per 3800 liters, about ten times the cost of water from terrestrial sources. Inland transportation of seawater desalinized near the coast also raises the cost of such water. Yet in parts of the world where water is scarce, the cost of desalinization is competitive with that of terrestrial water. Further, as pollution makes water of good quality more difficult to obtain, its price will rise. Combined with advances in desalinization technology and subsequent reduction in costs, fresh water production from seawater will undoubtedly become more widespread.

A kilowatt hour is a measure of energy. A 100-watt bulb burning for 10 hours expends 1 kilowatt hour (100 watts times 10 hours = 1000 watt hr.).

4–5 Sea Harvest

A significant fraction of the world's protein comes from the sea, averaging 25 percent on a global basis. In the United States, marine foods comprise only 5 percent of our total protein because we consume so much beef, poultry, and other meats. Even though we depend less on marine protein than other nations, we take more than our share of the fish harvest. While we represent 6 percent of the earth's population, the United States consumes 11 percent of the fish caught, 35 percent of the shrimp, and 44 percent of the tuna.

So long as world population grows, more and more fish will be taken from the seas. In the mid-1950s, 30 million metric tons of fish were caught annually; by the mid-1970s, that figure more than doubled, to approximately 70 million metric tons. During these last two decades most of the increase came from extensive fishing activity by Peru, Japan, China, the Soviet Union, and Norway, among other nations. United States production has fluctuated around 5 million metric tons per year, and to maintain our fish consumption, we have had to expand our imports. Twenty years ago we caught three-quarters of the fish we consumed, whereas today we can supply only one-quarter of our needs. Almost half of the world fish harvest is converted into fish flour for poultry and hog feed.

Marine food chains

Most of the fish we take from the sea are near or at the top of the marine food chain. Phytoplankton feed the zooplankton that feed herring, sardines, anchovies, and shrimp. The latter feed tuna, halibut, salmon, cod, and swordfish. The amount of commercial fish harvested thus depends on the primary productivity of phytoplankton, which need sunlight and nutrients. This fundamental dependence on light and nutrients locates most world fisheries in shallow coastal waters or in areas of strong vertical mixing from upwelling currents; in these places nitrates and phosphates are continually replenished.

Efficiency of food transfer from one level or link in the food chain to the next varies from 10 to 20 percent. For example, 500 kilograms of phytoplankton are converted to 50–100 kilograms of zooplankton, which are transformed into 5–20 kilograms of small fish, which are converted into a few kilograms of tuna. After cleaning and processing, these tuna will yield about three small cans of tuna fish. So roughly 500 kilograms of phytoplankton are required for a couple of tuna casseroles or a week's supply of tuna sandwiches. Thus the production of "quality" commercial fish that are several steps up the food chain amount to only a few hundredths or thousandths of the primary productivity of phytoplankton.

Predicting the fish harvest

Given these relationships and knowledge of the average rate of primary productivity in the oceans, marine biologists can estimate the maximum productivity of commercial fish stocks. In the open oceans, away from coastal margins and areas of upwelling, there are about five links in the marine food chain from phytoplankton to humans. Out here, away from coastlines, the number of links is larger because of an interesting phenomenon, which is illustrated in Figure 4–13. Phyto- and zooplankton in the open ocean are smaller sized than in coastal regions, so more links, or feeding steps, are required to produce fish large enough for humans. Also, each link has a lower efficiency of energy transfer. The result is that, while the open ocean offers wide areas of total primary productivity, the amount of harvestable fish is disproportionately small. In coastal regions and in zones of upwelling, the plankton are larger and efficiency of energy transfer greater; these areas, although only a small portion of the world's oceans, produce about one-half the total fish harvest.

The total maximum productivity of harvestable fish throughout the oceans is 242 million metric tons per year, as detailed in Table 4–4. (Marine biologists using different assumptions have estimated from 200 to 300 million metric tons.) Only about 50 percent of this total actually can be harvested. Some fish are devoured by sea predators other than

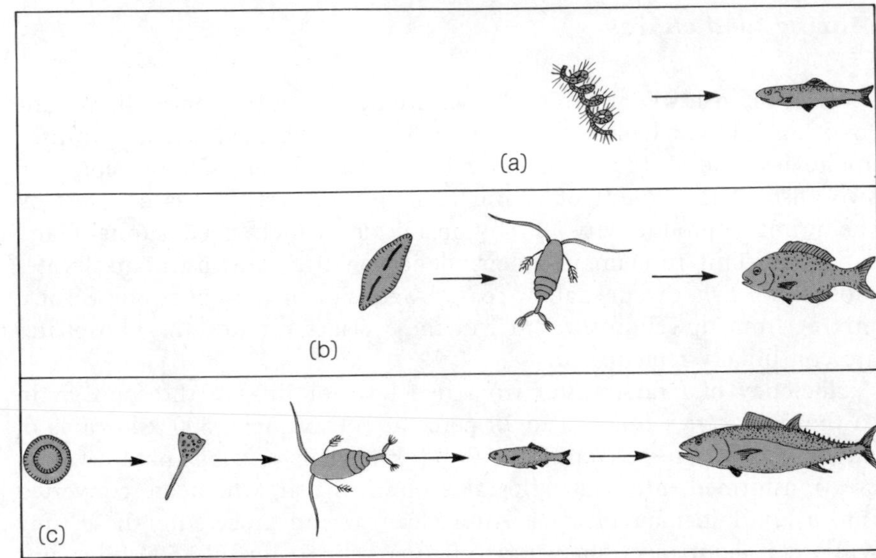

Figure 4-13

Marine food chains. (a) In zones of upwelling currents that bring abundant nutrients to the surface, the phytoplankton are large, aggregate masses of diatoms that support harvestable fish. Consequently, the food chain is very short, averaging about 1.5 links. (b) In coastal waters away from upwellings, the food chain is longer and averages about 3 links. (c) In the open ocean, away from coasts and upwellings, the phytoplankton are dispersed widely as single separate cells. Not only is the food chain longer, about 5 links, but the efficiency of transfer is less. (From "Marine Farming" by Gifford B. Pinchot. Copyright © 1970 by Scientific American, Inc. All rights reserved.)

humans, and some must be left behind to reproduce new fish in subsequent years. Consequently, the most realistic limit to the annual fish haul is between 100 and 150 million metric tons—roughly double the current catches. But any food increase resulting from larger catches of commercial fish will be compensated for by the doubling of the world's population in the next thirty-five years. Furthermore, expanding the fish catches beyond 50 percent of the standing crop would offer only a temporary advantage, with long-term disastrous results. As our experience with whales has demonstrated, populations of overfished marine species decline drastically. Some may become extinct altogether.

A greater proportion of protein exists lower down in the marine food chain. And if humans were to change their dietary preferences from tuna, mackerel, and salmon to phytoplankton and zooplankton, then hundreds to thousands of times more food would be available from the sea. However,

Table 4-4 Maximum Marine Productivity

Oceanic Region (percent of total area)	Primary Phytoplankton Productivity (tons of organic carbon)	Food Links between Phytoplankton and Humans	Efficiency	Fish Production
open ocean (90)	16.3 million	5	10	1.6 million
coastal (9.9)	3.6 million	3	15	120 million
upwellings (0.1)	0.1 million	2	20	120 million
			Total	242 million

it would be less palatable. Plankton contains too much silicon and common salt to be digested easily by humans. To make things worse, large-scale harvesting of plankton would severely diminish the preferred fish stocks at the higher end of the food chain.

If we want to harvest food from the seas in any reasonable way (that is, faster than population grows), we'll need an "aquacultural" revolution equivalent to the agricultural revolution ten thousand years ago, when humans shifted from hunting and gathering to the deliberate raising of crops and livestock. One cloud that darkens the whole prospect of unlimited food resources from the sea is marine pollution. Effluents like lead and mercury compounds, herbicides and pesticides, and oil may well diminish the ocean's already-strained biological productivity.

Viewpoint

M. Grant Gross

M. Grant Gross is Director, Chesapeake Bay Institute, Johns Hopkins University. Prior to his current activities, Dr. Gross studied the impact of liquid and solid waste disposal in New York harbor. In this Viewpoint, Dr. Gross discusses some of the problems arising from widespread dumping of wastes in the oceans.

Using and Misusing the Ocean

For a long time we have been using the ocean as a source of food and fuel and as a natural defense. But our approach to the ocean is still surprisingly primitive. In fact, we could compare our attitude toward the sea with the cave man's view of the land around him. The cave dweller saw the land as a place to hunt game (when he could find it), to collect a few odds and ends, and to protect himself from hostile bands.

Compare this attitude with your knowledge of modern land use. Today we cultivate crops extensively and produce far more than the nuts and berries available to a primitive collecting society. Carefully tended domestic animals provide protein and other desirable products, and industry extracts a wide range of fuels and minerals from the land. Ownership and user rights are so well established that banks are willing to lend money for developing natural resources.

Our use of the ocean is much closer to that of the cave dwellers—in this realm we are still hunters and gatherers. We hunt marine organisms by means of primitive detection techniques and we depend on our experience to know where to look for fish. Despite the value of marine resources, the legal status of the ocean's wealth is often poorly defined. Thus, bankers are unwilling to commit large amounts of money when it is unclear who really owns the minerals involved. Furthermore, only a few semi-domesticated species of seaweeds and animals (such as oysters and shrimp) provide the yields desired and permit more than rudimentary aquaculture (farming the sea). In short, we have scarcely begun to tap the ocean's resources.

Because of our primitive view of the ocean and our unregulated draining of its resources, we have carelessly damaged both. Prolonged and heavy fishing has consumed rich sources. Uncontrolled hunting of whales has greatly reduced their numbers, and some scientists fear that several species may be near extinction. Changes in currents and ocean climate combined with overfishing have nearly destroyed the major anchoveta fishery off Peru, which produced about one-fifth of the world's fish catch in the early 1970s.

So far we have looked at extraction of ocean resources, but there is another service the ocean provides that we often forget—waste disposal area. For centuries the ocean has received society's wastes. And our failure to recognize the effects of this marine pollution has destroyed fisheries, damaged coastal resources, and caused disease.

Let's look at waste disposal in the ocean. Basically, there are two philosophies for waste management: one favors the dilute-and-disperse method and the other the concentrate-and-contain method. Although both systems have been used, the first is far more common in the ocean because it is easier and cheaper. The dilute-and-disperse approach depends on ocean currents, usually tidal currents, to carry away the wastes. It relies on the volume of ocean waters to dilute the wastes to acceptable levels. Industrial and municipal wastes are frequently disposed of in this way. More toxic wastes such as highly radioactive materials or toxic chemicals are first concentrated, then placed in barrels or other containers that are weighted to sink to the ocean bottom. There the wastes will remain out of reach of human activity for long periods. Eventually the containers rust through and the wastes slowly seep out and disperse in the deep ocean waters. We hesitate to resort to the concentrate-and-contain method, however. We are still wrestling with questions about the long-term safety of certain substances in an environment where these materials can be neither observed nor controlled.

The public-health pioneers of the nineteenth century viewed piping of sewage and other wastes to the sea as the ideal solution to their problem of ridding cities of water-borne diseases such as cholera and typhoid fever. They wanted to remove human wastes from the streets and public water supplies. What could be better than dumping these wastes into the ocean? The tides would carry them out to sea and they would never be seen again.

This solution has been widely adopted. For many years New York City dumped its street sweepings, garbage, and other wastes offshore from New York Harbor. This worked well for the city; the wastes were disposed

The ocean is a valuable source of many raw materials, such as glass, iron, salt, rubber, plastic, and surplus naval equipment.

of at relatively low cost. But New Jersey objected strongly. The currents that took New York's wastes to sea deposited bottles, wood, and garbage on New Jersey beaches. After years of court battles and various efforts to control the problem by seasonally moving the disposal sites, the Supreme Court finally forbade further ocean dumping, and the last "honey barge" loaded with New York garbage went to sea in June 1934.

The second part of the dilute-and-disperse problem is that only a small volume of ocean water is easily accessible. Most wastes are not dumped in the open ocean where there is a vast reservoir for dilution. Instead, wastes from many cities and industries flow into estuaries where river water and seawater mix. Estuaries are generally small and cannot adequately dilute large volumes of waste. Problems develop when the dissolved oxygen in the water is consumed by decomposing wastes. One result of the decomposition process is that a strong odor pervades these estuaries in summer. Another difficulty is that estuaries are effective traps for solids and many chemicals dissolved in the water. Wastes caught in the estuary are usually deposited with the sediments that accumulate in navigation channels, boat basins, and wetlands; there they cause additional problems. Frequently dredging is required to remove this debris so that ships do not go aground in the harbor.

Coastal cities in California, New York, and New Jersey have chosen to discharge sewage a mile or so from the shoreline to avoid some of the problems associated with sewage disposal in the bays. On the continental shelf, the sewage can mix with larger volumes of water. Unfortunately, we do not know how much waste these coastal ocean waters can absorb before they too become overloaded.

Clearly we need to know more about the ocean in order to protect it from the adverse and conflicting effects of waste disposal and food production. It would be comforting to some to limit all further use of the ocean until we could determine how best to protect it. Unfortunately, the world doesn't work this way. Political considerations often dictate that remedies be tried long before we've had a chance to identify and thoroughly investigate the effects. Even if the time for research were available, the money needed is rarely on hand.

How do we break out of this cycle in which the solution to today's problem becomes tomorrow's crisis? The first step is to recognize that we are not dealing solely with scientific questions. There are strong social components to all the problems we have discussed, and any solutions proposed must be phrased in socially understandable and acceptable terms.

Secondly, we must begin to apply what we already know about the solution of problems. Usually, scientific solutions are known but have not been translated into large-scale projects that prove the merits of the concept to public officials. In this effort to employ what we know, we may be able to shorten the time between scientific discovery and application.

Finally, we need more scientists willing to work on "dirty" problems. We also need more citizens who are aware of the scientific basis and limitations of the solutions proposed for marine environmental problems. Without committed experts and an informed citizenry, any efforts to move beyond our primitive approach to the ocean will be slow-moving and more and more costly.

Summary

Seventy-one percent of the earth's surface lies beneath its oceans, which average 4000 meters in depth. The topography of the sea floor is as varied as that of the continents, with submarine ridges, deep trenches, and abyssal plains. Continental slopes mark the transition from the continents and the deep ocean basins, while the continental shelves are merely seaward extensions of the continents. The shelves thus contain the same sorts of metal and fossil fuel deposits found on land. Nearshore metal and nonmetal deposits will be increasingly exploited as land resources dwindle. Deep sea, metal-rich nodules, like those carpeting large portions of the Pacific Ocean's abyssal plains and the metal-enriched sediments of the

Red Sea, offer potential new sources of major mineral wealth. Oil and gas, too, will be tapped increasingly in offshore areas of the continental shelves as the difficulty of locating new petroleum deposits on land comes to outweigh the problems of recovering fossil fuels from beneath the sea.

The tremendous volume of ocean water, with its huge store of dissolved salts, is a valuable source of fresh water and a few concentrated elements. The recovery of most elements in minute concentration is still a long way off; mainly, the energy required to remove these substances is too costly. The fish that can be harvested from the sea can be doubled, at most, but with human population doubling in 35 years, this increase will hardly affect net food supply. The sea's potential as a major source of food is limited by our hunting-and-gathering fisheries technology. If, however, the sea is farmed deliberately, as the land has been since the rise of agriculture, then food obtainable from the sea could multiply considerably.

World marine resources are thus like any land-based resource: their ultimate value depends less on how much is out there and more on our ability to recover them at a reasonable cost. To whatever extent we do exploit the sea's resources, we must take care not to upset its natural systems—especially its biological activity, upon which we may then heavily depend.

Glossary

conservative elements Major elements dissolved in seawater—chlorine, sodium, sulfate, magnesium, calcium, and potassium—whose proportions relative to each other remain the same, even though the total ocean salinity may vary.

continental shelf Submarine extension of the continent that slopes very gently toward the deep ocean.

continental slope Sea floor that dips from the edge of the shallow continental shelf down to the deep ocean basin.

estuary The lower part of a river valley where river water and seawater mix.

midocean ridge Broad ridge, mostly submarine, of volcanic rocks intruded and extruded at diverging plate boundaries; usually, but not always, lying within the central part of the world's oceans.

minor elements Seawater constituents whose individual abundance ranges from 1 to 100 parts per million and include bromine, carbon, strontium, boron, silicon, and fluorine.

nonconservative elements Elements dissolved in seawater (as minor and trace elements) whose proportions relative to each other fluctuate from place to place and with varying salinity.

seamount Isolated, submarine mountain peak that does not reach the surface; many are flat-topped by wave erosion, and most are extinct volcanoes.

sedimentation cell Circular to elliptical pattern of marine currents that transport nearshore sediments to the deep sea via submarine canyons cutting across the continental shelf and slope.

trace elements Seawater constituents dissolved in amounts of 1 part per million or less.

turbidity current A current of muddy, sediment-laden water that moves within a body of surrounding, nonturbid water.

Reading Further

Cloud, P. 1969. "Mineral Resources from the Sea." In *Resources and Man.* San Francisco: W. H. Freeman, pp. 135–158. A more pessimistic (realistic?) view of the sea's resources.

Gross, M. G. 1972. *Oceanography.* Englewood Cliffs, N.J.: Prentice-Hall, 581 p. A readable, but fairly comprehensive, treatment of oceanography.

Mero, J. 1964. *The Mineral Resources of the Sea.* New York: American Elsevier, 312 p. An optimistic treatment of the mineral wealth of the oceans; almost half of the book discusses manganese nodules.

Pinchot, G. 1970. "Marine Farming." *Scientific American,* vol. 223, no. 6, December, pp. 15–21. Discusses how the sea may be farmed rather than merely used for hunting-and-gathering food production; cautiously optimistic about the sea's fertility.

Ricker, W. 1969. "Food from the Sea." In *Resources and Man.* San Francisco, W. H. Freeman, pp. 87–108. A careful estimation of the limits of the sea's biological productivity; good discussion of marine food chains.

Ross, D. 1970. *Introduction to Oceanography.* New York: Appleton-Century-Crofts, 384 p. An introductory text on the subject; the last chapter reviews the chemical, physical, biological, and geologic resources of the sea.

Ryther, J. 1969. "Photosynthesis and Fish Production in the Sea." *Science,* vol. 166, pp. 72–76. Another analysis of the ultimate production of food from the sea; presents important ecological factors upon which all projections must depend.

Skinner, B. and K. Turekian. 1973. *Man and the Ocean.* Englewood Cliffs, N.J.: Prentice-Hall, 149 p. A short, concise, up-to-date review of marine resources; includes a chapter on marine pollution.

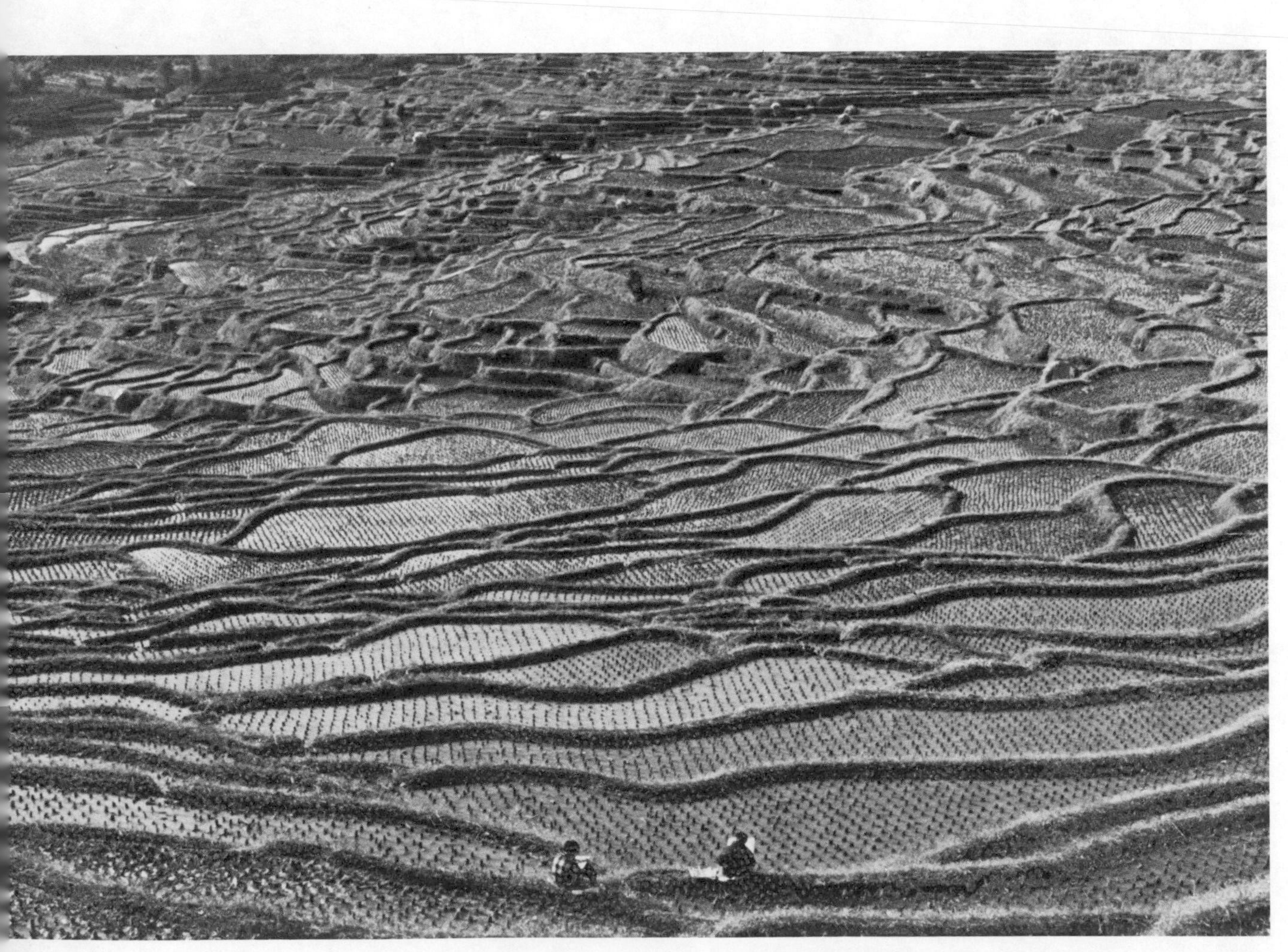

Soils 5

Most people, unless they come from a farming family, do not immediately think of soil as a valuable resource. Instead, they usually equate soil with "dirt," something to be swept off the floor and kept out of food. But after a moment's reflection, we realize the many ways that soil supports life. From it, we get vegetables and fruits, meat, cotton and wool, lumber, paper, and even much of our aluminum. Like other resources we've discussed so far, the various types of soil are products of everyday geologic processes, they vary in their economic value, and they can be irretrievably lost if mismanaged.

Earth to earth, ashes to ashes, dust to dust.

Psalms, c. 500 B.C.

The U.S. Soil Conservation Service defines *soil* as a mixture of fragmented and weathered grains of minerals and rocks with variable proportions of air and water; the mixture has a fairly distinct layering; and its development is influenced by climate and living organisms. This definition is similar to the geologist's concept of soil as essentially a product of mineral and rock weathering, and to the civil engineer's, as most anything that can be excavated without blasting. To put it simply, the critical aspect of soil for the farmer is that it is a medium for plant growth; for the geologist, that it is a weathered product of rock and sediment; and for the engineer, that it is loose, unconsolidated earth.

In examining soils, we'll avoid the many complexities involved in naming specific soils and will focus instead on texture, composition, and formation, along with methods of classification. We consider the physical and chemical soil properties that determine their strength, water-retention ability, and fertility. Because of the key role that soil plays in food production, we discuss the agricultural uses of soil and its ultimate capacity to feed the world's expanding population. Finally, we look at soil as a nonrenewable resource and explore how this resource is diminished in value by erosion, loss of fertility, and conversion to nonagricultural uses like supporting urban sprawl.

The Viewpoint by Hunt elaborates on these various definitions of soil.

5-1 What Is Soil?

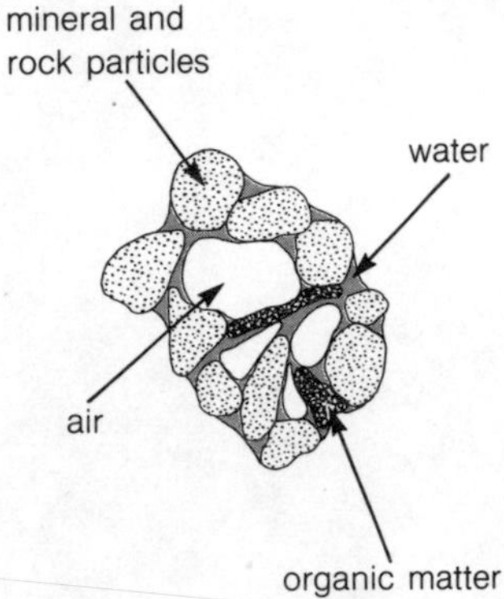

Figure 5-1

Major components of soil. Weathering of rocks and sediments produces solid mineral and rock particles; water and air circulate through the pores among the solid particles and support the organisms that live within the soil. Particles of organic matter also accumulate within the soil and after their decomposition supply nutrients as well as acids that leach the soil's inorganic solid particles.

The loose, unconsolidated material called soil is composed of mineral grains and rock fragments, air and water, and organic matter, as illustrated in Figure 5-1. Solid, inorganic soil particles are the products of physical and chemical weathering of rocks and sediments at the earth's surface. Water and air from the atmosphere seep into the pore spaces between these particles and support not only the plants growing there, but also the numerous microorganisms contributing to soil formation. Organic matter added by these plants and microorganisms accounts for the third essential soil ingredient. The proportions in which all these substances are mixed determine the soil's properties and uses.

Will it hold water?

There are 10 millimeters to 1 cm; a dime is about 1 mm thick.

Geologists, on the other hand, define sand as particles whose diameter lies between 2 and 1/16 mm, silt between 1/16 and 1/256 mm, and clay less than 1/256 mm.

Soil texture refers to the size of a soil's component particles. If we follow U.S. Department of Agriculture terminology, soil texture ranges from very coarse to very fine, according to the amount of *gravel* (particles more than 1.0 mm in diameter), *sand* (1.0 mm to 0.5 mm), *silt* (0.5 mm to 0.002 mm), and *clay* (less than 0.002 mm). Coarse-grained soils have proportionally less pore space among their grains than do fine-grained soils. For example, a gravelly soil has about 30 percent porosity by volume compared with about twice that for clay soil. The pores in coarser soils, however, are larger and better interconnected; thus coarse-grained soils are more permeable than finer soils, and air and water can circulate better in them.

When soil particles are all about the same size and are well-rounded, soil porosity and permeability are further affected. If particles are well-sorted according to size, porosity and permeability are greater than if they are poorly sorted; with poor sorting, smaller grains fit into the pores of larger ones. In a similar way, if particles are irregularly angular, they fit together like pieces of a puzzle and close up the pore space. Thus poorly sorted and poorly rounded soils have less porosity and less permeability than well-sorted and well-rounded soils with comparable grain sizes; refer to Figure 5-2. Sorting and rounding take place when the parent materials of the soils are transported by wind and water.

Soil texture is critical because it determines how much water a soil can hold. If soil is too permeable to hold water, it will not support many plants. Sandy soil composed of well-sorted and well-rounded quartz grains drains so well that it retains almost no water. For this reason, sand dunes even in areas of high rainfall can support only sparse vegetation. (The constant shifting of the sand also inhibits plant growth.) At the other extreme are clay soils whose porosity is so great that they are often too water-logged to support many plants.

Variations in water content explain the differences in support that each of these soils provides. Sandy soil particles pack tightly, and each rounded sphere holds up several others; these soils can thus support loads. Conversely, clay soils have so much water between the grains that they are oozy and compact easily when a load is placed on them. (Compare running on a wet, sandy beach with slogging through a clay-rich mud.) For agriculture, it is best to have soil with an intermediate texture—the so-called *loams,* which contain almost equal amounts of sand and silt and somewhat less clay. This kind of soil has just the right amount of porosity and permeability for good drainage: air can circulate within the soil, yet enough water is retained to support luscious plant growth. Variations in texture are indicated with names like silty clay, sandy loam, and loamy silt; Figure 5-3 further describes the texture-porosity-permeability relationship.

A rough approximation of loamy texture is to squeeze a clod of damp soil and let it drop on the ground. If the clod completely disintegrates, the soil is too sandy; if it holds completely together, it is too clay-rich. If, however, the clod breaks into a few, smaller pieces it is probably loamy.

In addition to completely filling pore spaces within soil particles, water can be retained by soil in the form of water molecules on the surface of the soil grains themselves. Water is an irregularly shaped molecule with each double-charged, negative oxygen atom linked to two single-charged, positive hydrogen atoms. These atoms are so arranged that, although the water molecule as a whole is electrically neutral, one side is a bit more positively charged than the other side, which is negatively charged; see Figure 5-4(a). Thus a water molecule can be attracted and attached to the surface of particles with slight, opposite electrical charges, in the same way iron filings are drawn to and held by a magnet, as shown in Figure 5-4(b). Clays in particular can attract and retain water molecules over

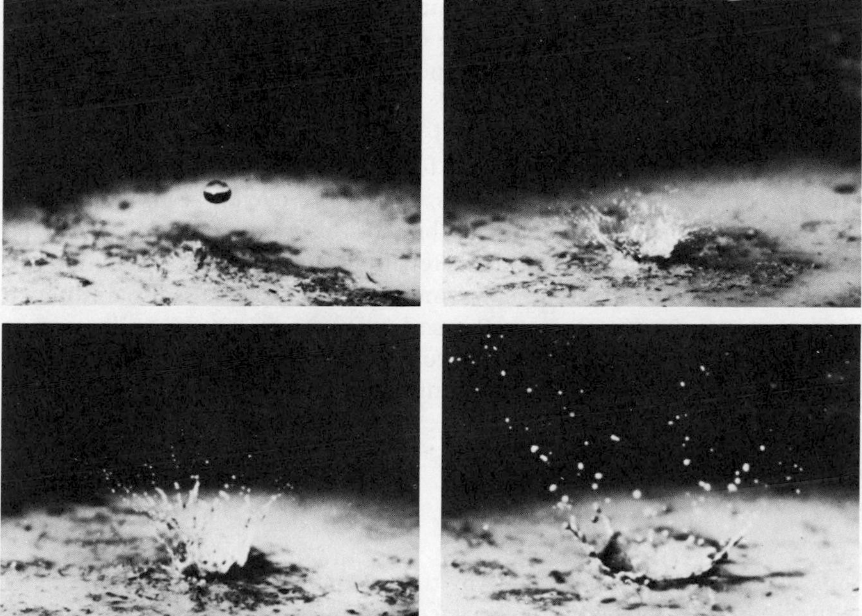

Raindrop striking wet soil—a 3 mm sphere of water traveling 10 meters per second. The force of the raindrop throws particles of soil and water outward to distances of 2 meters.

Clays also attract and adsorb positively charged metal ions. For this reason many fine-grained sedimentary rocks are relatively enriched in metals.

their entire surface. This capacity to hold water within the grains' pore spaces and on the grains themselves explains in large part the impermeability of clay-rich soils. The electrical attraction of water molecules inhibits the flow of water within such soils. No wonder then that clay soils, with their high porosity and impermeability, are often waterlogged.

A potpourri of soil components

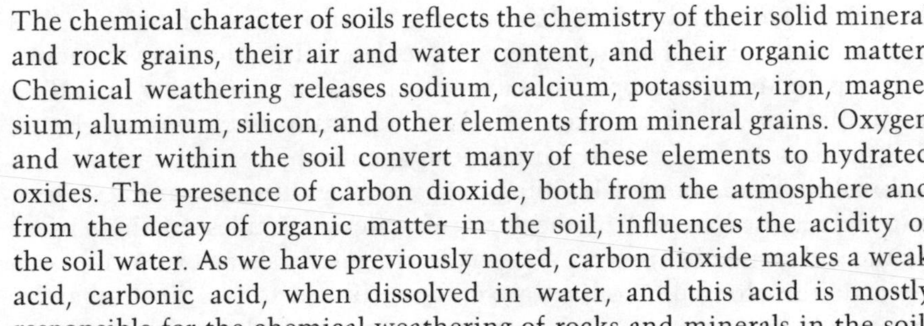

(a)

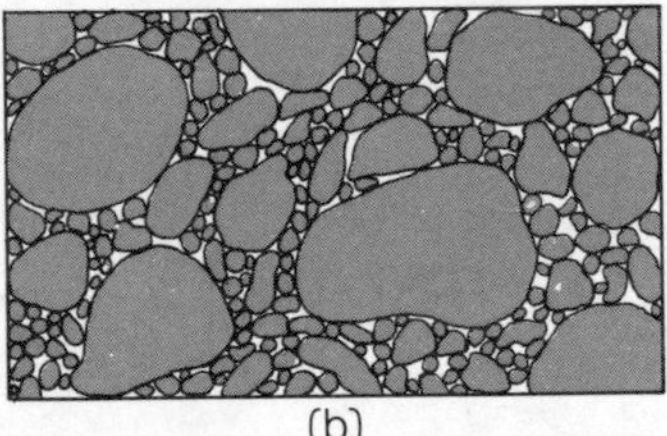

(b)

Figure 5–2

Variations in soil texture and porosity. (a) Well-sorted soil, in which all the soil particles are approximately the same size. The porosity of such soil is good, and results in relatively more room for water and air among the soil particles. (b) Poorly sorted soil, in which the soil particles are many different sizes. The porosity of such a soil is poor, because the little particles fill in the spaces among the larger particles and there is less room for water and air.

The chemical character of soils reflects the chemistry of their solid mineral and rock grains, their air and water content, and their organic matter. Chemical weathering releases sodium, calcium, potassium, iron, magnesium, aluminum, silicon, and other elements from mineral grains. Oxygen and water within the soil convert many of these elements to hydrated oxides. The presence of carbon dioxide, both from the atmosphere and from the decay of organic matter in the soil, influences the acidity of the soil water. As we have previously noted, carbon dioxide makes a weak acid, carbonic acid, when dissolved in water, and this acid is mostly responsible for the chemical weathering of rocks and minerals in the soil.

Many organic substances are contributed to the soil by plants and animals living within and on it. Plant leaves, stems, and roots accumulate in the upper soil layers, as do insect remains, animal droppings, worm castings, and so on. Nutrients in this accumulated organic matter, having been previously extracted by living organisms, are returned to the soil through the action of decomposing microorganisms like bacteria and fungi. Nitrogen, phosphate, and potassium which are chemically bound up in organic matter are useless to plants until microorganisms have decomposed them into simpler compounds. The decomposed organic matter in soils is called *humus* and largely determines a soil's natural fertility. Some soil microorganisms also can take gaseous atmospheric nitrogen (N_2) and convert it into nitrogenous compounds for easy assimilation by plants. Many nitrogen-converting microorganisms live in nodules in the roots of plants called *legumes,* including peas, beans, alfalfa, and clover. Legumes are thus cultivated not only as food crops, but also as cover crops that can be plowed back into a field to restore its fertility because of their high nitrogen content. Larger organisms like worms and other animals also influence fertility by burrowing through the soil; this maintains the soil's porous structure by allowing water and air to circulate through it, which in turn help to support other organisms living there.

5–2 How Soils Form

Soils, as we indicated, are created by the weathering of rocks and especially sediments lying on the earth's surface. Although hard, consolidated rock

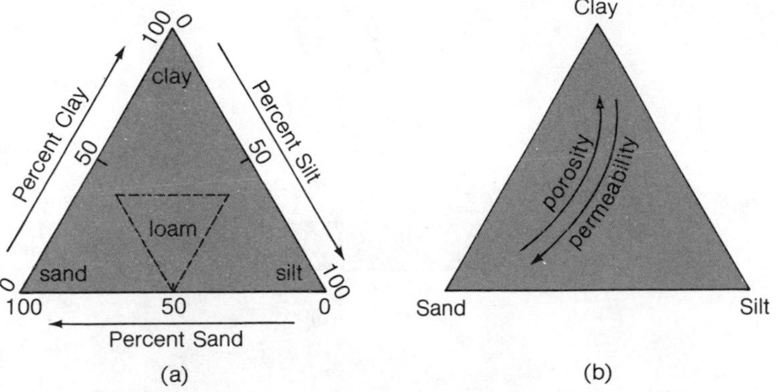

Figure 5–3

Textural variations in soil. (a) Names for different soil textures depend on relative proportions of sand, silt, and clay. Loam that contains roughly equal amounts of sand and silt, along with slightly lesser amounts of clay, makes the best agricultural soil. (b) Variations in porosity and permeability reflect soil texture. In general, the coarser grained soils are less porous and more permeable than the finer grained soils which are more porous and less permeable.

like granite, schist, or limestone can weather and eventually form a residual soil, almost all soils are formed from the weathering of loose, unconsolidated sediments transported by wind, water, or ice.

Weathering processes begin at the boundary between the rock or sediment and the atmosphere, and work progressively downward into the fresh, unaltered parent material below. This downward penetration of soil-forming processes creates a horizontal layering in the soil. If we look at the thickness, texture, and composition of each layer, we can see a vertical soil profile which reveals the kind of material being weathered as well as the nature of the weathering process itself.

Most soils take hundreds to thousands of years to develop–rates that are extremely slow by human standards. For this reason they must be considered nonrenewable resources, although they can be used over and over again. This reuse is analogous to the recycling of metals obtained from nonrenewable ore deposits.

Parent materials

Geologic materials on the earth's surface that become soil either form in place or are transported from elsewhere. *Residual soils* develop on outcroppings of all kinds of bare rocks exposed to physical and chemical weathering. Such soils usually form rather slowly, so they are not very thick, unless the rocks have been at the earth's surface for a long time. Along much of the Atlantic, Gulf, and Pacific Coasts, for instance, the local bedrock has been deeply weathered for millions of years and has left behind thick, residual soils reddish in color from the presence of iron oxides. Also rich in aluminum silicates, these soils are essentially the insoluble residues left behind by long-term chemical weathering. Some soil scientists believe, however, that such thick residual soils may have formed relatively rapidly under optimal weathering conditions in certain locations.

Some residual soils retain the structures of the parent rock. So even

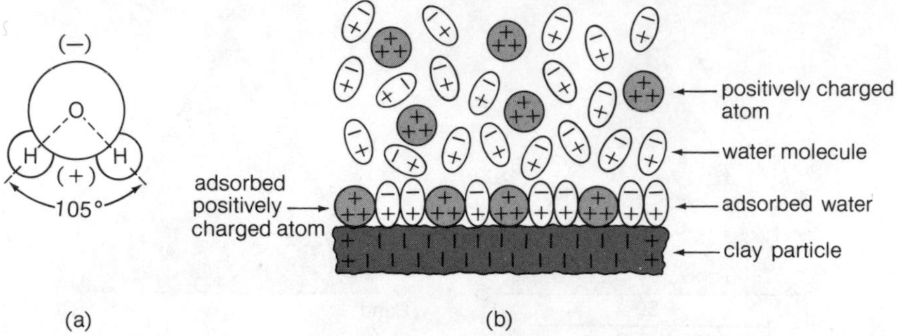

Figure 5–4

Electrical attraction of water and clay particles. (a) The asymmetrical arrangement of positively charged hydrogen atoms around the negatively charged oxygen atom. Although the water molecule is electrically neutral, its asymmetry results in one side of the molecule being slightly negative and the other slightly positive. (b) The faces of a clay particle are slightly negatively charged, whereas the edges are slightly positively charged. Consequently, water molecules and other charged atoms are attracted and held to the clay particle. Clays thus have water within their pores as well as a thin layer of adsorbed water and other charged atoms on their surfaces. Much of the impermeability of clay-rich soils is caused by soil water tightly held by the clay particles within the soil. Organic particles behave in a similar way.

after a hard rock has been altered to an unconsolidated soil, we can still see structures like veins, cross stratification, and the outlines of larger mineral crystals or rock grains. Residual soils which preserve the primary internal structures of the parent rock are called *saprolites.*

But, as we know, not all of the earth's surface is composed of solid rock that formed in place. In fact, most areas are covered by loose, unconsolidated sediments deposited by glaciers, streams and rivers, mass wasting, and wind. Extensive deposits of gravel, sand, and silt were laid down by the Pleistocene glaciers that covered large portions of northeastern North America, northwestern Europe, and the British Isles. As the glacial ice traveled southward, it removed the existing soils, sediments, and some of the bedrock. When the glaciers eventually melted, they left a veneer of sediments that had been incorporated into the ice. This mantle of glacially deposited sediment, called *glacial drift,* includes rock debris left behind by the ice itself, as well as sediment deposited by glacial streams and lakes fed by the melting ice, as pictured in Figure 5–5. Thickness of glacial drift varies widely, ranging from less than a meter to several tens of meters or more.

Another important source of transported parent material is the sediment laid down in stream and river valleys. The vast, fertile lands bordering the Ohio, Missouri, and Mississippi Rivers in the Midwest and the Sacramento and San Joaquin Rivers in California are composed of thick, rich soils formed from sediments deposited in the rivers' floodplains. Debris conveyed down hillsides by mass wasting (creep, solifluction, slumps, and slides), as well as wind-blown silts and volcanic ash, are additional transported surface deposits that generate soils.

Transported surface deposits generally make better agricultural soils than do residual deposits. By the time a residual soil is thick enough to be farmed, most of its valuable nutrient elements have been dissolved and removed by water moving down through the soil. By contrast, transported surface deposits are usually much thicker to begin with and have a loamy texture and good organic content; thus they make excellent agricultural soils relatively soon after being deposited.

Soil profile

Soil formation processes are largely controlled by the gravitational flow of surface water into the parent material. Surface water transports oxygen and carbon dioxide, together with acids and nutrients, and consequently exerts a strong control on the progress of soil formation. As the downward flow of water moves under the pull of gravity, soils develop a layering that parallels the contours of the ground surface.

Figure 5–5

Alpine glacier in Switzerland; dark linear bands on ice are composed of rock debris and sediment washed down mountain slopes and carried along by the glacier. When such materials are melted out of the glacier, they form glacial drift.

A soil contains several horizons, or layers, that together are referred to as the *soil profile*. The uppermost layer, at the ground surface, is the *O horizon,* rich in organic matter and humus from plant and animal remains. Below the O horizon is the *A horizon,* where surface water that percolates downward dissolves or leaches many of the soil's mineral substances. Below the A horizon is the *B horizon,* a layer of precipitation where some or all of the substances leached from the A horizon are deposited. The *C horizon* marks the transition from the B horizon and the fresh, unweathered parent material below in the *D horizon.*

In humid regions with abundant rainfall and vegetation, soil water is acidic. Consequently, this water leaches the upper soil layers and carries many of the dissolved materials to the groundwater below, as in Figure 5–6(a). Soils in these regions are rich in the less soluble aluminum and iron compounds that are left behind after leaching. In arid regions, where rainfall and vegetation are less abundant, soil water is neither so plentiful nor acidic, and there is less leaching of the soil. Whatever is dissolved near the ground surface in the A horizon is precipitated a little further down in the B horizon. Here there is not enough surface water to carry dissolved substances all the way down to the groundwater. The precipitated substances are carbonate salts of various sorts, especially calcium carbonate

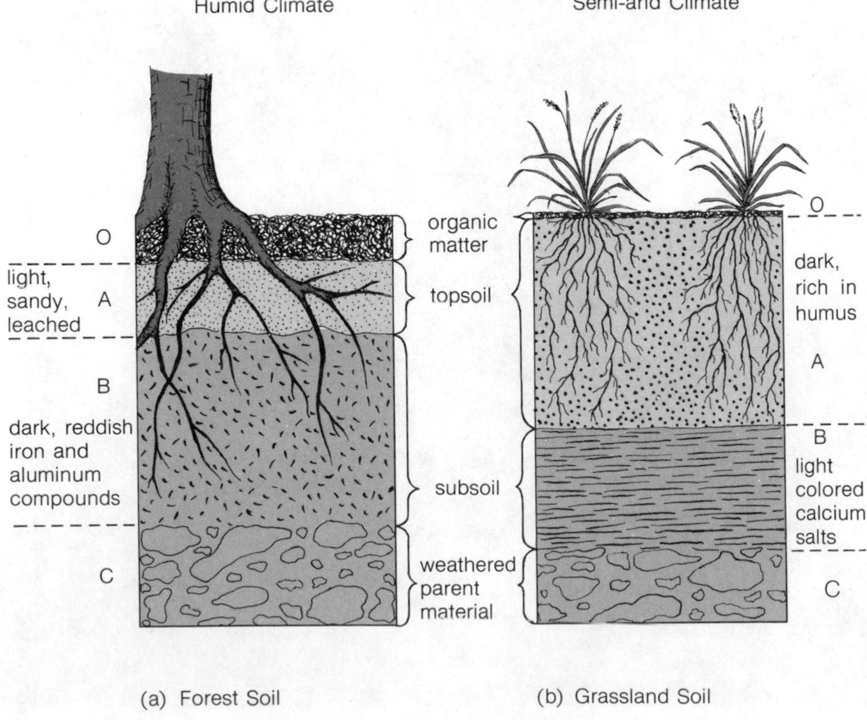

Figure 5–6

Soil profiles in humid and semi-arid climates. (a) Abundant precipitation allows water to leach much of the topsoil's mineral matter in the A horizon. In the O horizon organic acids in the surface litter of plant debris facilitate the leaching process. The B horizon contains some of the more insoluble iron and aluminum silicates, but it too loses many of its soluble compounds to the groundwater. (b) In semi-arid climates water scarcity results in deposition in the B horizon of compounds dissolved from the A horizon. Note the differences in thickness of the A and B horizons in these two profiles.

($CaCO_3$), and they make the B horizon more limy and alkaline than acidic, as explained in Figure 5–6(b).

5-3 Classifying Soils

Soils may be grouped into three major categories, according to the extent of mineral leaching by surface water loaded with organic acids from decaying vegetation. Regional climate thus is central to soil classification because precipitation and temperature determine the amount of water and plant matter within a soil. Further subdivisions within each of these main categories are related to variations in texture and composition of local parent materials.

Pedocals, pedalfers, and laterites

Scientists recognize three major soil types that reflect the degree of mineral leaching: pedocals, pedalfers, and laterites. The *pedocals* are soils that develop in climates with low precipitation (less than 50 cm per year) and moderate-to-high temperatures—regions generally characterized by prairie, grassland, scrub, or desert vegetation. The relative lack of soil water does not permit much leaching of the A horizon, and any mineral matter that is removed precipitates into the B horizon below. The soil water dissolves some of the lime in the upper part of the soil and deposits it in the lower part, but there is not enough water to flush out the soil minerals and carry them to the underlying groundwater. (The term "pedocal" comes from *pedon,* which means soil in Greek, and *cal*cium; thus it alludes to the limy condition of these soils.)

Many plants in semi-arid prairies and grasslands have deep roots that can extract minerals from the B and C horizons. The plants eventually replace most or all of the minerals leached from the A horizon when they die and decompose at the surface, and consequently, prairie and grassland soils are quite fertile. In truly arid regions, there is so little water that soil leaching hardly occurs. Although soils there may be rich in minerals, the lack of water prevents much vegetation growth. During the daytime in arid areas, when ground temperatures are high, soil moisture evaporates and the dissolved salts in this moisture are precipitated within the soil. Hence, the carbonates and other salts deposited in desert soils are as much the result of soil water evaporation as of water trickling down from the surface. The sparse vegetation in arid regions does not allow much humus to accumulate or mineral matter to recycle by plant growth and decomposition.

Pedalfers are soils that form in high-precipitation areas (more than 50 cm per year), usually with lower temperatures—regions generally forested with coniferous evergreens or deciduous hardwoods. The abundant soil water is rich in organic acids generated by plant debris decaying on the surface. Soil water leaches the A horizon of almost everything but quartz grains; the B horizon is also heavily leached of most mineral substances, but the more insoluble silicates of iron and aluminum accumulate there. Enough water is available to flush out the leached minerals and carry them to the groundwater below. (The term pedalfer alludes to the iron and aluminum content of the soil: *ped*on, soil; *al*uminum; and *fer*rum, Latin for iron.) In deciduous hardwood forests, trees are deeply rooted and therefore can replace some leached minerals, as in prairies and grasslands. Also, the decay of dead leaves returns minerals to the soil surface.

The leaching process that produces the pedalfer group of soils is called *podsolization*, a word whose root, *podzol*, comes from Russian and means ashlike. Pedalfer topsoil often is light gray and sandy—hence ashy; many soil types within the pedalfer group have the podzol designation.

The third major group of soils are the *laterites*, usually found in the wet tropics. Laterites have been leached of virtually all their soluble mineral matter and contain residues of hydrated iron and aluminum oxides. The Latin word for brick, *later*, is used to designate these soils because of their bricklike color and hardness. Extreme lateritization is responsible for formation of aluminum-rich bauxite ores. Refer to Table 5-1 for a summary of the soil-forming processes and the resulting soil groups.

This soil process is similar to secondary enrichment, discussed in Chapter 1.

Soils for agriculture

Soils best suited for raising crops and grazing livestock are the pedocals of prairies and grasslands. These fertile soils have naturally high humus content, a loamy texture, and sufficient moisture. The acidic pedalfers make less favorable agricultural soils, but if lime is added regularly, their fertility can be maintained. For further description of the relations between soil type and agriculture, see Figures 5-7 and 5-8. With the introduction of irrigation and artificial fertilization, many soils otherwise unsuited for farming or pasturage have become valuable agricultural land. For example, in parts of California like the Imperial Valley, the use of irrigation and fertilizers has made that state the nation's leading agricultural producer. Most tropical soils are nutrient-poor pedalfers, and agriculture in these regions is of the slash-and-burn type: the forest is cut over, burned for minerals contained in the ash, farmed for a few years, and then abandoned as the nutrients become depleted.

Besides being fertile, loamy, and well watered, soils must be thick enough to allow plowing, cultivation, and root growth. In New England, for instance, most soils on the glacial drift are too thin and stony for large-scale, mechanized agriculture. What farming there is, is concentrated in the thicker soils of major river valleys like the Connecticut. This valley has been an important local source of farm products since the colonial era.

Table 5-1 Major Soil-forming Processes

Leaching →

Process	Calcification	Podsolization	Laterization
precipitation	low	high	very high
temperature	moderate to high	low	high
vegetation	grassland	cool forest	tropical forest
soil reaction	basic to neutral	acid	acid
topsoil (A horizon)			
color	dark brown	light grey	red
texture	loam, friable	sandy	clay, loam
principal minerals	various	silica	iron, aluminum
humus content	high	low	low
fertility	high	low	low
subsoil (B horizon)			
color	whitish	red	red
texture	loam, friable	heavy clay	heavy clay
principal minerals	calcium	iron, aluminum	iron, aluminum
Soil Group	**Pedocals**	**Pedalfers**	**Laterites**

The final two factors determining the quality of agricultural land are its drainage capability and slope. Soils that drain poorly, either because of their texture or because of their topography, become too waterlogged for good plant growth. Land that slopes too steeply is vulnerable to serious soil erosion once cultivation disturbs the natural vegetative cover.

According to criteria of slope, drainage, soil depth, texture, and natural fertility, the U.S. Soil Conservation Service has developed a land-use capability classification described in Table 5-2. This classification defines eight categories of land suitable for cultivation in varying degrees. Of the 920 million hectares of land in the United States, 405 million hectares (44 percent) are most suitable for cultivation. At present, about half is being used, as you can see in Figure 5-9. Of the 400,000 hectares of land being urbanized by cities each year, 80,000 are land most suitable for agriculture: categories 1–3 in Table 5-2.

The close correlation between vegetation, soil type, and parent materials makes possible the mapping of regional geology by satellite images of vegetation on the ground.

5-4 Building on Soil

So far in our discussion of soils we've emphasized their properties as a plant-growing medium. Soils are more than an agricultural resource; they

Figure 5-7

Relations between climate, vegetation, soil type, and agriculture. The best agricultural soils are in the pedocal group of soils. In cooler climates, the pedalfers are used for dairy farming, pasturage, and some crops.

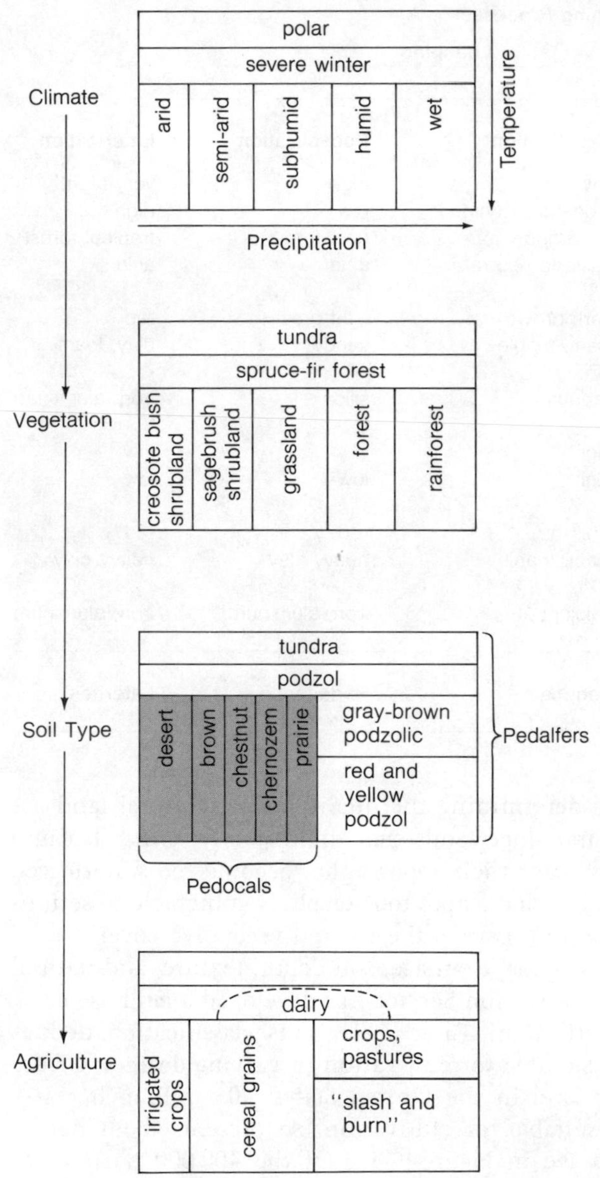

also serve as foundations for highways and buildings and as fill for all kinds of construction. As we turn from an agricultural to an engineering context, we must consider soils in a somewhat different light. That is, we must pay more attention to their ability to support heavy loads, their tendency to expand or contract, and their capacity to hold or drain water.

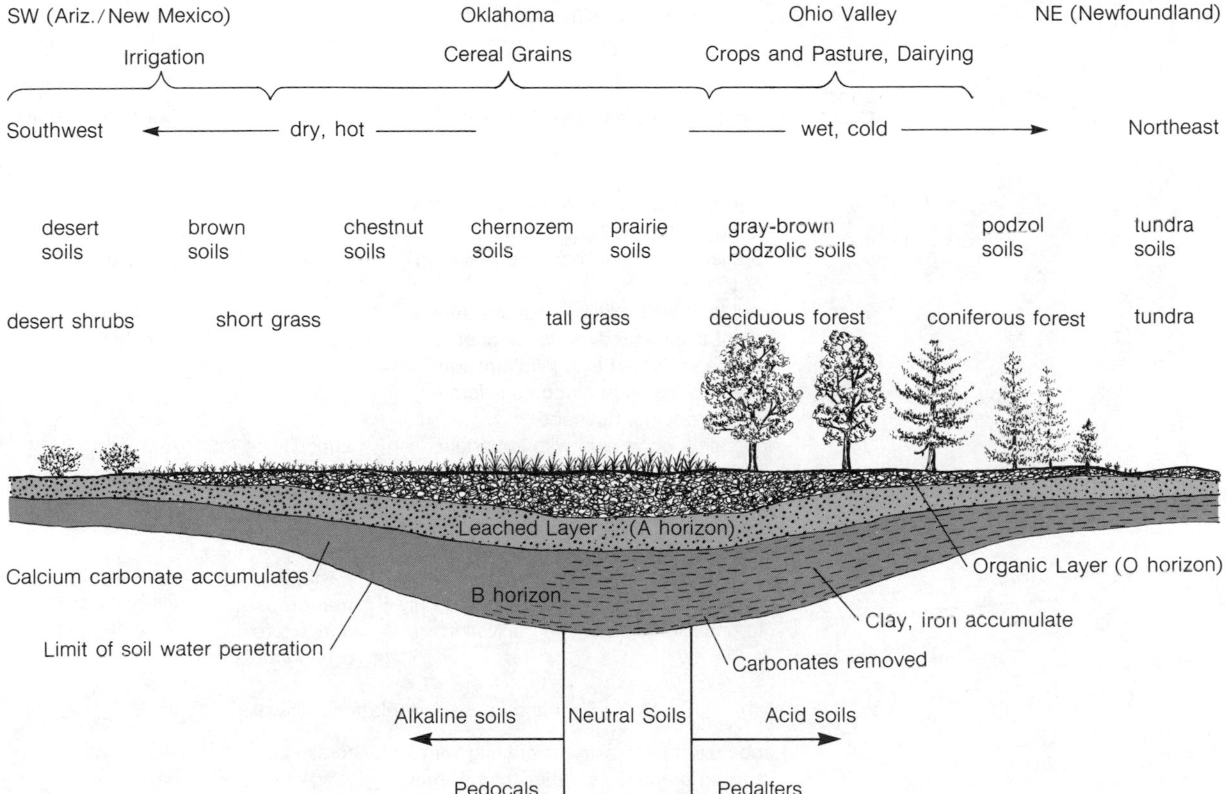

Figure 5–8

Changes in soil profiles across North America. Variations in climate and vegetation, along a diagonal line from the southwestern United States to southeastern Canada, result in systematic changes in soil type and agriculture. Pedalfer soils are found in the eastern portion of North America, and they become less acidic and more alkaline going west. The change from pedalfer and pedocal soils occurs around the 100th meridian, where annual precipitation averages about 50 centimeters. To the west of that longitude annual precipitation averages less than 50 cm; to the east, more than 50 cm.

From an engineering viewpoint, soil is simply the loose, unconsolidated earth material that lies on hard, consolidated bedrock. Soil horizons, nature of parent material, and fertility are of little concern.

Engineering properties

All man-made construction—houses, skyscrapers, factories, highways, airports, dams, and others—need a supporting foundation. Hard, consolidated

Table 5-2 Land-use Classification

Land Class	Land-capability and Use Precautions	Primary Uses	Secondary Uses
	Group I Lands More Suitable for Cultivation		
1	Excellent land, flat, well drained. Suited to agriculture with no special precautions other than good farming practice	agriculture	recreation wildlife pasture
2	Good land with minor limitations such as slight slope, sandy soils, or poor drainage. Suited to agriculture with precautions such as contour farming, strip cropping, drainage	agriculture pasture	recreation wildlife
3	Moderately good land with important limitations caused by soil, slope, or drainage. Requires long rotation with soil-building crops, contouring or terracing, strip cropping, or drainage	agriculture pasture watershed	recreation wildlife urban-industrial
4	Fair land with severe limitations caused by soil, slope, or drainage. Suited only to occasional or limited cultivation	pasture tree crops agriculture urban-industrial	recreation wildlife watershed
	Group II Lands Less Suitable for Cultivation		
5	Land suited to forestry or grazing without special precautions other than normal good management	forestry range watershed	recreation wildlife
6	Suited to forestry or grazing with minor limitations caused by danger from erosion, shallow soils, and so on. Requires careful management	forestry range watershed urban-industrial	recreation wildlife
7	Suited to grazing or forestry with major limitations caused by slope, low rainfall, soil. Use must be limited, and extreme care taken	watershed recreation wildlife forestry range urban-industrial	
8	Unsuited to grazing or forestry because of absence of soil, steep slopes, extreme dryness or wetness	recreation wildlife watershed urban-industrial	

rock obviously provides the strongest foundation. Yet surface distribution of hard bedrock is more common in regions of steep topography and high relief, where construction is more difficult and costly. In areas of gentle topography and low relief, ground surface is mostly loose, unconsolidated materials, either the weathered products of hard rock or transported sedi-

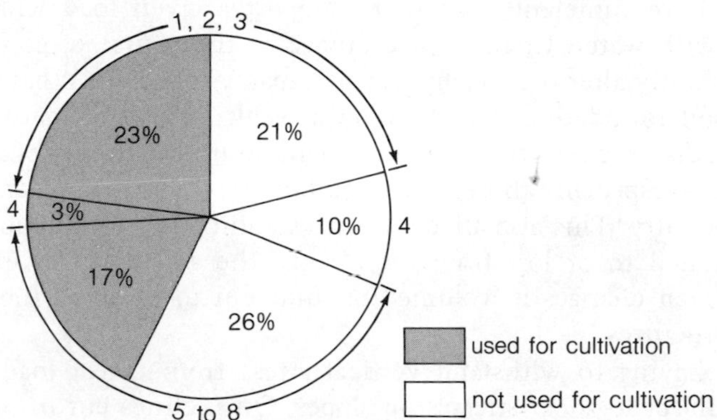

Figure 5–9

Relative proportions of various land-use capability classes in the United States. Total land area is 920 million hectares (2.3 billion acres), of which 44 percent is classified as most suitable for agriculture (categories 1–3). The shaded portions indicate relative amounts actually being used for cultivation. Note that while some of the best agricultural land lies fallow, some of the less suitable land is being cultivated.

ments which are glacial, alluvial, or from mass wasting. Although several physical properties determine a soil's suitability for construction, we'll consider only the most important ones: its *bearing strength*, or ability to support heavy loads; its capacity to hold or lose water; its tendency to swell and expand when wet, or shrink and contract when dry; and its stability on a sloping surface, like a roadcut.

Soil texture largely determines its ability to support a heavy load. Fine-grained soils are more porous and therefore more easily compressed and compacted when loaded than coarse-grained soils. Gravelly textured soils have good bearing strength since the individual particles of hard rock are in contact with and support each other. Mixtures of sand and gravel are stronger still because the sand particles fill the pore space of the gravel particles and provide additional support. For bearing strength of other types of soil, see Table 5–3.

Even if they are the same grain size, soils vary in bearing strength according to the composition of individual particles. A gravel composed of limestone particles is weaker than one composed of granite particles because limestone is an intrinsically weaker rock than granite. Moreover, if the gravel contains some water, the limestone particles can be slowly dissolved whereas the granite particles can not. Thus acidic groundwater moving through a limestone gravel can dissolve and reduce the size of the solid particles, causing the gravel to compact and settle. Sometimes, though, groundwater or soil water may precipitate mineral matter around grains and weld them together, and in this way significantly increase a soil's bearing strength.

Coarsely textured soils drain better than fine-grained soils because of their greater permeability. Soils that do not drain well will compact when surface loads squeeze water from among the soil particles. That is, water keeps the particles apart until pressure is applied. Upon loading, the solid particles crowd together and occupy a smaller volume than before; the ground surface settles as the soil compacts. So some soils that might otherwise have sufficient strength to support a given load will settle if saturated with water. Changes in drainage in the course of construction can significantly alter the weight-bearing capacity of a soil. What was once a strong soil foundation may become a weak one when natural water drainage is disturbed during construction and water accumulates around it.

Some soils, especially those rich in certain clays, expand when wet and shrink when dry. This also affects a soil's stability as a foundation. When water is added to or lost from these soils, the soil particles expand or contract. Such changes in volume are sufficient to threaten the stability of most structures.

Beyond having to withstand vertical stress from direct loading, soils are also subject to shear stresses on slopes. On inclines cut in soil—along a highway embankment, for example—the solid particles try to move downslope under the pull of gravity. Frictional forces among the soil particles may be greater than the downslope force, and so the slope remains in place. But the slope may be so steep that the gravitational force is greater than the internal frictional resistance of the soil; then the soil shears off and moves downhill. Or, the slope may be stable when dry, but when the soil particles are wet, the water reduces friction among the particles and adds weight to the soil, and the soil slides downhill.

Fortunately, all these engineering soil properties—and many we haven't discussed—can be routinely measured before construction by soil tests that determine bearing strength, compressibility, volume changes when wet or dry, and so on. Because soils do have widely ranging mechanical behavior dictated by their intrinsic properties and external conditions, we shouldn't be so eager to build on flat, easy-to-excavate soil without first inquiring how the soil will change once the structure is built.

Table 5-3 Allowable Bearing Capacities of Earth Materials

Material	Allowable Bearing Capacity (metric ton/0.1m^2)
medium-soft clay	1.5
medium-stiff clay	2.5
loose fine sand	2
loose coarse sand; compact fine sand; loose sand-gravel mixture	3
loose gravel; compact coarse sand	4
compact sand-gravel mixture	6
exceptionally compacted or partially cemented gravels or sands	10
sedimentary rocks, such as hard shales, sandstones, limestones, and siltstones	15
foliated rocks, such as schist or slate	40
massive bedrock, such as granite, gneiss, and basalt	100

5-5 Soil Erosion

Soil-forming processes are incredibly slow from a human standpoint. Many hundreds to thousands of years pass before a thick, rich soil forms from transported sediment or on bedrock. Some soils in the northern Midwest which developed on loose, unconsolidated glacial drift are a meter or more thick, and took 15,000 years to form. In nearby areas, where limestone bedrock was laid bare by glaciers and not buried by glacial drift, only a few centimeters of soil (most of it windblown loess) have been generated during the same time. When agriculture and urbanization disturb the land, soil is lost by erosion much faster than new soils can form. For this reason, soil is a recyclable resource but not a renewable one.

Urban construction strips about 1600 km² annually in the U.S. And each square kilometer yields roughly 1800 metric tons of sediment.

(a)

(b)

(c)

(a) Cloudburst flooded a spinach field, leaving behind erosion gullies and sediment. (b) Drought and strong winds combine to erode fine-grained soil particles in Colorado. (c) Soil conservation in Australia where stakes and willow branches have been placed on steep slopes laid bare by construction. The willow branches will take root, stabilize the slope, and inhibit erosion.

Erosion from agriculture

Wind, water, and ice continually erode the land—with or without human intervention. But human activities have significantly accelerated the erosion rate. In their natural, undisturbed state, soils differ in erodability mainly according to their vegetative cover and the amount of rainfall; this relationship is detailed in Figure 5-10. On a continent-wide basis, the current average erosion rate of the United States is about 6 cm per thousand years. Some geologists have calculated that this rate represents twice the average for the half-billion-year period before humans came on the scene.

The destructive human influence on soil erosion rates arises from removal of protective vegetative cover. Plant roots and organic litter on and within the soil maintain its cohesion and inhibit erosion by wind and water. The porosity of undisturbed soil allows water from rain, melting snow, and ice to be stored there temporarily rather than flowing immediately overland and eroding as it moves downslope. Undisturbed vegetated soils thus reduce flooding and recharge the groundwater reservoir by holding water back, giving it time to percolate gradually downward into the less permeable rocks. Once the natural vegetative cover is disturbed, the soil begins to erode. Thinner soil holds back less water, and so erosion proceeds ever faster until the landscape is bare rock. Thus, by destroying the vegetative cover, we enable more water to flow and erode soil; the ensuing soil erosion causes still more water to run off and erode still more.

As shown in Figure 5-11 the amount of sediment eroded from watersheds in Mississippi varies according to whether the land is cultivated for agriculture, lies fallow, or remains in its natural, undisturbed, wooded condition. Sediment yields from cultivated watersheds were found to be 100 times or more greater than those from undisturbed woodlands. In

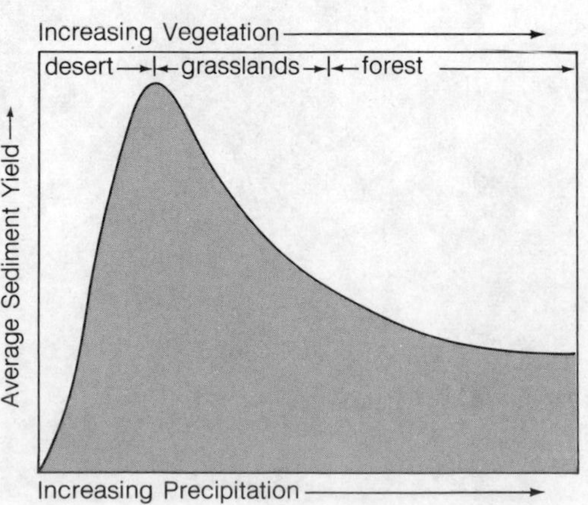

Figure 5-10

Erosion varies with differences in precipitation. Erosion is measured in terms of average annual sediment yield from the land surface. Notice that erosion increases rapidly with precipitation in desert environments and then decreases in grassland and forested environments, owing to the increasing vegetative cover which is itself dependent on rainfall. Data are from some 100 stream sampling stations in watersheds averaging 3900 square kilometers.

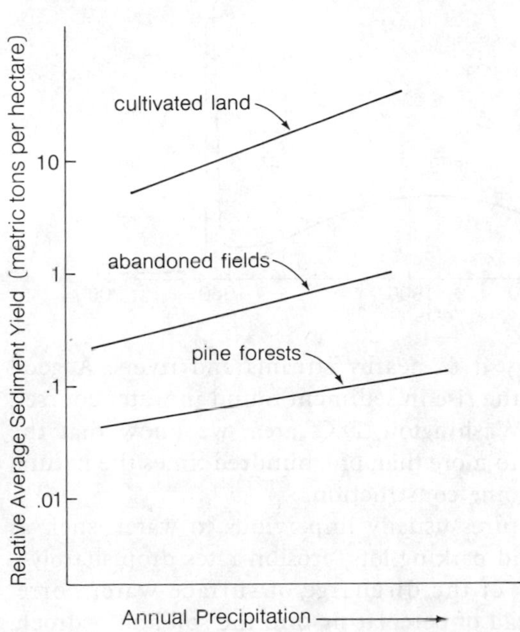

Figure 5-11

Variations in sediment yield from watersheds in northern Mississippi, with differences in precipitation and land use.

another study, geologists examined temporal changes in erosion near Washington, D.C., as the region changed from untouched forest to farmland to pasture and woods, and finally to a heavily urbanized area. As seen in Figure 5-12, erosion rates progressively increased with cultivation, decreased when land returned to woods, and rose sharply with construction. Following construction, erosion rates dropped because much of the region is covered with impervious structures like buildings, roads, driveways, and parking lots.

Erosion from urbanization

Three percent of the United States' total land area lies within urban and built-up areas. Every year an additional 400,000 hectares (one million acres) are urbanized, of which 80,000 hectares are land most suitable for agriculture (categories 1-3 listed in Table 5-2). In California, the leading farm state, more than 36,000 hectares of farmland are lost each year to suburban expansion, freeways, airports, and industry. Already, approximately 1,500,000 hectares of California farmland have been converted to nonagricultural use, an amount equal to more than three percent of the state's total area.

Figure 5-12 indicates that soil erosion is greatest during construction because large expanses of ground are stripped of vegetation, and excavations leave huge volumes of loose soil lying exposed. Wind and especially water

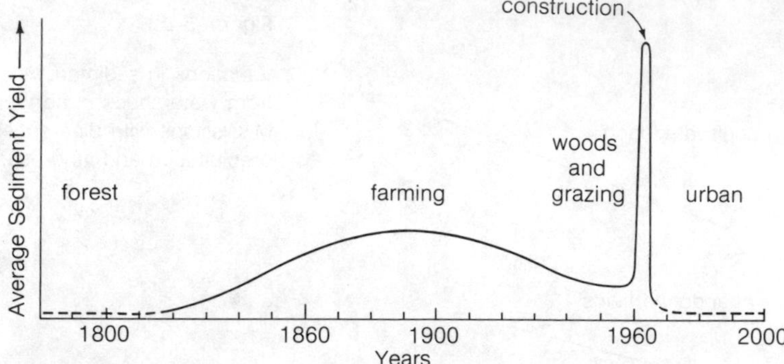

Figure 5–12

Historical changes in erosion in the Washington, D.C. area.

easily erode the soil and carry it to nearby streams and rivers. A good measure of growing erosion is the rise in sediment found in water courses. From data in the Baltimore–Washington, D.C. area, we know that the sediment load jumps from ten to more than one hundred times the natural amount in watersheds undergoing construction.

Upon construction of structures usually impervious to water, such as buildings, roads, driveways, and parking lots, erosion rates drop sharply—look again at Figure 5–12. Yet the discharge of surface water correspondingly rises, because instead of percolating into the soil and bedrock, the water flows freely across these impervious surfaces and eventually reaches local streams. For this reason, streams and rivers surrounding urbanized areas receive much more water after construction than before; the added discharge erodes stream and river channels and raises their sediment load. Thus the net effect of urbanization on soil erosion is more erosion during construction, in the immediate locality being urbanized, and more erosion after construction, in the region surrounding the newly built-up area, as described in Figure 5–13.

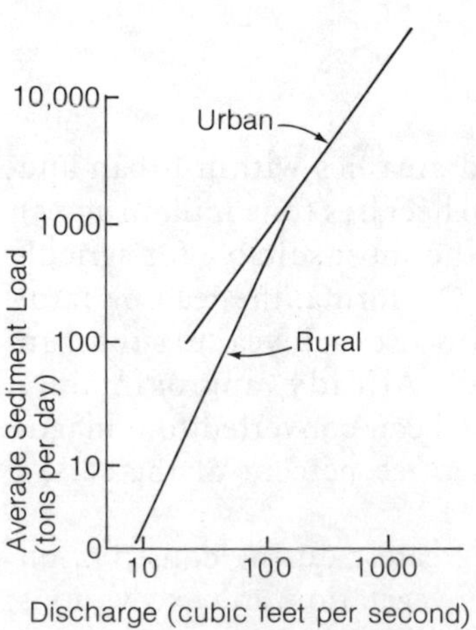

Figure 5–13

Variations in sediment production in a rural area compared with an urban area. The discharge increase in an urban area results in a significantly higher sediment load in local streams.

Viewpoint

Charles B. Hunt

Charles B. Hunt is Professor in the Department of Geography and Environmental Engineering, Johns Hopkins, Baltimore. Mr. Hunt's research has been concerned with the origin of landforms in the United States and the geology of its soils. In this Viewpoint Mr. Hunt demonstrates the various meanings that different types of scientists apply to "soil" and the need for better coordination of ideas and interpretations for the all-important ground around us.

What Does "Soil" Mean?

The term "soil" is ambiguous, for it has very different meanings to different people, depending on whether one's interest is agricultural, geologic, or engineering. To understand the differences in usage, we need to distinguish between the loose, unconsolidated surface deposits that mantle the ground and their weathered upper layers, which are "soil" as that term is used by agriculturalists.

Most surface deposits are sediments weathered from bedrock in one area and transported by water, wind, or glacial ice to another area. They are much younger than the underlying bedrock and generally are unrelated to it. They are older than the soil because the parent material for the agriculturalists' soil developed by weathering of their surface layers. The deposits may be alluvium, that is, sediments that have been deposited by running water. They may be wind-blown deposits—dunes or loess. They may be glacial deposits, and so forth. Other surface deposits are not transported but formed *in situ*, or in place, as a result of weathering of bedrock; they are residual deposits.

Weathering of surface deposits causes the development of distinctive layers more or less parallel to the ground surface. These are the layers in which plants anchor their roots and from which they derive the nutrients and water necessary for growth. At the surface is a layer of litter, or dead plant material. Below this is a layer containing older, decayed organic matter usually called *humus*. The soil below these organic layers is composed largely of weathered mineral matter. As rainwater seeps through the organic layers, it reacts with the carbon-rich material to produce carbonic acid. This acid enables the rainwater to dissolve some of the mineral matter in the upper layers of the soil, move the material downward in solution (some also in suspension), and redeposit it deeper in the ground. These several weathered layers form the agriculturalists' soil. These soil layers are the zone in which plants root, and generally amount to a thickness of no more than two or three feet, although in some places roots may go much deeper. Such soil layers are still developing as present-day weathering continues. Few changes take place below the evident

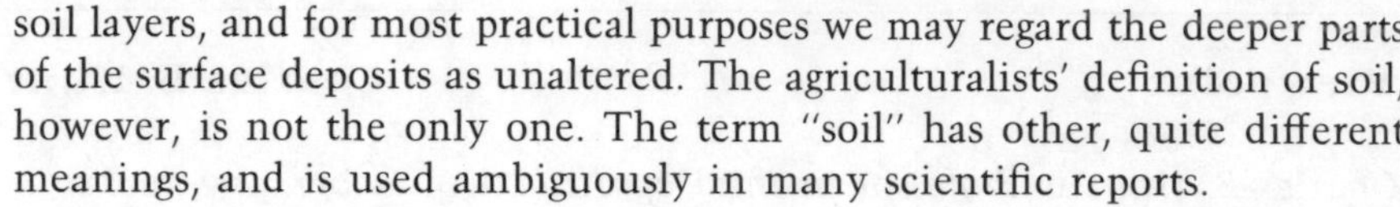

soil layers, and for most practical purposes we may regard the deeper parts of the surface deposits as unaltered. The agriculturalists' definition of soil, however, is not the only one. The term "soil" has other, quite different meanings, and is used ambiguously in many scientific reports.

Geologists use the term "soil" in a broad sense to refer to all materials produced by weathering *in situ*, regardless of their depth or utilization by plants. Geologists thus consider residual deposits as soils. Such soils may be buried by unweathered, younger transported surface deposits, or they may be the deep part of a residual deposit produced by ancient weathering far below the present root zone. Thus, in the specialized sense of the agriculturalist, "soil" on a residual deposit may be only the surface part of an older, deeply weathered zone or "soil" in the geologic sense of the term. That is, a geologist would recognize two soils—a young soil, which is still undergoing development, and an older and deeper soil that is parent material for the young one. To geologists, the older soils are indicators of past weathering processes and climates.

Engineers have a still different usage, one that is highly empirical. In engineering, "soil" refers to ground that can be excavated by earth-moving equipment without blasting; the term has about the same meaning that "surface deposit" has to a geologist.

Such different usages arise because those who study our subject—the agriculturalists, the geologists, the engineers—generally belong to separate organizations; whether they work in universities or in government agencies, they are separately housed. Still a fourth group are the chemists who in their laboratories have directed their attention to clays and organic matter lying in the earth's surface layer. They, too, have much to contribute to our understanding of soil. With all these specialists so scattered, there has been inadequate interdisciplinary exchange of ideas and approaches. For too long, the experts—geologists, soil scientists, and engineers—have worked each in his own cell without the benefit of the knowledge that the others could provide. It is my hope that scientists in each of these fields will make a greater effort in the future to exchange ideas about the ground around us.

Summary

Weathering of rocks and especially sediments exposed on the land surface produces soil of varying texture, composition, and thickness. Water percolating through the soil circulates oxygen and carbon dioxide and supports plants and animals within it. These organisms in turn contribute to soil-forming processes, especially by decomposing accumulated organic matter.

The latter returns nutrients to the soil and adds acids to soil water that leaches it. Minerals are leached in the upper layers by water seeping down through the soil, and are either deposited in lower layers or carried away to the groundwater.

Pedocal soils are those in which the lower soil layer, or B horizon, is enriched in calcium carbonate and other salts dissolved from the upper layer, or A horizon. Pedalfers are soils in which many of the more soluble minerals are leached away, leaving less soluble iron and aluminum compounds in the B horizon. Laterite soils are extreme conditions of the podsolization which forms pedalfers, in that laterites are completely leached and only hydrated iron and aluminum oxides remain. Soil-forming processes thus produce different horizons within the soil that ultimately depend on local conditions of temperature and rainfall.

The best agricultural soils have a loamy texture and are rich in nutrient elements; such soils are typically within the pedocal group of soils. Engineers define soil more generally than agriculturalists, and include all the unconsolidated surface materials that lie on hard, consolidated rock. For construction, such materials must support heavy loads and remain stable. Consequently, soils that are stable after construction must resist compaction, shrinking or swelling when dry or wet, and internal shear.

Given the importance of soils—especially for raising crops and livestock—they must be conserved by careful management and use. Humans expose soils to erosion when they remove the natural protective vegetative cover for farming or construction, often magnifying natural erosion rates tens to hundreds of times. Urbanization not only prevents land from being used to produce food, fibers, and lumber, but also accelerates water runoff from built-up areas. Such runoff erodes local stream channels faster and thereby compounds soil losses.

Glossary

humus Partially decomposed organic matter within soils.

laterite Soil enriched in iron and aluminum and from which most other compounds have been leached away.

loam A particular soil type that has roughly equal amounts of sand and silt, and somewhat less clay, making the soil of just the right porosity and permeability to drain well and yet retain enough water to support vegetation.

pedalfer An acidic soil in which iron and aluminum have been leached from the A horizon and deposited within the B horizon.

pedocal An alkaline soil in which calcium carbonate has been leached from the A horizon and deposited in the B horizon.

podsolization Soil process in which leaching of iron and aluminum occurs in the A horizon and their deposition in the B horizon, forming the acidic, pedalfer group of soils.

residual soils Soils that form in place on bare, exposed rocks over a long period of weathering.

saprolite Residual soils retaining internal features or structures of parent rock.

soil Mixture of mineral and rock grains, organic matter, air, and water. To the farmer a medium for plant growth, to the geologist a weathering product from sediment or rock, and to the engineer loose, unconsolidated earth.

soil profile Horizontal layering in soil that results from physical, chemical, and biological processes.

soil texture Soil characteristic defined by the size, shape, and sorting of its constituent grains or particles.

Reading Further

Dasmann, R. 1968. *Environmental Conservation.* New York: John Wiley, 375 p. Excellent short chapter on "Agriculture and soil" that explains soil characteristics and classification, with emphasis on those factors important in conserving soils.

Basile, R. M. 1971. *A Geography of Soils.* Dubuque, Iowa: Wm. C. Brown, 152 p. Concise review of soil classification and distribution.

Guy, H. 1970. *Sediment Problems in Urban Areas.* U.S. Geological Survey Circular 601-E, 8 p. Washington, D.C. Brief review of the problems of soil erosion and sediment loading in streams that result from urbanization.

Hendricks, S. 1969. "Food from the Land." Chapter in *Resources and Man.* San Francisco: W. H. Freeman, pp. 65–85. Discussion of the arable land throughout the world and its potential for providing food for increasing global populations.

Hunt, C. 1972. *The Geology of Soils.* San Francisco: W. H. Freeman, 344 p. A comprehensive and well-written account of the processes that form soils, how soils are classified, and the uses to which they are put.

Judson, S. 1968. "Erosion of the Land." *American Scientist,* vol. 56, pp. 356–374. Interesting general discussion of how the natural processes of erosion and sedimentation are altered by human activities on the land; summarizes many useful data.

Leopold, L. 1968. *Hydrology for Urban Land Planning—A Guidebook on the Hydrologic Effects of Urban Land Use.* U.S. Geological Survey Circular 554, 18 p. Washington, D.C. Brief, technical review of the changes in stream discharge and sediment load that accompany urbanization. Useful graphs for predicting the consequences of construction on the behavior of streams.

Landscape in Jordan, overgrazed by goats.

Resource Issues 6

The optimist proclaims that we live in the best of all possible worlds; and the pessimist fears this is true.

James B. Cabell, 1926

What can we now conclude about the future availability of earth resources? Having examined the formation, distribution, and abundance of metallic ores, fossil and nuclear fuels, water for industry and irrigation, metals and food from the sea, and soils for agriculture and construction, there are several questions we want to pose. Will we have enough of these things to maintain our way of life indefinitely? Is there enough to go around so that all the peoples of the world might reasonably expect to improve their living standards in the next few generations? In short, what is the future supply of earth resources and what sort of demand for them will there be?

In this chapter, we look at some of the principal factors influencing the supply and demand for earth resources. Although not the stuff of which earth science texts are usually made, these issues must be considered if we are to think intelligently about our natural resources and formulate rational plans for their use.

6-1 Will the Sky Fall?

Any discussion of resource issues hinges on two crucial elements: their probable supply and the predicted demand. We have already suggested this duality in earlier chapters by comparing current estimates of available resources with projections of the future population that will need them. The usual result of such a comparison is the conclusion that there will not be enough. However, this disturbing result is mitigated by an awareness that similar calculations made years ago did not pan out—a situation reminiscent of Chicken Little in the children's story who ran about shouting "the sky is falling, the sky is falling," but the sky didn't fall. At least, not yet.

The Chicken Little position

In 1798, Thomas Malthus, a clergyman and part-time economist, predicted that the rapidly growing world population would soon outstrip the earth's potential food supply. As Malthus saw it, the human population increases geometrically, whereas food production can increase only arithmetically; his theory is expressed in Figure 6–1. Malthus foresaw widespread famine, disease, and war as an inevitable consequence of unchecked population growth.

It was Malthus's prediction that led Thomas Carlyle to label economics as the "dismal science."

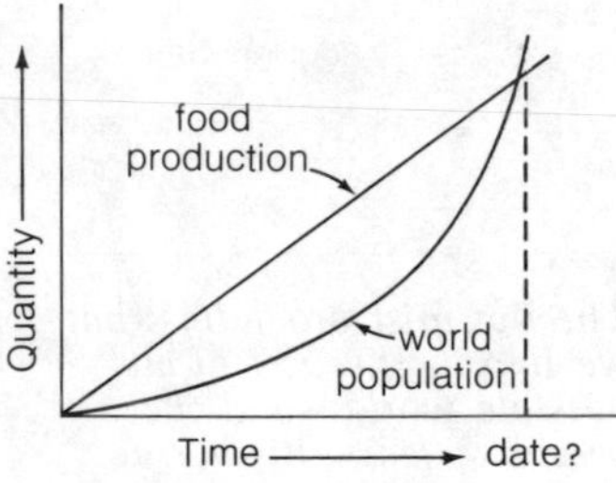

Figure 6–1

The original Malthusian prediction. In 1798, Thomas Malthus stated: "Assuming, then, my postulata as granted, I say that the power of population is indefinitely greater than the power in the earth to produce [food] subsistence for man. Population, when unchecked, increases in a geometrical ratio. Subsistence increases only in an arithmetical ratio."

The Malthusian prediction never quite came to pass—at least in the way it was predicted—because while population did continue to grow ever faster, the technology ushered in by the eighteenth-century Industrial Revolution enabled food production to keep pace with population growth. Certainly, there have been wars, disease, and famines since Malthus, but on the average the human situation has not deteriorated as Malthus thought it would. Many, in fact, would argue that it has improved immeasurably since then. Although it was never vindicated, many still accept and vigorously reiterate the Malthusian argument today, particularly in terms of the earth's resources. Modern Malthusianists, like Chicken Little, constantly remind us that world resources are limited and, given the exponential rise in population, will indeed be exhausted before long.

What these dire predictions usually fail to take into account are the factors that continually influence the supply of a given resource and the demand for it. The assumption is made that supply and demand are unalterably fixed, simply because earth resources are fixed; but instead, we can view the situation as a dynamic relationship between the two elements of supply and demand. Changes in one directly influence the other, and this interaction tends to keep the system in balance, rather than crashing and breaking down completely as predicted.

The Can-Do position

Rather than looking into the future and estimating the limits of our resources, the Can-Do school points backward and argues that what we did before we can do again. For example, Malthus was not able to predict the technological advances in food production and distribution made possible by the combustion engine and the advent of mechanized farming. Can-Doers remind us that dire predictions have been made regularly, and just as regularly they have failed to occur. Like Henny Penny, the Can-Doers pay no attention to Chicken Little. But what if this time, *just this once,* Chicken Little is right, and the sky will fall? Anyone who has looked at the earth's resources might indeed feel uneasy about optimistic claims that more and more resources can be discovered and utilized. After all, the earth is a finite physical body, and by implication so are its resources. Moreover, there must be a point where the world's population will exceed the capacity of these resources to support it. If nothing else, the space available for people is limited, let alone space for feeding them or supplying them with water and other materials.

What are we to do? We can throw up our hands and give up. Or we can try to examine more carefully what influences the supply of earth resources and the demand for them. Such an analysis will not settle these resource issues once and for all, but it will help us understand more clearly the complexity of issues involved so that we can begin to deal with them. Mere reliance on the aphorisms that "earth resources are limited" or "if we can put a man on the moon, we can fix anything" is at best simple-minded, at worst irresponsible.

The Viewpoint by Ridker that concludes this chapter deals with this sort of false dichotomy with respect to economic growth.

6–2 Factors Influencing Supply

To understand the dynamic interaction between supply and demand, we have to recognize the influences on the supply of earth resources. In general, there are four factors: market price, which reflects demand and provides an incentive to explore for and develop a resource; current technology for extracting and marketing it at a competitive price; basic geologic knowledge of how and where resources are likely to occur; and finally the natural abundance upon which its availability depends in the first place. Significant changes in any one of these factors has a marked impact on relative supply and demand.

Price incentives

The cost of exploring, extracting, refining, and transporting a resource must be less than the price that resource brings in the marketplace. Only wealthy eccentrics would spend money to find, develop, and market an earth resource that sells for less than it costs to produce. For example, some offshore oil deposits of sufficient volume could be tapped, but the total cost of recovery and transportation to onshore refineries is less than the current market price. Individuals or organizations with enough capital to underwrite these production costs find that their money can earn a better return if invested in a savings and loan association, real estate, or stocks than in oil production. Let's say that an oil producer pays $2 million for a 2000-hectare (5000-acre) lease in 50 meters of water, and discovers an oil-bearing sandstone on the edge of a subsurface salt dome. Using the figures in Table 6–1, he estimates the total oil reserve at 16,000,000 barrels, of which 13,300,000 can be recovered. So he drills seven wells in addition to the discovery well, and all turn out to be good producers. A completed well costs $664,000; the eight total $5,316,100. Outlay for the lease and the wells means a total investment of $7,316,000.

Obviously, the potential profitability of this oil field would be greatly improved with a sharp rise in crude oil prices as experienced in the early 1970s.

With 93 barrels of oil per well per day withdrawn, the estimated life of the reserves is sixty-six years; the time required for an even return on the initial investment is twenty-six years. Gross income over the sixty-six years will be $36,666,600 and total expenses, $28,466,500, yielding a profit of $8,200,100.

Table 6–1 Hypothetical Example of a Geologic Success and an Economic Failure

Gross reserves	16 million barrels
Recoverable reserves	13.3 million barrels
Allowable production rate	93 barrels per day per well
Lease allowable	271,200 barrels/year
Depletion period	66 years
Payout after production starts	26 years
Gross income	$36,666,600
Operating expense	$20,240,000
Income tax	$ 2,004,400
Capital investment (net after U.S. income taxes)	$ 6,222,100
Total expenditures	$28,466,500
Gross profit undiscounted	$ 8,200,100
Profit discounted at 3%	zero
Profit discounted at 6%	(–$2,961,000)

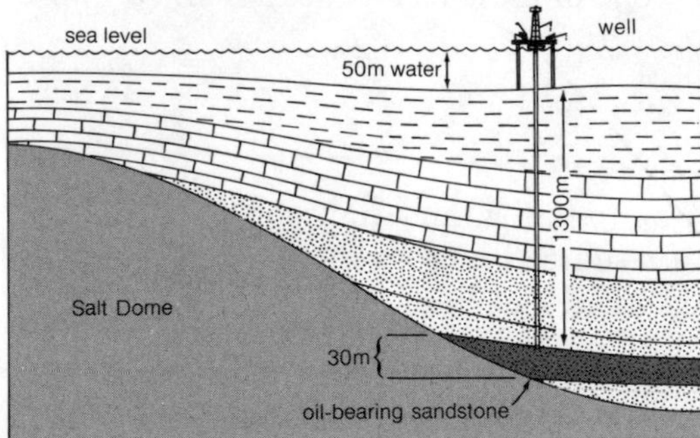

Cross section of hypothetical oil wells discussed in Table 6–1. Oil bearing sandstone, 30 meters thick, occurs along flank of subsurface salt dome. Offshore wells standing in water depths of 50 meters drill 1300 meters into sea floor to tap oil.

If he had invested his money in some other financial venture at 3 percent annual interest over the same interval, he would have made a similar profit. But if he had put his money into a financial venture returning 6 percent interest, it would have produced a greater return–$2,961,000 more than in oil speculation. Clearly, then, mere geologic success in discovering an earth resource does not guarantee a profit. And if there is no profit, there's little motive for recovery.

If a resource is especially critical to the national economy, a state or federal government may provide public capital to recover the resource.

In that case, the public decides to underwrite the production costs with taxes. In the United States, though, virtually all resources are developed with private rather than public capital. However, if public institutions control the market price, they can manipulate the price to encourage private development of a resource. For instance, the U.S. Atomic Energy Commission (AEC) controls the market price of uranium, and during the 1950s, set it at a level that encouraged private uranium exploration, as indicated in Figure 6-2. This action led to large-scale discoveries of the ore throughout the western United States. After it became clear to the AEC that these newly discovered deposits would meet projected national needs for several decades in the future, the price of uranium was lowered. Later the AEC announced that it would not automatically purchase any newly discovered uranium, but instead would individually negotiate their future purchases. So, clearly, one important factor controlling the supply of an earth resource is the price incentive to the potential producer of that resource.

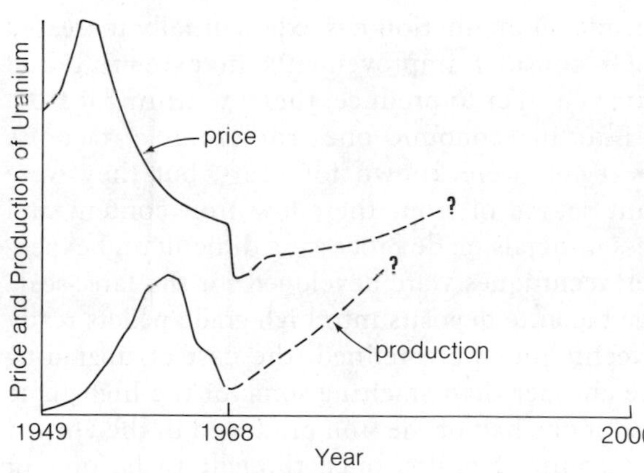

Figure 6-2

Relation between price and production of uranium. Government control of the market price of uranium has stimulated and depressed production of this ore, and indicates the role that price plays in influencing the supply of earth resources. Increased future demand for uranium will be met when the price of uranium is allowed to rise, thus encouraging increased exploration and recovery.

Role of technology

Knowing that a million tons of a certain earth resource exist somewhere out there is not enough. We also require a method of recovery and processing to bring the resource to potential consumers. As methods of discovery and withdrawal improve, additional resources become available, as shown in Figure 6-3. The natural character of a resource does not change; what does change is our ability either to find it or exploit it.

To illustrate this point, we need only examine the relationship between oil production and technological advances in petroleum exploration. Starting with simple exploration techniques of studying surface geology and locating natural oil seeps, and advancing to complex methods of geophysical

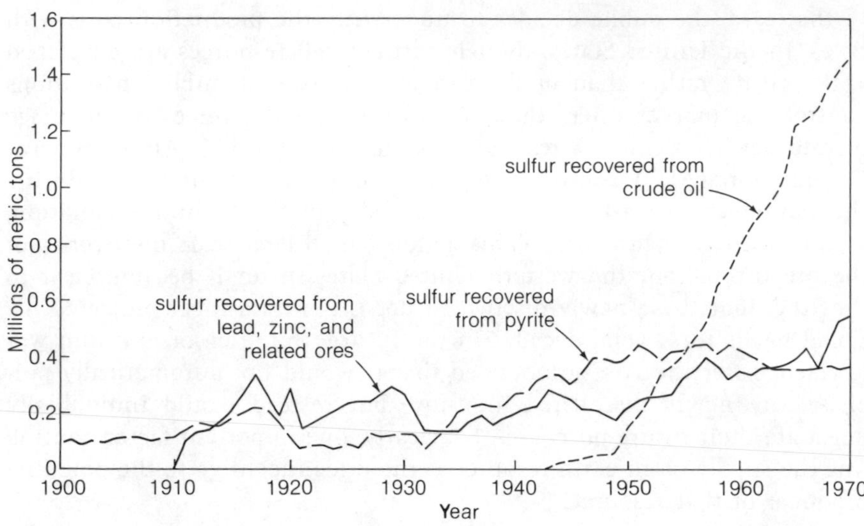

Figure 6-3

Changing patterns in sulfur production. Sulfur was initially recovered from pyrite, an iron sulfide. During World War I, additional sources of sulfur came from smelting lead and zinc sulfide ores. In the last several decades, crude oil has become a major source of sulfur. This is a good example of how technologic innovation can increase the supply of an earth resource.

and offshore prospecting, crude oil production has exponentially increased in the last half-century. Or consider improvements in extracting and refining that make a resource cheaper to produce, thereby turning it from an uneconomic resource into an economic one. For example, taconite ores in the Lake Superior region were known for years, but they were not considered a significant source of iron; their low iron content and high proportion of worthless minerals made processing difficult and expensive. In the 1950s, however, techniques were developed for the large-scale transformation of low-grade taconite deposits into high-grade pellets ready for the blast furnace. As techniques were refined, the cost of upgrading low-grade taconites became cheaper than smelting some of the high-grade iron ores. Consequently, about one-half of the iron produced in the United States today comes from taconite deposits, once thought to be ores of last resort. Moreover, the proved reserves of these low-grade ores are enormous: vast quantities exist throughout the world. There is a hitch, however. Enormous quantities of waste rock must be disposed of in taconite mining. In the early 1970s, one such mining operation was dumping more than 60,000 tons of solid waste into Lake Superior each day, an amount roughly equivalent to 45,000 loaded freight cars each year.

Undoubtedly, there are limits to what technology can achieve in discovering and recovering earth resources—if only because we cannot find and exploit what is not there. Nevertheless, past experience shows that improved methods of exploration and exploitation can considerably alter the supply of earth resources. In this regard, the Earth Resources Technology Satellite (ERTS) program, which takes high-altitude photographs of the entire earth, marks another major step in resource exploration. Such widespread photoreconnaissance will undoubtedly reveal new mineral resources.

(a)

(b)

Contrast in technology of oil delivery. (a) Laying a crude oil pipeline by hand at the turn of the century in Pennsylvania. (b) Modern oil loading jetty in the Persian Gulf, where as many as ten tankers can be filled at an overall rate exceeding a half million barrels every hour.

Growing geologic knowledge

The search for valuable concentrations of earth resources cannot be a random one; it must be guided by an understanding of how the earth produces them and where they are most likely to exist. As new knowledge is gained, we can re-evaluate resource prospects in regions with known deposits and predict completely new areas where they might be found.

Perhaps the best illustration of this need for knowledge is the recently developed concept of plate tectonics, which has enlarged our understanding of how some metallic mineral deposits form. Entirely new metal-bearing provinces may be revealed by this concept, as well as insights into al-

As large an amount of oil as this is, it would last a little more than 8 months at the current rate of U.S. ***energy*** *consumption, which is equivalent to approximately 40 million barrels of oil per day.*

ready-known provinces. Another example—unverified—relates to the discovery of 10-billion-barrel oil fields on Alaska's north coast. As the story goes, most petroleum companies initially avoided large-scale prospecting there because they knew that the sedimentary rocks were all Triassic in age. From past experience, they also knew that rocks of this age were notoriously poor oil producers. Thus the chances for finding oil or gas were slim. Once petroleum was discovered in Alaska, in Triassic sandstones covering an area the size of the state of Massachusetts, many of the same companies rushed to lease land for further exploratory drilling. If true, this story certainly demonstrates how geologic knowledge or lack thereof influences decisions about where to look for new earth resources.

Estimating resources

When geologists estimate resource quantity, they must consider both the uncertainty of discovery and the economics of recovery. The U.S. Geological Survey defines four categories of resources according to feasibility of economic recovery and uncertainty of discovery: reserves, conditional, hypothetical, and speculative, as diagramed in Figure 6–4.

The most reliable category of earth resources is termed *reserves,* which exist in identifiable, proven quantities and can be recovered economically. We are as sure of the existence of *conditional resources* as we are of reserves, but currently we cannot exploit conditional resources profitably. The dividing line between reserves and conditional resources is an economic one and can shift with changes in a resource's market value or in its recovery costs. Aside from fluctuating economic factors, both reserves and conditional resources are *identified resources;* that is, we know for

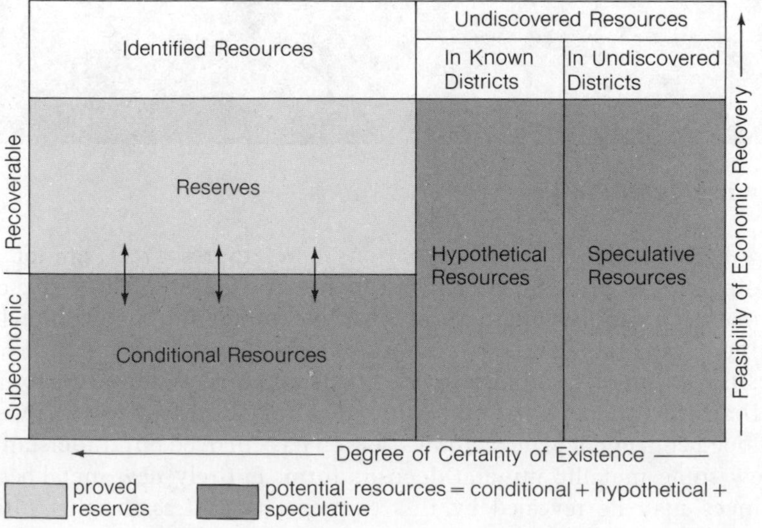

Figure 6–4

Resource categories developed by the U.S. Geological Survey for classifying national mineral resources. Two qualifications defining these categories are degree of certainty as to their existence (amount, distribution, quality) and feasibility of recovering them economically. The boundary between reserves and conditional resources is economic and hence can fluctuate with changes in economic conditions.

sure that they exist. For instance, we may know the size, distribution, and ore grade of a gold field in Nevada, but whether we regard it as a reserve or conditional resource depends on the current market value of gold and the present costs of extracting and refining it.

Undiscovered resources are of two kinds: *hypothetical resources,* or those presumed to be in an area where some have already been found, and *speculative resources,* or those thought to be in regions that haven't yet produced such a resource. To give an example, until oil was located on the north coast of Alaska, petroleum resources there were purely speculative and based on limited geologic knowledge of that part of the world. Once petroleum companies found oil and gas in several wells there, and once they gained some idea of the extent and thickness of producing and nonproducing strata, they could make new estimates of the region's oil and gas resources. The greater certainty of the new estimates allowed speculative resources to be termed hypothetical resources. Undiscovered resource categories can be further subdivided on the basis of feasibility of economic recovery.

The boundary between identified resources and undiscovered resources is established by our geologic knowledge, which does not fluctuate as economic factors might. Moreover, movement from one to another of these resource categories is for the most part one-way and irreversible. For instance, speculative resources may become hypothetical resources or proved reserves as we gain geologic information; identified resources cannot revert to unidentified resources, nor can hypothetical resources revert to speculative ones. However, the boundary between reserves and conditional resources is reversible and does fluctuate as economic conditions vary. All economic geologists do not uniformly employ the resource terms used by the U.S. Geological Survey, but the two principal criteria of degree of uncertainty about a resource's existence and feasibility of its economic recovery are invariably applied.

6-3 Factors Influencing Demand

Turning to demand, we find a similar array of determining factors. Four major variables influence the demand for earth resources. First, market price discourages or encourages consumers to purchase the resource and can switch the market to (or from) another resource more favorably priced. Second, as population grows, there are more and more people who want the resource. Third, each person may consume more of the resource; so even if population remains constant, individuals use more of it. Finally, technological change or improved living standards call for more of the resource. If any one of these factors varies significantly, it will exert a definite impact on the balance of supply and demand.

Rising prices

Can you think of earth resources whose demand curves might match those shown in Figure 6–5(b)?

Other things being equal, consumer demand for a resource—a ton of aluminum, a barrel of oil, one million liters of irrigation water, a hectare of farmland—varies according to its price, as illustrated in Figure 6–5. Although many economic complexities enter into the picture, for our purposes we can assume that as rising demand forces prices up, one or more of the following will result. Producers may feel pressure to supply more of the resource from their proved reserves. They may also discover that they can supply more of the conditional reserves because costs of recovery may now be more than met by the new, higher prices. Alternatively, the producer may not be able to expand the supply; then some consumers because of the higher price may decide to do without it or to use something else in its place. Others will decide that they can afford the higher price and will pay it. Because some consumers do not buy, the demand for the resource may fall off.

Let's consider a simple example. Suppose that the demand for copper rises sharply as consumers come to desire much more copper than can be supplied. Copper prices will rise correspondingly because individual consumers will try to outbid each other for the available copper. Those who decide that the prices have soared higher than they want to pay will substitute another metal for the copper, presumably one whose price is more reasonable. Or perhaps they will just do without. If demand keeps prices up, copper producers may conclude that it is economically worthwhile to develop some of their conditional resources, perhaps deep mines, because now the higher cost of subsurface mining will be more than met by the higher prices. The producers may even channel increased profits

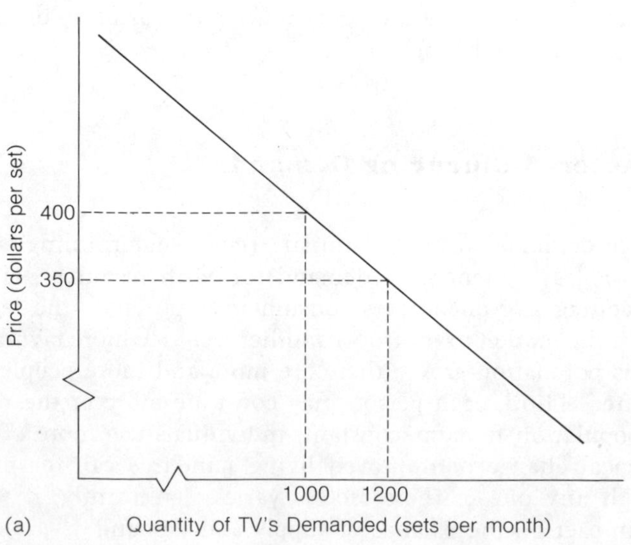

Figure 6–5

Demand curves of the economist showing relationship between prices and quantity of goods sold per unit time. (a) Demand for a particular brand and model of TV as measured by the quantity sold each month decreases with increasing price. The rate of decrease in demand per unit price increase depends on how important the consumer judges the commodity to be.

from the higher copper prices toward exploring for additional copper.

Even though the economist would find this analysis oversimplified, it clarifies why Malthusian doomsday predictions do not come to pass, at least to the extent forecast. Economic forces in the market place tend to curb rising demand by a change in price structure. Well before rising demand exhausts a resource, prices rise and put a damper on demand. In addition, higher prices provide incentives for producers to increase supply and for consumers to use a resource more efficiently, substitute a cheaper one, or do without it completely. The real difficulty with Malthusian predictions is that because they never seem to happen, we are lulled into ignoring the real resource issues: higher prices, wasteful resource utilization, problems of substitution, failure to convert conditional resources into reserves, and ignorance of how and where earth resources occur in the first place.

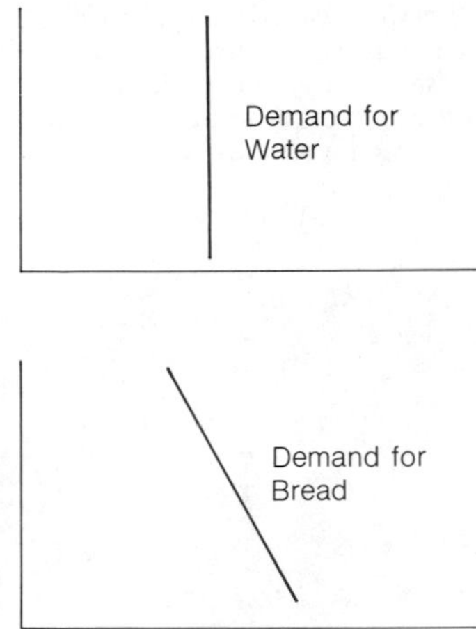

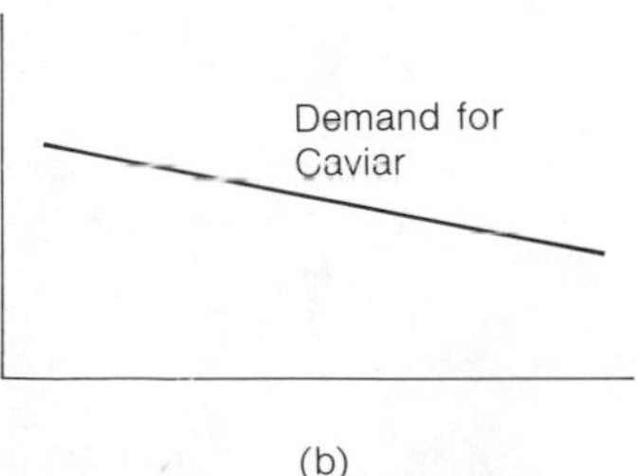

(b)

(b) Three different demand curves showing the varying importance of a commodity to its consumers. People will continue to purchase water, whatever its current price. In this case the demand is referred to as being inelastic, because the quantity demanded does not change with any change in price. The demand for bread is somewhat inelastic, as the quantity demanded will vary somewhat with price. The demand for caviar is relatively elastic, because the quantity demanded fluctuates widely with price.

Growing demand from a growing population

Increase in global population every year creates a greater demand for resources because more people need the energy, water, and goods that the earth supplies.

Let's look at the total rise in population. The net increase in the number of people living on the earth is determined by subtracting total deaths from total births. The medical revolution has steadily reduced the death rate among most nations of the world; this reduction is not usually accompanied by a proportional decline in the birth rate. Because the number of annual births is a certain percent of current population, the total population grows year by year. Such population growth is geometric, analogous to compound interest rates. In nonhuman populations growth is also geometric, but only temporarily so because at some point growth levels off owing to limited resources. This type of growth is called *logistic,* and its leveling-off phase is more or less in balance with the *carrying capacity* of the environment. That is, the environment can support, or carry, a maximum number of individuals. In nonhuman populations, the birth and death rates are in equilibrium, with no long-term net rise in total population. Humans, however, are still in an exponential phase of growth because technologic advances in medicine and resource utilization have permitted the population to continue multiplying. Sometime in the future, human population growth will level off, if only because there won't be enough land for everybody to stand on. No doubt, well before then the population boom will have been checked by deaths from mass starvation, disease, or war, or by deliberate birth control.

We've just made another one of those Malthusian predictions, but one that most people accept. Disagreement arises as to *when and how the leveling will occur.* As an example, the average world food requirement per person per day is 2354 calories, and right now 2420 calories are available.

This leveling should not be confused with ZPG, zero population growth, for it takes about one generation (65 years) for total population to level off after ZPG is reached.

One food calorie equals 1000 heat calories, with each of these calories equivalent to the amount of energy required to raise 1 gram of water 1 degree Celsius.

(Needless to say, in some parts of the world people get more or less than what they require, but we will consider only the world average here.) The world's carrying capacity in terms of food resources can, at best, increase eightfold: the amount of farmland can double, the productivity of farmland can double with existing agricultural technology, and technological innovations can achieve still another doubling in productivity itself. These three doublings can, at most, expand food resources eight times what they are now.

How long before the world's population reaches this optimistic carrying capacity? At present rates of world population growth, with total population doubling every 35 years, we will reach this predicted carrying capacity in 105 years—when the earth's population is around 30 billion people, eight times the present amount. So sometime in the latter half of the twenty-first century food supply and people demand will top out. Malthus finally will be vindicated. The timing of his prediction is way off, only because he could not foresee the exponential rise in food production that has so far kept pace with exponential population growth. But this new prediction might not come to pass if aquaculture can be raised to the level of agriculture. In terms of other earth resources, for the last two centuries the consumption of resources like copper, lead, and zinc has been exponential, too, paralleling the world population; see Figure 6–6. But just as with food and population, these exponential curves will have to level off ultimately.

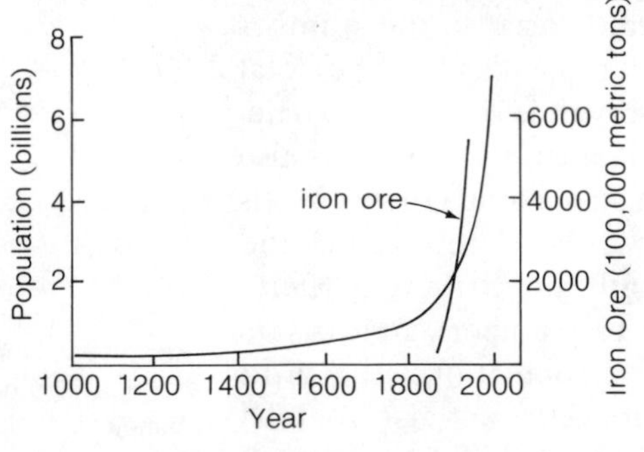

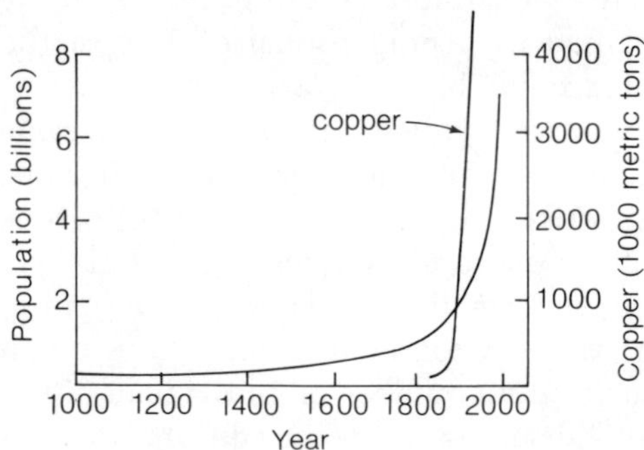

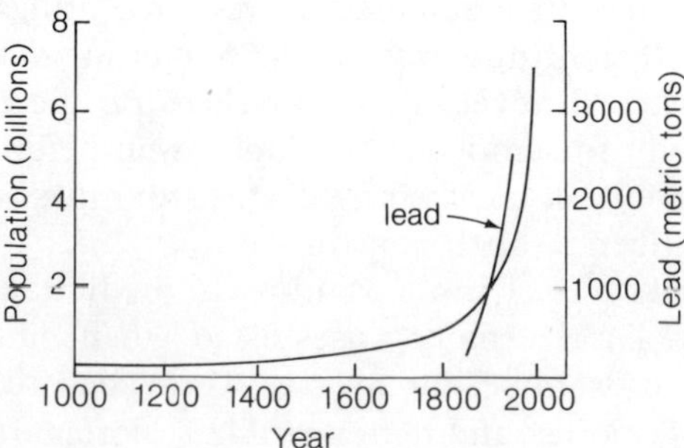

Figure 6–6

Exponential consumption of iron, copper, and lead paralleling the growth of the world population.

Increasing per capita consumption

While population growth has stimulated resource demand, there has also been an acceleration in per capita demand for many of the earth's resources. For instance, in the United States the number of automobiles per person has steadily climbed in the last several decades, from one car per thirteen persons in 1920 to one car per two persons in 1980. If this trend continues, by the year 2000 every three persons will have two cars. Here again, there must be some limit to exponential per capita growth, but in the meantime the demand for energy to power these cars and the raw materials to build them correspondingly accelerates. Table 6–2 shows, for example, the raw materials required just for one automobile. Or consider the United States per capita demand for electricity and water, which doubles every ten and forty years, respectively. Assuming that growth rates of the early 1970s are maintained, in the fifty years it would take the nation's population to double, total electricity use would jump thirty-two times and total water use (exclusive of transportation and recreation) would more than quadruple. Resource consumption thus grows not only with total population but also with per capita consumption, thereby compounding total consumption.

You might try to calculate how much rock waste will be generated just to produce the copper needed for the projected number of automobiles in the year 2000.

Table 6–2 Composition of an Automobile (U.S.)

As Fabricated Materials	As Raw Materials
1017 kg iron and steel	2250 kg iron ore
22.5 kg copper	2250 kg copper ore
22.5 kg lead	900 kg lead ore
22.5 kg zinc	900 kg zinc ore
211.5 kg rubber and plastics	405 kg crude oil
157.5 kg glass	315 kg oxides for glass
31.5 kg aluminum	126 kg bauxite
90 kg miscellaneous	225 kg miscellaneous
1575 kg, worth about $500	7371 kg, worth about $50

More resources to meet technology and life style

Our last major factor influencing demand for resources comes under the general heading of technology and life style and explains, at least in part, the per capita growth in demand that we've just discussed. Much of the escalating demand in the United States for aluminum, for instance, reflects a shift away from iron for construction, beverage containers, aircraft, and a host of other products. Not only has aluminum consumption grown, but fifteen times more energy is required to produce a ton of aluminum than the same amount of steel. In a similar way, a switch from packaging materials with paper, cardboard, and metal to putting them in plastics of all sorts has increased consumption of petroleum, from which the latter are made. Once again, significantly more energy is needed to produce the newer, petrochemical goods than the materials they replaced.

Higher living standards have a similar impact on resource consumption. With greater affluence, Americans now eat more beef than they did several decades ago. From the early 1940s to early 1970s, annual per capita beef consumption has more than doubled, going from 25 kg to more than 52 kg per person. In the same interval, total United States population has climbed 57 percent. So total beef consumption in the United States has tripled in the last three decades. We might point out here that rising beef demand was accompanied by sharp price increases, so eventually the demand slowed and prices declined. Rising beef consumption has other implications, too. As more cattle are raised in feedlots, larger amounts of animal waste are generated, most of which end up in surface waters. We could go on and on with similar examples, but essentially all would demonstrate that changes in technological production and life style accompanying rising living standards raise the demand for earth resources.

The wastes currently produced by livestock are tremendous, roughly equivalent to a national population of 2 billion people.

6-4 Balancing the Equation

If we look again at the factors influencing resource supply and demand, we find that all but one can be manipulated through ingenuity, planning, and effort, however difficult and complex that might be. Prices can be controlled to stimulate supply or limit demand. Technology can facilitate economic production of low-grade, nonrenewable resources as well as their recycling and reclamation. Technology also can help to replace artificially those resources consumed faster than they are renewed naturally. More comprehensive geologic information can be garnered through more vigorous efforts in geologic research and applied earth science. Population growth can be stabilized by controlling and limiting birth rates. Prior assessment of technologic innovation can anticipate possible booms in resource demand resulting from that innovation. And people can be educated and persuaded or legally and economically restricted from adopting life styles that put too heavy a strain on earth resources. But admittedly, achieving all this to bring resource supply and demand into balance will be extremely difficult, although theoretically possible.

None of these efforts, however, can affect the most crucial factor of all: the natural abundance of earth resources. No amount of human effort can create a resource that does not exist. As emphasized in the U.S. Geological Survey report on national mineral resources:

Imbalance between demand and supply. Accelerating growth of vehicles created huge demand for gasoline that could not be met during Middle East oil embargo in late 1973 and early 1974.

At some time, however, the pressures of both economic and geologic factors will meet in crisis. Economic factors may be altered rapidly. Changes in demand and use alter patterns of production and consumption; new deposits are sought elsewhere; substitutes will be sought; and new technology will be developed as the ingenuity of man is focused on solving the problems. But there is no economic availability if there is no geologic availability. Of the two factors, geologic availability is the more fundamental because without it economic availability is not pertinent. Just as no biological miracle can make it possible to extract blood from a turnip, neither technological magic nor astronomic dollar value can make it possible to extract gold or aluminum or borax or mica from rocks in which they are not present. Geologic availability, therefore, is the ultimate determinant of mineral potential. . . . (USGS Professional Paper 820, p. 6)

The equation

So far, we have discussed supply and demand qualitatively, examining the determining factors. A particularly useful, more concrete expression of these factors' relationship has been given by Dr. Vincent E. McKelvey, Director of the U.S. Geological Survey:

$$L = \frac{R \times E \times I}{P}$$

That is, a society's living standard *(L)* is a function of its consumption of earth resources or raw materials *(R)*, times its consumption of energy *(E)*, times its economic, political and technologic ingenuity *(I)*; all divided by the number of people *(P)* sharing the total product. This relationship indicates the point we have been stressing, namely, that we can manipulate or regulate ingenuity and population but not raw materials and energy. Consequently, in the long run, living standard is ultimately dependent on the raw materials and energy available to and produced by a society. Moreover, we can see that uncontrolled population inevitably diminishes *L*, as does failure of ingenuity.

Which brings us to the most important and pressing realization: resources are limited, and most are finite. Furthermore, when we ask, "Will there be enough?" are we thinking of our own generation, our children's, or their children's? What will we leave for all those who come after us? What is our responsibility to them? Everybody might agree that we ought to conserve our resources, but on what time scale?

The issues raised in this chapter are real, serious, complex, and global. Dealing with them will require energy, insight, compromise, restraint, understanding, tenacity, and cool. No specific solutions have been offered here, but just to enumerate what is required to balance supply and demand helps to clarify the nature and extent of resource problems. Such an enumeration sidesteps the polarized views of the Chicken Little and Can-Do schools of thought. Instead, it enables us to see the complexities of resource issues and define the areas where we can begin to deal with, if not solve, those issues.

Viewpoint **Ronald G. Ridker**

Ronald G. Ridker is a resource economist with Resources for the Future, Inc., Washington, D.C. Dr. Ridker's research interests center on the interconnections of population, resources, pollution, and the environment. In this Viewpoint Dr. Ridker argues that debates about future national economic growth—to grow or not to grow—widely miss the mark because the relevant question is, instead, how to channel and redirect economic growth to serve better humanity's needs.

To Grow or Not to Grow: That's Not the Relevant Question

It is fashionable these days to assert that there are two points of view on the question, "Must we limit economic growth?" On the one side is the progrowth, or business-as-usual, school, which is based on the implicit belief—stated more in actions than in words—that, as a social goal, material economic growth should take precedence over equity in the distribution of income, wealth, and privilege and over concerns about the social and environmental costs of growth. At the other extreme is the no-growth, or scrap-the-system, school, which at times comes close to assuming that these problems will all disappear if only growth disappears.

I believe that both viewpoints are wrong—indeed, that they border on the irresponsible. There can be no doubt that the fruits of economic growth will make the resolution of the social and environmental problems we face much easier to solve. That fact makes it irresponsible to argue for zero economic growth in a world still dominated by poverty. It is equally irresponsible, however, to use this fact as a rationale for the continual postponement of efforts to resolve basic social problems, both domestic and international. The relevant question is not whether to grow or not to grow, but how to channel and redirect economic output, and any accompanying production increases in ways that will make our economy better serve humanity's needs. If this is done, growth will probably be restrained. That is as it should be. But such reductions will be far less than the reductions that would be needed to solve the same problems through attacks on growth per se.

What about those persons who remind us that the earth is finite, that if growth continues we will eventually run out of resources and environmental carrying capacity? Should we not stop growth in the consumption of materials and energy before that day comes? Are not these problems so serious that any attempt to correct them, short of stopping all material economic growth, can only be considered a palliative?

If we rule out the possibility of importing materials and energy from outside the earth on an ever-increasing scale, this argument must ultimately be correct. The second law of thermodynamics, the entropy law, makes this certain. Indeed, this same law makes it certain that even a constant rate of economic activity cannot be maintained forever, unless that level of activity is sufficiently low to permit mankind to live within the limits imposed by the flow of solar energy he is able to tap. Technological breakthroughs may make it appear possible to continue growth forever. But this illusion arises from man's myopia. No amount of scientific knowledge can repeal the laws of nature; they can only postpone their consequences. No matter how closely we approach it, there is no such thing as a perpetual motion machine.

But knowledge that growth must eventually cease is of no practical significance by itself. The relevant question is *when?* It makes an enormous difference for policy today whether the "we" who must limit growth is mankind alive today or some far-off, future generation. Will the law of entropy catch up with us in 100, 1000, or 100,000 years?

While no one has an answer to this question for the world as a whole, the results of a study undertaken by Resources for the Future for the Commission on Population Growth and the American Future can be used to shed at least a little light on it. (U.S. Commission on Population Growth and The American Future, *Population, Resources, and the Environment,* R. G. Ridker, ed. [Washington, D.C.: Government Printing Office, 1972], vol. 3.) Concentrating mainly on the United States and only on the next 50 years, it reviews the prospects for more than 20 resources and 14 pollutants and can be interpreted as saying that, if some costs are paid and some adjustments made, no catastrophe is likely to result from continued growth during the next half-century. Indeed, at least as far as the United States is concerned, the results are fairly sanguine. We appear to have the resources and the know-how both to continue growing and to cope with the problems of that growth, if we are willing to adjust our lifestyles a bit. This is not to say that there will be no serious shortages during the next 50 years, but that these shortages are unlikely to arise solely as a consequence of population and economic growth.

For most of the problems associated with economic growth, direct attacks are probably better than indirect ones. For example, the study mentioned above indicates that direct attacks on pollution dominate over restrictions on population and economic growth as means of reducing pollution emissions. To assert otherwise is a bit like junking the family car because the tires have worn out or reducing a boy's food consumption because the sweets are giving him acne. Why use a meat ax when a scalpel will do better?

There are two important exceptions to this general principle. First, in the interest of humanity and world peace, it makes sense for the richer countries of the world to tax themselves and transfer the proceeds to the poorer countries. But this is not the same thing as saying that worldwide economic growth should be restricted. Obviously, if worldwide economic growth did stop, the chances of bringing about such a transfer would be far lower than they are today. Second, some of the costs of growth—particularly those outside the resource and environmental fields—may not be amenable to a direct attack. How can the regulations needed to control the negative spillovers of growth, the hecticness of modern life, and the superficiality of personal relationships that growth seems to generate, be controlled without reducing growth itself? It seems to me that the advocates of no-growth would have a better case if they were to focus their attack on these consequences of growth rather than on the resource and environmental consequences, which, in very large measure, can be managed by other means.

Of course, direct attacks on the resource and environmental consequences of growth will themselves reduce the growth rate, thereby helping to reduce the more general and pervasive costs of expansion. If these latter costs are not then reduced sufficiently for our taste, let us agree to restrict our economic growth by a larger amount. Over time, as we learn more about the earth's reserves and what is technologically possible, and as our tastes and preferences change, the situation will require reassessment. By proceeding in this step-by-step fashion, we will do ourselves and future generations less harm than by applying generalized, meat-ax approaches.

It is true that we do not know what kinds of disasters we may be letting ourselves in for by permitting economic growth to continue. But it should be remembered that we are also ignorant of possible technological and institutional breakthroughs that may eventually come along, breakthroughs that might not only save future generations from disaster but might make them substantially better off than the current generation. In light of our total ignorance about both positive and negative developments that may occur, what is the prudent course? It is not obvious that the prudent course is to save resources for future generations, at least not obvious to any but the most affluent on this earth.

The analogy of stopping the ship until one knows what lies ahead in the fog is an interesting one, conjuring up a picture of passengers sitting comfortably in their staterooms waiting for the fog to lift. It is a rich man's image. The poorer two-thirds of the world's population cannot wait, particularly when it is not clear that future generations will be worse off than people today. If the poor are to wait, the prudent course would be to share the stateroom—that is, the available resources—with them.

Your end is sinking!

These conclusions follow only if we do take advantage of the available opportunities, and directly attack the problems associated with growth. If political and institutional constraints make it impossible to apply direct measures forcefully, we are likely to be faced with an accumulation of very serious problems; in that situation, reductions in economic as well as population growth begin to make more sense. Those who advocate reductions in growth may believe that we will not apply such direct measures with sufficient force. I believe they can be proved wrong. But to do so will require stepping outside the intellectual constraints of the debate over growth and no-growth. As I indicated at the outset, proponents of growth tend to argue that solutions to the world's social and environmental problems should be postponed because economic growth will make them easier to solve, while the proponents of no-growth sometimes appear to argue the reverse, that no-growth will solve our problems or somehow make them easier to solve. Both schools, it seems to me, are copouts. What we must do is get on with the solution to the problems that obviously and directly face us. And the sooner the better.

Summary

The quality and scope of human life largely depend on the supply of earth resources. Availability of these resources is determined ultimately by their natural, geologic abundance. Thus we must husband these resources as much and as long as possible to extend their availability for future generations. Visionary schemes predicting low-cost nuclear power that will provide an unending supply of low-grade resources may or may not come true. More important is the shorter-term concern with supply and demand for higher-grade, less abundant resources.

In addition to natural abundance, factors influencing resource supply include profit incentives for discovery and recovery, technological advances that facilitate their economic exploitation, and expanded basic and applied geologic research into how resources originate. Estimating the abundance of proved reserves and potential resources depends on how feasible economic recovery is and how certain their geologic availability is.

Factors influencing demand for earth resources include their price, the total population that needs them, and per capita use. Changes in technology and life style also significantly affect the demand.

Overly optimistic or pessimistic predictions about the future supply of resources are usually based on unrealistic assumptions and oversimplified analyses that fail to consider complex factors controlling supply and demand. Resource issues need, on the contrary, careful definition, detailed analysis, and deliberate planning. Cries that the "sky is falling" or "we did it before and can do it again" are distracting and counterproductive.

Glossary

carrying capacity Total amount of life that a particular habitat can sustain with its given resources.

conditional resources Resources whose existence is known but which cannot, under current economic conditions, be profitably exploited.

hypothetical resources Additional resources presumed to exist in areas where such resources have already been found in some quantity.

identified resources Resources known definitely to exist, including both reserves and conditional resources.

logistic growth curve Increase in numbers of individuals in a population that starts off slowly, rises sharply, and then slows down and levels off as carrying capacity of the environment is reached.

reserves Resources known to exist in specified amounts and recoverable at a profit.

speculative resources Resources thought to exist in areas that have not, as yet, yielded such resources.

undiscovered resources Resources presumed to exist, including both hypothetical and speculative resources.

Reading Further

Boulding, K. 1968. "The Economics of the Coming Spaceship Earth." In *Beyond Economics.* Ann Arbor: University of Michigan Press. Important essay outlining how the national economy must shift from a "cowboy economy" of unlimited horizons to a "spaceship economy" in which resources are viewed as limited and finite.

Brobst, D. A., and W. A. Pratt. 1973. Introduction in *United States Mineral Resources.* Washington, D.C.: U.S. Geological Survey Professional Paper 820, pp. 1–8. Short but cogent review of factors that control the availability of mineral resources.

Commoner, B. 1971. *The Closing Circle.* New York: Alfred A. Knopf. Full-scale treatment of the "environmental crisis" with particular attention to the way in which technological changes have been responsible for rapidly rising demand for earth resources.

Hardin, G. C., Jr., and K. Mygdal. 1968. "Geologic Success and Economic Failure." Tulsa, Oklahoma: American Petroleum Association Geological Bulletin, vol. 52, pp. 2079–2091. Indicates how economic factors determine whether an earth resource can be profitably recovered; emphasizes that the geologic success of discovering an earth resource does not guarantee its feasibility of economic recovery.

McKelvey, V. E. 1973. "Mineral Resource Estimates and Public Policy." In U.S. Geological Survey Professional Paper 820. An important essay by the present director of the U.S. Geological Survey indicating the relationship between living standards and consumption of energy and mineral resources; explains the concepts of reserves and potential resources as a function of degree of certainty and feasibility of economic recovery.

Park, C. F., Jr. 1968. *Affluence in Jeopardy: Minerals and the Political Economy.* San Francisco: Freeman, Cooper, 368 p. A comprehensive discussion of the role that minerals and energy play in modern industrial economies. Clarifies how economics and politics influence resource production.

Conversion Tables (Approximate)

English to Metric

When You Know	Multiply by	To Find
inches	2.54	centimeters
feet	0.30	meters
yards	0.91	meters
miles	1.61	kilometers
square inches	6.45	square centimeters
square feet	0.09	square meters
square yards	0.84	square meters
acres	0.40	hectares
square miles	2.6	square kilometers
cubic inches	16.4	cubic centimeters
cubic feet	0.27	cubic meters
cubic yards	0.76	cubic meters
cubic miles	4.19	cubic kilometers
ounces	28.3	grams
pounds	0.45	kilograms
tons	0.9	tons
fluid ounces	30	milliliters
quarts	0.95	liters
gallons	3.8	liters

Metric to English

When You Know	Multiply by	To Find
centimeters	0.39	inches
meters	3.28	feet
meters	1.09	yards
kilometers	0.62	miles
square centimeters	0.15	square inches
square meters	11	square feet
square meters	1.20	square yards
hectares	2.47	acres
square kilometers	0.38	square miles
cubic centimeters	0.06	cubic inches
cubic meters	0.37	cubic feet
cubic meters	0.13	cubic yards
cubic kilometers	0.24	cubic miles
grams	0.04	ounces
kilograms	2.20	pounds
tons	1.1	tons
milliliters	0.033	ounces
liters	1.06	quarts
liters	0.26	gallons

Energy

1 barrel of crude oil = 42 gallons

7 barrels of crude oil = 1 metric ton = 40 million BTUs

1 metric ton of coal = 28 million BTUs

1 gram U_{235} = 2.7 metric tons of coal = 13.7 barrels of crude oil

1 BTU (British Thermal Unit) = 252 calories = 0.0002931 kilowatt-hour

1 kilowatt-hour = 860,421 calories = 3412 BTU

General Glossary

---

aquifer Permeable sediment or rock layer that transports underground water.

asthenosphere Weak layer within the mantle lying below the lithosphere that behaves as a viscous liquid.

biosphere The shell of all life that lies between the fluid shells of the atmosphere and hydrosphere and the solid shell of the crust.

capacity The amount of sediment a stream or river can carry past a certain point over an interval of time.

competence Maximum size of sediment particles that a stream or river can carry at a given velocity.

core Central portion of the solid earth composed of iron and nickel. The inner portion is solid, the outer half is liquid.

crust The outermost solid earth shell composed of rocks rich in sodium- and potassium-aluminum silicates.

crystal A solid whose constituent atoms have a regularly repeating arrangement.

discharge Volume of flow of a stream or river past a certain point over an interval of time.

dynamic equilibrium A state of balance within many geologic systems such that, if some conditions of the system change, the balance or equilibrium will shift in a direction to restore the original conditions.

ecologic niche Place within the economy of nature that a particular species of plant or animal occupies. Often described as the way an organism makes its living.

ecology Study of the physical, chemical, and biological factors that control the distribution and abundance of organisms.

ecosystem The totality of interacting phenomena—animal, vegetable, and mineral—within a life habitat that determines the numbers and kinds of organisms present. The ecologic system is usually considered closed in that the necessary energy and nutrients are continually recycled within it.

epicenter Point on the earth's surface directly above the focus of an earthquake.

extrusive rocks Igneous rocks that solidify from magmas that spill out onto the earth's surface.

fault Plane of breakage within the earth along which rocks have moved differentially.

feedback Process in which a cause produces an effect that in turn influences the cause itself. Positive feedback increases the initial causal force whereas negative feedback diminishes it.

focus Point of initial rupture within the earth that results in an earthquake.

food chain Transfer of energy, in the form of food, from the sun through primary producers (plants) to primary and secondary consumers (animals). *Food webs* are overlapping food chains.

fossil Traces or actual remains of a prehistoric plant or animal found in sediments or sedimentary rocks.

gradient The slope of a stream or river channel along its length.

granitization Formation of igneous rocks of granite composition by the partial melting of preexisting sediments and rocks.

half-life Amount of time it takes for a radioactive substance to decay to one-half its original amount.

hydrologic cycle Interconnected processes that move water throughout the earth's hydrosphere, including evaporation, precipitation, and surface and underground flow.

igneous rocks Solids formed from magmas that crystallize within or on the surface of the earth.

intrusive rocks Igneous rocks that solidify from magmas intruded into the crust below the earth's surface.

isostasy State of balance in the earth's crust and mantle whereby rocks achieve different elevations according to their relative densities.

isotope Chemical element having the same number of protons in its nucleus as another element, but a different number of neutrons. Isotopes of the same element thus have the same atomic number and almost identical chemical properties, but they differ in their atomic masses and physical behavior.

limiting factor That physical, chemical, or biological requirement that is in shortest supply within an ecosystem.

lithification Processes by which loose sediments become hard, coherent rocks, including compaction, recrystallization, and cementation.

lithosphere Strong layer within the crust and upper mantle above the asthenosphere that behaves as a rigid solid.

load Amount of sediment that a stream or river carries in solution, suspension, and along its channel by traction.

magma Molten material rich in silicates that crystallizes into igneous rocks of all types.

magmatic differentiation Derivation of different igneous rock types from a single parent magma.

mantle Solid earth shell lying between the core and crust, which is rich in iron-magnesium silicates.

mass wasting Downslope movement of surface soil, sediment, and rock by gravity; includes soil creep, solifluction, slides, slumps, rock falls, and mudflows depending on rate of movement and water content of materials.

metamorphic rocks Rocks that have new compositions or textures owing to the heating and squeezing of preexisting sediments or rocks. Also includes rocks formed by chemical reaction of preexisting rock with chemically active fluids like magma.

mineral Naturally occurring solid of specific chemical composition and internal arrangement of constituent atoms.

orogeny Formation of mountain systems, particularly by folding, faulting, and igneous activity.

oxide A chemical compound of negatively charged oxygen with a positively charged metallic element.

permeability Ability of sediments or rocks to transmit fluids within their pore spaces.

photosynthesis Chemical reaction carried out by plants using solar energy to make carbohydrates from carbon dioxide and water.

plates Individual portions of the lithosphere that diverge, converge, or shear past one another as they ride along the underlying asthenosphere.

porosity Proportion of pores, or open spaces, within sediments and rocks.

radioactive isotopes Isotopes that spontaneously break down into other isotopes or elements, yielding radiation as they do so.

residence time The average amount of time a particular substance spends within a designated earth system. The residence time is inversely proportional to the rate of movement within the system and directly proportional to the size of the system.

respiration Process by which plants and animals release energy bound up in food, producing water and carbon dioxide.

sedimentary rocks Solids formed on the earth's surface from sediments that accumulate as loose particles or precipitate directly from solution from natural waters.

silicate Chemical compound of two or more oxides, one of which is always silicon dioxide (SiO_2).

species Group of organisms whose members are similar to each other and that can interbreed to produce fertile offspring.

subduction zone Region where one plate pushes down below another plate as the plates converge.

tectonics Structural behavior of the earth's crust and mantle including plate movements, earthquakes, orogeny, and crustal uplift and subsidence.

weathering Chemical alteration and physical disintegration of earth materials in contact with air, water, and organisms.

Credits

Photographs

Page 1: Kennecott Copper Corporation.

Chapter 1 Page 2: Canadian Government Office of Tourism. Page 9: F.A.O. Page 14: Israel Government Press Office. Page 15: Dr. Brian Skinner, Yale University. Page 19: Woods Hole Oceanographic Institution. Page 26: P. D. Snavely, Jr., U.S. Geological Survey. Page 27: U.S. Geological Survey. **Chapter 2** Page 32: Japan National Tourist Organization. Page 36: Bethlehem Steel Corporation. Page 41: A. Leipzig, Texaco. Page 48: Riverton Ranger, Riverton, Wyoming, Atomic Energy Commission. Page 50: William Henry Jackson, Yellowstone National Park. Page 51: Pacific Gas and Electric Company. Page 53, left: Courtesy of Georgia Institute of Technology; right: Swiss National Tourist Office. **Chapter 3** Page 62: Japan National Tourist Organization. Page 78, top: Bureau of Reclamation; bottom left: Israel Government Press Office; bottom right: State of California, Department of Water Resources. **Chapter 4** Page 90: Heyward Associates, Inc., courtesy of The Portuguese National Tourist Office. Page 94: Duke University Marine Laboratory. Page 95: Centre Océanologique de Bretagne. Page 99: National Science Foundation. Page 102: Exxon. **Chapter 5** Page 120: Japan National Tourist Organization. Page 123: U.S. Department of Agriculture, Photo by Naval Research, Bureau Yard & Docks. Page 127: Swissair. Page 137, top left: U.S. Department of Agriculture; top right: U.S. Department of Agriculture, Soil Conservation Service; bottom: Australian Information Service. **Chapter 6** Page 146: F.A.O. Page 153, top: Exxon; bottom: Standard Oil of California. Page 161, left: EPA-Documerica-David Falconer; right: Elihu Blotnick, BBM.

Viewpoints

Chapter 5 Pages 141–142: Adapted from *Geology of Soils: Their Evolution, Classification, and Uses* by Charles B. Hunt. W. H. Freeman and Company. Copyright © 1972. **Chapter 6** Pages 162–165: Copyright © 1973 by the American Association for the Advancement of Science.

Line Drawings

Chapter 1 Fig 1-7: After A. Bateman, *The Formation of Mineral Deposits,* New York: Wiley, 1951, p. 210. Fig 1-8: After B. Skinner, *Earth Resources,* Englewood Cliffs, N.J.: Prentice-Hall, 1968, p. 35. Fig 1-10: After F. Sawkins, "Sulfide Ore Deposits in Relation to Plate Tectonics," *Journal of Geology,* vol. 80, 1972, p. 392. Fig 1-11: After U.S. Geological Survey Professional Paper 820, 1973, p. 410. Fig 1-12: After E. Cameron, ed., "The Mineral Position of the United States, 1975–2000," Madison: University of Wisconsin Press, 1973, p. 18. Fig 1-13: After U.S. Geological Survey Professional Paper 820, 1973, p. 10. Fig 1-14: After B. Skinner, *Earth Resources,* Englewood Cliffs, N.J.: Prentice-Hall, 1968. **Chapter 2**

Fig 2–1, Fig 2–3: After U.S. Geological Survey Professional Paper 820, 1973, pp. 10, 135. Fig 2–4: After C. Dunbar and J. Rodgers, *Principles of Stratigraphy*, New York: Wiley, 1957, p. 155. Fig 2–5: After U.S. Geological Survey maps, "Coal Fields of U.S. and Alaska," sheets 1, 2. Fig 2–8: After E. Cameron, ed., "The Mineral Position of the United States, 1975–2000," Madison: University of Wisconsin Press, 1973. Fig 2–10: After U.S. Geological Survey Professional Paper 820, 1973, p. 456. **Chapter 3** Fig 3–4, Fig 3–5: After A. Piper, U.S. Geological Survey Water-Supply Paper 1797, 1965, plates 1, 2. Fig 3–9, Fig 3–10, Fig 3–11: After C. Murray and E. Reeves, U.S. Geological Survey Circular 676, 1972, pp. 5, 6, 8. Fig 3–12(b): After G. Aron and V. Scott, "Dynamic Programming for Conjunctive Water Use," *Journal of the Hydraulics Division, Proceedings of the American Society of Civil Engineers*, Paper 8145, May 1971, p. 711. Fig 3–14: After T. O'Riordan and R. Moore, "Choice of Water Use," in *Water, Earth, Man*, R. Chorley, ed., London: Methuen, 1969, p. 550. **Chapter 4** Fig 4–3: After D. L. Inman and B. M. Brush, "The Coastal Challenge," *Science*, vol. 181, pp. 20–32, Fig. 10, 6 July 1973. Copyright 1973 by the American Association for the Advancement of Science. Fig 4–4, Fig 4–7: After D. Ross, *Introduction to Oceanography*, New York: Appleton-Century-Crofts, 1970, pp. 301, 113. Fig 4–9: After K. Turekian, *Oceans*, Englewood Cliffs, N.J.: Prentice-Hall, 1968, p. 77. Fig 4–11, Fig 4–12: After M. G. Gross, *Oceanography*, Englewood Cliffs, N.J.: Prentice-Hall, 1972, pp. 402, 399. Fig 4–13: After G. Pinchot, "Marine Farming," *Scientific American*, vol. 223, no. 6, December 1970, pp. 15–21. Copyright © 1970 by *Scientific American*. All rights reserved **Chapter 5** Fig 5–6: After R. Dasmann, *Environmental Conservation*, New York: Wiley, 1968, p. 107. Fig 5–7, Fig 5–8: After C. Hunt, *The Geology of Soils*, San Francisco: W. H. Freeman, 1972, pp. 173, 183. Fig 5–10, 5–12: After S. Judson, "Erosion of the Land," *American Scientist*, vol. 56, 1968, pp. 362, 366. Fig 5–13: After L. Leopold, U.S. Geological Survey Circular 554, 1968, p. 13. **Chapter 6** Fig 6–2: After *Mineral Facts and Problems*, U.S. Bureau of Mines Bulletin 650, 1970, pp. 231, 234. Fig 6–3, 6–4: U.S. Geological Survey Professional Paper 820, 1973, pp. 608, 4. Fig 6–6: After C. F. Park, Jr., *Affluence in Jeopardy*, San Francisco: Freeman, Cooper, 1968, pp. 12, 14.

Tables

Chapter 1 Table 1–1, Table 1–2: After "U.S. Mineral Resources," U.S. Geological Survey Professional Paper 820, 1973. Table 1–4: Modified after J. Gilully, A. Waters, and A. Woodford, *Principles of Geology*, 3rd ed., San Francisco: W. H. Freeman, 1968, p. 550. Table 1–5: After U.S. Geological Survey Professional Paper 820, 1973. Table 1–6: After National Research Council, National Academy of Sciences, *The Earth and Human Affairs*, San Francisco: Canfield Press, 1972, p. 62. **Chapter 2** Table 2–1: After U.S. Geological Survey Professional Paper 820, 1973, p. 140. Table 2–2: American Petroleum Institute. Table 2–3: After M. K. Hubbert, *Resources and Man*, San Francisco: W. H. Freeman, 1969, p. 209. Table 2–4: After U.S. Department of Interior, *United States Energy: A Summary Review*, 1972. **Chapter 3** Table 3–1, Table 3–4: After G. P. Kalinin and V. D. Bykov, "The World's Water Resources, Present and Future," in *Impact of Science and Society*, vol. 19, no. 2, Paris: UNESCO, April–June 1969, pp. 135–150. Table 3–2: After R. Garrels and F. Mackenzie, *Evolution of Sedimentary Rocks*, New York: Norton, 1971, p. 101. Table 3–3: After J. Giddings, *Chemistry, Man, and Environmental Change*, San Francisco: Canfield Press, 1973, p. 285. **Chapter 4** Table 4–1: After J. Mero, *The Mineral Resources of the Sea*, New York: American Elsevier, 1964, p. 180, and U.S. Geological Survey Professional Paper 820, 1973. Table 4–2: After B. Skinner and K. Turekian, *Man and the Ocean*, Englewood Cliffs, N.J.: Prentice-Hall, 1973, p. 61, and U.S. Geological Survey Professional Paper 820, 1973. Table 4–3: After U.S. Geological Survey Professional Paper 817, 1973, tables 13, 14. Table 4–4: After J. Ryther, "Photosynthesis and Food Production from the Sea," *Science*, vol. 166, p. 74. **Chapter 5** Table 5–1, Table 5–2: After R. Dasmann, *Environmental Conservation*, 2nd ed., New York: Wiley, 1968, pp. 109, 127. Table 5–3: After P. Flawn, *Environmental Geology*, New York: Harper & Row, 1970, p. 75. **Chapter 6** Table 6–1: After G. C. Hardin, Jr., and R. Mygdal, "Geologic Success and Economic Failure," American Association of Petroleum Geologists Bulletin, vol. 52, p. 2088. Table 6–2: After National Academy of Sciences, *Mineral Science and Technology*, Washington, D.C., 1969, p. 25.

Index

Page numbers in **boldface** type indicate glossary entries.